# Data Warehousing
## Using the Wal-Mart Model

# Data Warehousing

## Using the Wal-Mart Model

**PAUL WESTERMAN**

Compaq Computers, Inc.

**MORGAN KAUFMANN PUBLISHERS**

AN IMPRINT OF ACADEMIC PRESS

A Harcourt Science and Technology Company

SAN FRANCISCO   SAN DIEGO   NEW YORK   BOSTON
LONDON   SYDNEY   TOKYO

| | |
|---|---|
| *Executive Editor* | Diane D. Cerra |
| *Production Editor* | Howard Severson |
| *Production Assistant* | Mei Levenson |
| *Assistant Editor* | Belinda Breyer |
| *Cover Design* | Yvo Rezebos |
| *Cover Image* | © Henry Sims/The Image Bank/PictureQuest |
| *Text Design* | Mark Ong |
| *Copyeditor* | Carol Leyba |
| *Proofreader* | Jennifer McClain |
| *Composition & Illustration* | Technologies 'N Typography |
| *Indexer* | Ty Koontz |
| *Printer* | Courier Corporation |

Designations used by companies to distinguish their products are often claimed as trademarks or registered trademarks. In all instances where Morgan Kaufmann Publishers is aware of a claim, the product names appear in initial capital or all capital letters. Readers, however, should contact the appropriate companies for more complete information regarding trademarks and registration.

ACADEMIC PRESS
A Harcourt Science and Technology Company
525 B Street, Suite 1900, San Diego, CA 92101–4495, USA
*http://www.academicpress.com*

Academic Press
Harcourt Place, 32 Jamestown Road, London, NW1 7BY, United Kingdom
*http://www.academicpress.com*

Morgan Kaufmann Publishers
340 Pine Street, Sixth Floor, San Francisco, CA 94104–3205, USA
*http://www.mkp.com*

*Library of Congress Cataloging-in-Publication Data*

Westerman, Paul
   Data warehousing : using the Wal-Mart model / Paul Westerman
      p. cm
   Includes bibliographical references and index.
   ISBN 1–55860–684-X
   1. Data warehousing. I. Title

QA76.9.D37 W47 2001
005.74—dc21                                                          00-043408

This book has been printed on acid-free paper.

# Contents

# Preface

There is a tangible value to effective decision making for organizations across all industries. Data warehousing requires that technology be applied to deliver business solutions. Unlike technology development of the past where technology departments worked in a near sterile environment, today, both technology and business people must work together to provide for the information needs of their company. Normally, when you read about data warehousing, it is from a very technical perspective. In this book, I have combined the retail business perspective with the technical perspective. The intention is to give you a broad understanding of data warehousing.

The key objective in data warehousing is to learn from the experiences of others. I have used my retail experience, starting as an employee of Wal-Mart Stores and continuing my career as a consultant at many premier retailers worldwide, as the basis for this book. Of course, I would have never anticipated that the database I built at Wal-Mart would have become famous around the world. I am told this database is approximately 70 terabytes today. If I had known, I would have taken careful notes. I have always felt that I am a normal person who was placed in extraordinary circumstances and succeeded. The reason for my success at Wal-Mart was the desire to learn and the drive to overcome both technological and business issues. The culture of Wal-Mart is very similar. They also have a drive to overcome both technological and business issues. They learn whatever they can from whomever they can. They apply what they think fits, and discard the rest.

The founder of Wal-Mart, Sam Walton, writes in his book *Sam Walton: Made in America*, "Most everything I've done I've copied from someone else." This is a strong part of the Wal-Mart culture. As you will read in my book, even the data warehouse encapsulates that type of culture. Furthermore, Wal-Mart's drive is harder and faster than all but a few companies that I have worked with. They try something and discard it before other companies begin an analysis. It is the results of this drive to learn and deliver business solutions, as well as continuous company support and investment from the business side, that has created this large enterprise data warehouse. The construction of their huge data warehouse is not an abnormality, it is a strategic investment in technology. Other companies can learn from their culture and their database. This is why I chose the title *Data Warehousing: Using the Wal-Mart Model*.

There are many data warehouse books that were written to dive into great depths about a specific area of data warehousing, such as technical issues, project management, or case studies. With this book, I worked hard to ensure that the breadth of information flowed from chapter to chapter. Consequently, each chapter will become more complex and build upon, and reference, previous chapters. I am not going to discuss every small detail about data warehousing. Some things, like basic project management, can be obtained in great detail elsewhere. Instead, I explain the subtleties and the needs that are specific for data warehouse development.

Chapter 1 explains the concept of data warehousing and gives a brief discussion of the evolution of the technology that drives the construction of data warehouses. This first chapter may be redundant for experienced data warehouse people, but it is needed for the people wanting to learn about data warehousing, and it will explain the terms that I will use throughout the book. Chapters 2 and 3 are entitled Project Planning and Business Exploration. The project planning chapter will discuss the key project elements that need to be in place during data warehouse's development. Chapter 4 is dedicated to building a business case study as well as measuring and documenting return-on-analysis (ROI) of the data warehouse. Chapter 5 will cover integrating a data warehouse into your organization. In Chapters 6 and 7, you will find the key technology points that should be considered for development and maintenance of the data warehouse. Chapters 8 and 9 are dedicated to sharing my experiences about building the Wal-Mart data warehouse. Of course, the retail business is discussed throughout the book but Chapters 10 and 11 are dedicated to some of the successful retail data warehouse analyses that I have been directly involved in building with retailers worldwide.

I hope you can learn from this book and enjoy reading it.

## ACKNOWLEDGMENTS

First and foremost, I would like to dedicate this book to my wife, Kelly, who not only reviewed and edited this book but has supported, encouraged, and endured my career decisions all while raising a wonderful family. I would like to thank my colleagues in Compaq EMEA for their support, sponsorship, and encouragement to pursue writing this book. I would like to thank my colleagues, Lucie Dermentzuglou, Stefan Kolmar, Dave Norris, Marcel Saxer, and Rhod Smith for spending their personal time to review the draft of the manuscript and provide valuable feedback. Thank you, Joerg Plegge, for the strong support and sponsorship that opened the door for my European assignment as well as putting me in contact with the people at Lebensmittel Zeitung. From the Lebensmittel Zeitung and Deutsher Fachverlag, there are many people who have been involved, and I would like to thank them for their efforts and support of this book-writing endeavor. This has been a great learning experience for me. Thank you.

# 1

# What Is Data Warehousing?

The concept of data warehousing is really quite simple. Data from older systems is copied into a new computer system dedicated entirely to analyzing that data. Normally, the data warehouse will store a substantial amount of historical data. Users of this system are able to continuously ask or query it to retrieve data for analysis. The intent of the data analysis is to better understand what is happening, or what did happen, within a company or organization. The value of better understanding is better decision making. There is a tangible value to better decision making for every organization across all industries. Many companies have already realized that their historic data will tell a story of both good and bad decisions made in the past. They wish to learn about their mistakes and improve on their successes. If there is any theme I would like this book to have it is this: Use your data to provide information to people in your company so they can make better, informed decisions faster. When better decision making is the goal of the data warehouse, it will be successful.

Of course, building a data warehouse is not as simple as the concept. Like every other technological implementation, a data warehouse implementation needs to align with the needs and goals of the organization. Ordinary project deliverables, milestones, timelines, project management, and the like still apply to the construction of the data warehouse. Good team building is as important as selecting the best technology. It is important to understand the differences between a data warehouse application implementation and a typical functional application implementation from a technological standpoint. For maximum business impact, it is also essential to understand the changes within your organization that will be needed to achieve better decisions. I will discuss these differences in this book, but the key point here is that data warehouse development is focused solely on information delivery, whereas classical computer applications are focused on functional efficiency.

> **Good team building is as important as selecting the best technology.**

As more companies have developed data warehouses, technical terms to describe a data warehouse implementation have proliferated. Everyone in the data warehousing industry can provide a definition that typifies a specific product offering. I prefer to craft a definition from a business perspective, then find the products that fit the business. From a business perspective, a data warehouse system is also called a *decision support system* (DSS). It enables and enhances the daily decisions that must be made. Enabling better decisions can require anything from a small amount of data with a simple analysis, to a very complex combination of data and analyses. The data can be from only one data source or from a combination of hundreds. The old classical applications are very good at providing analysis from one source of data. In contrast, the real strength of building a data warehouse is the flexibility to combine the disparate data sources into a single combined system. From a business perspective, the most successful data warehousing implementation I have been involved in is called an *enterprise data warehouse*. This is a more advanced implementation of a data warehouse. The reason this is better is simple: it provides more business value than other implementations. To fully understand an enterprise data warehouse, it is important to understand the evolution of data warehousing. This chapter will describe how information usage evolved from information centers to the full-blown enterprise data warehouse. In this chapter, I will discuss the technology leading up to the data warehouse, the types of data warehouses, and the key components of a data warehouse. Finally, I have included a retail example showing how the data of a retailer is combined to make a data warehouse and an enterprise data warehouse.

> The real strength of building a data warehouse is the flexibility to combine the disparate data sources into a single combined system.

## EVOLUTION LEADING UP TO THE DATA WAREHOUSE

The computer evolution leading up to the data warehouse progressed through three basic steps in application development (Figure 1.1). The first applications implemented were for the automation of mundane tasks. Most of these systems were data entry applications that used a keyboard and a text-only, normally green, display screen. During the second step, after these tasks were automated, computers were used to control and make basic decisions. These applications still used the text-only green screens, but were used to manage, control, or change something in the business. Inventory management is a good example of a controlling application because it is not data entry but is still process-centric. The third step in application development entailed a fixed type of data presentation. This fixed presentation was informative but basically only displayed the data in the database. This data had been captured from the first two, functionally focused computer system implementations. Sometimes the data was summarized but remained primarily organized and used in the exact same way as in the functional systems. Originally, the data presentations used only the green text-only screens, but they soon began to utilize color screens. If they were "really advanced," they could display bar graphs. These latter systems were often called *executive information systems* (EIS). All three of these systems were time-critical *on-line transaction processing*

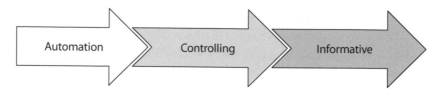

**Figure 1.1** Development of OLTP applications.

(OLTP) systems that required from the computer a very fast, normally subsecond, response time. The people that used these systems expected a fast response time, too.

## Executive Information Systems

So the first step taken toward data warehousing was the fixed presentation of data that was built on top of automation and controlling applications. These executive information systems (EIS) started simply enough but rapidly began to grow in complexity, fueled by the value of the information they provided to company executives. This happened in retailing as well as across all other industries. As executives became more dependent on the valuable information these systems provided, they requested more and more complex analyses from their information technology departments. EIS implementations began the process of combining data from different functional systems into a separate cohesive system for business executives. An EIS tied critical components from each functional system together and enabled the executive to search through the data within a defined data hierarchy and thus to better analyze the company. For example, with an EIS the executive could review the value of open orders for each department, then select a specific department to see the purchase order, and then select the purchase orders to see the line items. This concept is called a *drilldown* because the executive could move down a logical hierarchy to see an increasing level of detail. Another important advancement was the development of cross-functional "drilling" capabilities through the

> The first step taken toward data warehousing was the fixed presentation of data that was built on top of automation and controlling applications.

data horizontally. This process, now called *drill-across* functionality, means that the executive could review information across different systems. For example, he could review the value of open orders and, instead of only going down to the line item, he could also review the suppliers that would fill the open orders for that department. Next he could review the articles for which that supplier was responsible. This executive could then review other data in the open purchase orders and finish by reviewing article data, passing through the supplier information.

The options to drill down or drill across were welcome features of these first EIS implementations. This same "drilling" capability is a fundamental requirement for a data warehouse. In this example, the EIS effectively joined data from three functional systems: the purchase order system, the supplier system, and the article system. Of course, this application was still using the data with each independent application from each of the corresponding systems. The EIS application typically required subsecond computer response times, also. These very structured executive information systems were the birth of the data warehousing concept, but there was still a problem with these executive applications: they did not provide enough analytical flexibility. More was demanded.

Wal-Mart created an EIS system on the IBM platform around 1988. (For the technical people, it was built using TSO's ISPF panels and used DB2 as the database.) As I have described above, it was very structured but allowed the business executives to drill down through the data. Most of the data concerned store operations, such as this year's sales compared with last year's sales, but there was some information about article sales, mostly at the company and department levels. They could start at the company level and see an overview of the company sales. Next they could drill down through to the store figures or down to the department figures. They could also scroll down a page and across a page to view more information. Most of these figures were updated nightly.

> **Wal-Mart created an EIS system on the IBM platform around 1988. It was very structured but allowed the business executives to drill down through the data.**

## Direct SQL Access

At Wal-Mart and other companies, technology departments reluctantly began to allow the more technically oriented business people to access the data directly, using a computer access method called *structured query language* (SQL). The development of fourth-generation languages (4GL) like SQL, along with its respective report writing tools, was a tremendous step forward toward data warehousing in terms of simplicity and flexibility, which had been lacking. Allowing business people SQL access to the data was helpful to those people who had acquired some technical knowledge and needed the data in order to improve their performance. These people are sometimes called *advanced users* or *power users* because they are more adept at using technology than others. Simply put, power users are more comfortable than their colleagues when it comes to using newer technologies. In a typical company, even today power users tend to comprise a very small minority. When PCs were just beginning to be used in the workplace, normally this was where they were used first. Wal-Mart's power users began downloading data from the operational system, using SQL, into their PCs. The PC was used to perform the data analysis, mostly using the newly invented spreadsheet. The spreadsheet was a huge innovation. The PC could, with relative ease, create complex graphs that allowed executives to see obvious trends more quickly than before. Better still, there might even be a color printer attached to these PCs! Many companies still do this today. This is essentially the same process that is followed during a data warehouse project, but with a substantial ease-of-use improvement (Figure 1.2).

This was still not the ideal solution because there were problems associated with direct SQL access to the database. To begin with, business people needed to be trained properly. This was a problem because they often had no previous computer exposure, and doing the simplest things required a substantial amount of technical guidance. Once they got over the first hurdle of basic operation, they needed to understand how to retrieve the data effectively. This was important because the SQL data retrieval process could cause contention with the operational and controlling applications. For example, it was not uncommon for the EIS system to interfere with the order entry system when the execu-

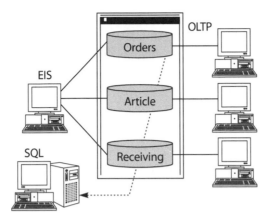

**Figure 1.2** Pre–data warehousing.

tive wanted to review outstanding purchase orders for a specific article. This request might require all records in the entire purchase order database to be read, causing the order entry application to wait or compete for the same data. The result was a slower response time for the order entry application, and this was not acceptable because the subsecond response-time expectations were clearly established for the purchase order entry system. If the response time went from under a second to two seconds, the order entry department was very quick to complain about the degrading response times.

Around 1990, there were essentially two ways to extract information using SQL at Wal-Mart. The first way was to use IBM's QMF (query management facility), and the other was a product called PC/SQL-Link by Micro Decisionware (which was later acquired by Sybase). The process for QMF was to create the SQL, run the query, save the data, export the data to a file on TSO, transfer the file to the PC, and then (finally) import the file to a spreadsheet. Because the volume of data was so large—in our view of things, at the time—this process had to be repeated many times to keep the file size small enough to ensure the file transfer would complete.

> Around 1990, there were essentially two ways to extract information using SQL at Wal-Mart.

This laborious process was simplified by PC/SQL-Link, which ran the query and performed the download automatically. But both methods required the user community to learn, create, and test their SQL. As I recall, BIM (basic inventory management) and the sales planning groups used the data most extensively. They spent a lot of time testing and waiting. It worked but it was very time consuming and laborious. The BIM group was doing year-out forecasting, and it was not uncommon for them to go through this process several times a day, for different data, and to download data for more than an entire week! Then they would start their forecasting processing!

Another problem with direct SQL access involved the format and consistency of the data. Business people were retrieving data from computer systems that was designed for data entry. These databases were not designed for high-level data analysis. This usually meant that the data was not consistent throughout a single database nor across different databases. For example, there might be some old records that the on-line system was able to identify as old because they contained zeros or low values in a specific date field. Therefore, the business people writing the SQL queries had to understand what appeared to be a strange data exception in their query. Not only was the data inconsistent, but the data types were not consistent for the same element. For the same element, the field length might be four characters in one database and six characters in another database. Once again, the people writing the queries needed to understand how to manage this transformation issue. They needed to "clean" and "transform" the data themselves.

## Data Warehouse

To solve the contention problems with the other applications, data in these systems was copied into an altogether different database, even onto a different dedicated computer. The innovative users were thus allowed complete access to the data without impacting the automation and controlling applications. Working within a separate database also gave users the chance to "clean" the data. This was essentially the birth of data warehousing, as there is one very clear differentiation between a data warehouse and an EIS: the data warehouse database is completely separate from the functional systems. This means that data is copied from the functional OLTP systems, cleaned, transformed, and duplicated into

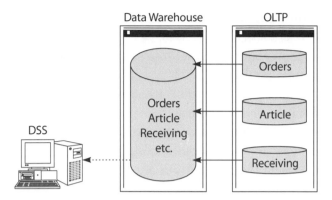

**Figure 1.3**  Data warehouse.

the data warehouse database. The data in that database can be designed to provide unrestricted read access for informational purposes (Figure 1.3). One factor that prevented this development earlier was the high cost of hardware. As the cost of hardware declined, however, the idea of utilizing a separate database for decision support became much more practical and affordable.

Early on, there were two main benefits of data warehousing:

1. no contention with the functional systems, and
2. historic data could be accumulated.

On the first point, a query (or request of information) would not interfere with the operational functions no matter how much data was required. There can be no contention with the OLTP systems when a copy of the data is being used. Secondly, the functional systems typically maintained only a limited amount of data (mostly because of performance considerations), whereas the data warehouse could maintain historic information. This encouraged the development of applications to show the graphical representation of historic trends—without the fear of impacting the OLTP applications.

Another interesting differentiation identified only later concerned response-time requirements. There were no subsecond response-time requirements for a data warehouse. Because the business people did not operate under the same procedural pressures as those using the OLTPs, they could afford to wait for an answer. They wanted accurate answers to their queries, so speed was secondary.

One final point about the difference between functional systems and data warehouses. Unlike the OLTP systems that simply displayed data values in their database, the data warehouse was used to *analyze* data from one database or many databases. This type of processing is now known as *on-line analytical processing* (OLAP).

Now that you are beginning to understand the concept of a data warehouse, it starts to get slightly more complicated because there are different types of data warehouses. I think the technology people began to make this simple concept more complex so they could maintain control of the technology! While I am joking, of course, technical discussions regarding types of data warehouses can be confusing to business people, who prefer to remain focused on business solutions. Still, in order to follow the discussions in this book, you need to know that there are now several types of data warehouses. There are four commonly used terms to describe the functionality of data warehouses: *data mart, data warehouse, enterprise data warehouse*, and *operational data store*. There are also other industry-related terms, such as *data mining*, which essentially implies there is a specialized function performed on a data warehouse database. These four types, however, are the most common.

## Data Mart

A data mart is a data warehouse but for a smaller subset of data elements. Most companies start their data warehouse project by building a data mart first. Using retail terms, I would call these the "convenience stores" of data warehousing. They normally comprise smaller sets, or a single subject area, of data designed for a special group of users. They may or may not be directly related to a larger data warehouse. They certainly can complement and enhance the functionality of a larger data warehouse.

> **Most companies start their data warehouse project by building a data mart first.**

They can be dependent on another data mart or data warehouse, or they can be independent. The fact that they contain a smaller subject area than a data warehouse does not mean they are cheaper or easier to build. A data mart can be just as complex and as time consuming to build as a data warehouse. A company can build many data marts, one for each subset of data. That would add complexity but can sometimes improve query performance and provide faster response times.

The degree of complexity also depends on how you "slice" the subject areas. If you consider the data in the data warehouse as a cube, you can slice the cube in many different ways. Normally, companies slice the data horizontally or vertically. For a retailer, a store might have a data mart with all data that that single store needs but no data about other stores. To find information about another store would require querying the other store's data mart or even the corporate data warehouse. Another way to slice this retail data is by department. Each department could have information on that department's articles and for all stores. This would work nicely for a group of buyers responsible for a specific department. They would have all the information regarding their department. If they wanted information from another department, they would have to query that other department's data mart or query the corporate data warehouse. It is important not to confuse volume of data with a smaller subset of data elements. As you might have already guessed, the data volume of a data mart can be quite large depending on how the data is sliced. You can build a data mart only to support the POS (point-of-sale) transaction basket-level analysis and this could be a substantial volume of data, but only one subject area.

We built many small data marts at Wal-Mart. The first was in IBM DB2, and the second was in IBM's VM/SQL. At the time, these systems could easily manage the smaller data volumes, but larger volumes of data were difficult to handle. Also, the technology department did not think much of these historical systems, considering them a waste of expensive disk space. When the new massively parallel processing (MPP) technology (the Teradata system) was introduced and used, it easily enabled Wal-Mart to manage all of the detailed article information in a single database. So, they built another data mart—a big one. The POS table at Wal-Mart was originally about 1.2 billion records. After we learned we could easily manage this very large amount of data, we began adding more smaller sets of related data. Within a half year it was turned into a data warehouse with several tables over 500 million rows. As I will describe later, the ability to analyze this volume of data made

Wal-Mart acutely aware of the need to effectively manage their global and local supply chain.

## A data mart should be built to solve a business problem, not a technical problem.

Sometimes a data mart, as opposed to a data warehouse, is created because of a real or perceived technical limitation, such as a large volume of data. This is not a good reason to build a data mart. Like a data warehouse, a data mart should be built to solve a business problem, not a technical problem. When multiple data marts are created solely in order to manage a large volume of data, unfortunately, the business usually suffers. There are other, proven technologies that can manage large data sets. I will discuss this technology issue more in depth in Chapter 6.

One good technical point about data marts is that they can bring data closer to the group that needs it. By this I mean there can be faster access to the data and fewer restrictions on it. For example, you can use the larger, more powerful data warehouse to calculate summary information and then copy that summary data to the data mart. The user may not even realize that the data mart exists, except for the reduced wait times. The wait times can be reduced because the data is closer to the user. That is, the data can be reformatted for a specific analysis, the data volume is much smaller, and there may be fewer users logged onto the data mart. In fact, using data marts is a great way to "off-load" requests from the data warehouse. For repetitive requests such as end-of-week analyses, this can substantially reduce the workload from the data warehouse.

If business units within a single company are substantially different, then constructing a data mart might be necessary. For example, a manufacturer may build a product as well as run an independent transportation company to distribute its products. That manufacturer may distribute another manufacturer's products, too. Together they complement their businesses but operate almost independently of each other. Because they have substantially different information needs, they may each need their own data mart or even their own data warehouse. Sometimes company security is the driving force that requires a data mart to be built. I have seen managers force distinct data boundaries within franchise organizations as well as in privately owned orga-

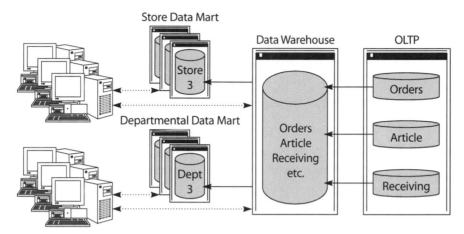

**Figure 1.4**  Data mart.

nizations. Some franchisees do not want other franchisees to see their information because they may be perceived as direct competitors. Some privately owned organizations don't want their financial results made public, so they allow only a few people access to all of their figures.

As with many things, the data mart's biggest asset is also its main flaw. And the biggest problem with data marts is that they are compartmentalized. Only one group of people can access that information. If that group wants additional data, it must be gathered from another data mart or data warehouse and brought to their data mart. When this begins to happen you can end up having multiple data warehouses to manage. My advice is to wait to build your data marts until after you have constructed the data warehouse. Then the flow of data becomes much less complex. It flows from the functional systems into the data warehouse and then on to the data marts (Figure 1.4). With this data flow strategy, you can easily and relatively quickly build data marts for those special groups of people with similar needs as well as maintain a centralized enterprisewide data warehouse. All of this should be done transparently to the user community. They should all be using the same graphical user interface

**Wait to build your data marts after you have constructed the data warehouse. Then the flow of data becomes much less complex.**

(GUI) workstation with which they are already familiar. They should not know that they are going to the data warehouse or the data mart to retrieve their data.

### Enterprise Data Warehouse

My favorite type of data warehouse is an enterprise data warehouse. An enterprise data warehouse is a data warehouse built for the entire (enterprisewide) company. For reasons I hope to clarify in this book, I believe the enterprise data warehouse provides the highest return on invest-ment (ROI) and most informational value to a com-pany, particularly if that company is centrally man-aged. An enterprise data warehouse is usually built at the central corporate office of a company. The ini-tial construction is normally a data mart and grows into a data warehouse. The difference is that the construction continues endlessly. An enterprise data warehouse grows with the organization. As the peo-ple in the organization need and require better in-formation faster, the enterprise data warehouse be-comes the place to maintain that data.

> **The enterprise data ware-house provides the highest return on investment (ROI) and most informational value to a company, particularly if that company is centrally managed.**

There are two essential features for building an enterprise data warehouse:

1. information from the entire company must reside in the data warehouse, and
2. newly created data is fed back into the operational systems.

The first point means that new data needs to be continually added to the data warehouse. Building on the retail example, a retailer creating a data warehouse will normally start with point-of-sale (POS) data, pur-chase order (PO) data, store receipt data, and inventory data. Then they will give a GUI application to their users so they can do their own anal-yses (Figure 1.5). But this is only the beginning. Other related subject areas must be continually added. It is a relatively easy task to add an-other subject area like marketing campaigns. For example, the market-ing group can benefit by directly measuring the results of a campaign

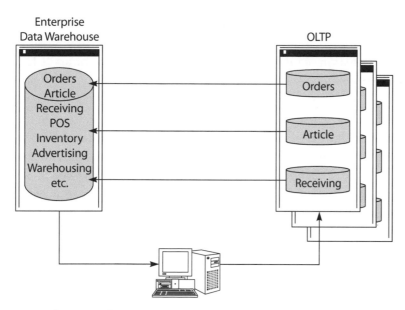

**Figure 1.5** Enterprise data warehouse.

by studying the article sales. The logistics department can use the data to determine a more accurate demand for specific articles during different times in the year. The buying organization can use historic information during price and quantity negotiations with a supplier. Even the department manager can use the data to locate articles in other stores. Wal-Mart has continued to add data since 1989. By now, I would guess that 99% of their data elements are maintained in their enterprise data warehouse. Many companies will stop development of the data warehouse after they have completed the first or second phase. The benefits that were achieved in the first implementation may have been large but I believe that continual developments can lead to

> **Wal-Mart has continued to add data since 1989. By now, about 99% of their data elements are maintained in their enterprise data warehouse.**

much greater results and return on investment. I will continue to discuss various aspects of an enterprise data warehouse throughout this book to help clarify the added benefits.

Regarding the second point—that newly created data from the data warehouse will be fed into other systems—this does not need to happen instantaneously but in a continuous loop. This is called a *closed-loop application.* The transaction mix in these applications can be a combination of OLTP and OLAP. (When the OLAP and OLTP need to be very fast or subsecond, this begins to define an *operational data store* described in the next section.) Continuing the closed-loop concept, planning applications probably present the best examples for understanding how to use data from the data warehouse to feed production systems. For instance, many retailers will build a business plan based on actual sales and the projected increase that is needed to reach a goal. By using the data in the data warehouse to develop an accurate representation of current movement, you can feed the planning system with detailed data and work from there—in other words, "bottom up" planning. This will not eliminate the "top down" planning; the two will be joined together in the middle. Let's say a department must increase profits by 20%. In the planning process, should they decide to buy more articles into a category, or can they manage this by improving the in-stock position over last year? If they know the historic sales and in-stock figures, the planning can be driven in an entirely new direction. This type of planning is normally not practical without a data warehouse.

Another area that can benefit from this combination of using data and creating data is new article introduction. Many retailers create, by educated guesswork, the initial allocation of a new article. Normally, this allocation is based on store size: larger stores get more, while smaller stores get less. Using the sales and inventory data of a similar product, a more precise allocation can be determined, with an allocation for every store, instead of the typical 10 groups of stores based on size. This is an allocation based on customer demand. When the proper store-level allocation is determined, the data is fed directly into the PO system at the most granular level—the store. The order is placed with a clearly defined store allocation.

The drawbacks of building an enterprise data warehouse are typically the cost and the complexity. Costs can generally be broken down into hardware, software, and people. The cost of the technology—hardware and software—is more of a timing issue because it is being reduced daily. For example, the first Wal-Mart data warehouse database cost around $20 million; it had 169 Intel-286 processors with over 600 gigabytes of disk space. Now, eight years later, a similar sized database will cost only about $750,000. This newer database may even be more powerful! Of course, an exact dollar-for-dollar price/performance comparison would be difficult because of the dramatic changes in technology. This certainly implies that the hardware cost is a relative issue that will decrease over time. This does not mean you should wait to build your data warehouse. Building a data warehouse should be based on the short- and long-term ROI. Software will follow a similar trend. This can actually be a good thing for companies that have not yet invested in data warehouse technology. They have the opportunity to implement with newer and more powerful technology than the early adapters of data warehousing. The technology has been more thoroughly tested, and it is now easier to implement a data warehouse solution. The complexity issue is very different. With complexity comes an added cost in human resources. This means you will have to hire or contract people to help build and maintain this database. This can be very expensive. Unlike the technology costs, the human resource costs continue to rise. Using the techniques that I will describe later in this book, the added costs of an enterprise data warehouse can be justified by measuring the ROI a year after implementation.

## Operational Data Store

There is another type of data warehouse called an *operational data store* (ODS). An ODS is a data warehouse that requires faster response time and update capabilities. Normally, it is used not so much to analyze historical data but to present an up-to-date, instant snapshot. The goal of the ODS is to be able to view and maintain large volumes of data, and when the data from a vast ODS database is viewed, it is typically updated. A good example of an ODS application is a customer call center—a database that can provide an instant view of all information about the customer who is on the phone (or the Internet) and the ability to be updated with the information from the current call. An ODS is a combination of analyses and updating. The transactions are very quick, and the volume of transactions is typically very high. From a business perspective, there is a fine line between an ODS and an enterprise data warehouse. Like a data mart, an ODS could certainly become an enterprise data warehouse over time. An ODS could also feed the data warehouse.

### Data Warehouse Is a Tool

While I have identified some types of data warehouses, I would not encourage you to become obsessed with the technical aspects of building a data mart, an ODS, or an enterprise data warehouse. Like Wal-Mart, you should be obsessed with providing business value to your company. The reason to build a data warehouse is to have the ability to make better decisions faster based on information using current and historic data. A data warehousing application can present data in a way that will provide information to individuals so they can make better decisions. If you can focus on the business decisions that need to be made and deliver the information that is needed to make better decisions, you should be able to call the system whatever you like. Then your data warehouse will naturally evolve into one of these. Focus on delivering the business solutions, and after some time, you will know which type of data warehouse you have built. A data warehouse is just a tool to enable better decision making.

> Like Wal-Mart, you should be obsessed with providing business value to your company.

From the purist perspective, only the database that is used to maintain this information is the data warehouse. But in reality there is more to a data warehouse than the database. There are software applications that will maintain the database and software applications that will present the data. There is also the *metadata*. Metadata is data that describes the data and usually constitutes another database. I simply call these things *data warehouse tools*. Every data warehouse project needs them. My philosophy on these tools has always been to find one that works and buy it. They are relatively inexpensive. Just buy what you need as you are building. You will need an evaluation period, but it should not be longer than a few weeks. Next year there will be a better tool. If you spend too much time waiting for the ideal tool to present itself, it will have been wasted time. You are not focusing on the business needs if you are in a constant evaluation period. Most companies I have worked with do not require a perfect tool. They require a tool that will solve their business problem. If you cannot buy what you need, then you need to plan on building it. The database itself is the tool to store the large volume of data. Loading tools will need to be purchased or created to maintain the data. The GUI tool will present the data as information to a person. Finally, the metadata will most likely have to be built. The person that will use these information tools can be a customer, an employee, or even a prospect. With the new Internet World Wide Web technology, the user can be just about anybody anywhere in the world. Publishing on the Web is simply another presentation tool. The business community will use all of these tools to better understand their own businesses. Therefore, keep the tool evaluation time frames short, buy what you can, and build what you need.

> **Keep the tool evaluation time frames short, buy what you can, and build what you need.**

## APPLYING THE DATA WAREHOUSE CONCEPT

Now that we have defined the data warehouse, we need to understand the difference between classical systems application development and a data warehouse application development. Classical application systems are based on functional processes. These functional processes are usually created to simplify, mimic, or streamline an existing functional process, usually a manually intensive process. Normally, the investment to build such a system is recovered by cost reductions. These cost reductions are usually based on time and/or material cost. Let us use an order entry system as an example. A functional system might be built to eliminate the time required to issue a purchase order. Let's say that a purchase order requires a minimum of two approvals, unless it is over $300,000, then it requires a third signature. This paper process takes approximately five days. With the "new" electronic order entry system, this can be reduced to only two days. This might be because there is no longer the delay of interoffice mail. Another benefit might be that the system can immediately determine if a third signature is needed and request approval concurrently. This simple example shows how computer technology has been used in the past and is still used today. The return on investment, in this case, is to reduce the costs (three days of time) of creating a purchase order. An additional benefit is the standardization and documentation of purchase orders.

A data warehouse application, by contrast, is about making better decisions. In addition to reducing cost, the business can actually earn money with a data warehouse implementation. This poses an interesting challenge for most information technology departments because they are used to delivering systems that reduce costs. How can a data warehouse earn money? Let's use an inventory management example. A merchandise manager, through the use of the data warehouse, is able to graphically view inventory levels, sales, and deliveries. Reviewing a historic chart (see Figure 1.6), she can see that the order frequency for a particular article is too long because there is a continual out-of-stock situation happening. The clear spikes and valleys of this chart, as opposed to smooth curves, visually illustrate an inventory flow problem. Knowing this, she takes action to increase the order review frequency from 14 days to 7 days, orders are placed more frequently, and the consequence is increased sales and profits! For retailers, this is why you want to implement a data warehouse. Of course, there are opportunities to reduce costs too. For example, the merchandise manager can identify stores that are overstocked with an article and move some of those articles into stores that are understocked, thereby reducing, delaying, or eliminating the markdown for that article. This action may simply reduce markdowns, but it could also increase sales and profits.

**At Wal-Mart, they did not have item-level sales information for each store available on-line, only on magnetic tape. The historical presentation of this information at the store/item/date level was also new.**

Another important way that a data warehouse distinguishes itself is by providing the company with new information. It is important to understand the difference between data and information. Data are the facts that are maintained in a database. Information is the palatable transformation and presentation of that data into a form that communicates a trend or concept. These are newly identified trends revealed by old data. Ultimately, the goal is that the business people will be able to make better, faster business decisions by reviewing the newly created information. In the previous example, the inventory

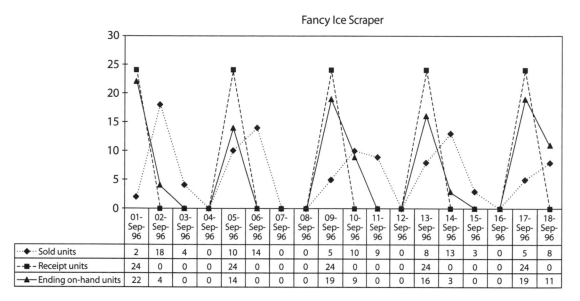

Fancy Ice Scraper

| | 01-Sep-96 | 02-Sep-96 | 03-Sep-96 | 04-Sep-96 | 05-Sep-96 | 06-Sep-96 | 07-Sep-96 | 08-Sep-96 | 09-Sep-96 | 10-Sep-96 | 11-Sep-96 | 12-Sep-96 | 13-Sep-96 | 14-Sep-96 | 15-Sep-96 | 16-Sep-96 | 17-Sep-96 | 18-Sep-96 |
|---|---|---|---|---|---|---|---|---|---|---|---|---|---|---|---|---|---|---|
| ◆ Sold units | 2 | 18 | 4 | 0 | 10 | 14 | 0 | 0 | 5 | 10 | 9 | 0 | 8 | 13 | 3 | 0 | 5 | 8 |
| ■ Receipt units | 24 | 0 | 0 | 0 | 24 | 0 | 0 | 0 | 24 | 0 | 0 | 0 | 24 | 0 | 0 | 0 | 24 | 0 |
| ▲ Ending on-hand units | 22 | 4 | 0 | 0 | 14 | 0 | 0 | 0 | 19 | 9 | 0 | 0 | 16 | 3 | 0 | 0 | 19 | 11 |

**Figure 1.6**
Sample inventory movement chart.

figures may have been available to the merchandising manager in another system or on tape. At Wal-Mart, they did not have item-level sales information for each store available on-line, only on magnetic tape. The historical presentation of this information at the store/item/date level was also new. The new information could be the presentation of the data in a graph instead of as a string of numbers. This is new presentation functionality, and it can be a very powerful tool. The new information could be easier to obtain, in three minutes on-line instead of five weeks for tape. The new information could be the combination of different systems, like sales, inventory, and purchase orders. It may actually be new data! Even better, the new data may be created from the data warehouse and then fed into another system. A successful data warehouse implementation will provide the decision makers with new information and better information than is currently available in other systems.

I have often been asked to define the difference between a data warehouse and statistics. A statistical analysis will show the same trends that the data warehouse will show. That is true. A statistical analysis will not cost much to produce. That is true, too. The difference is time, flexibility, and margin of error. A statistical report normally requires a statistician with a special skill at producing these accurate reports. To build a new statistical report requires that you work with this person to create the report. Once the report is defined, it has to be created. After it is created, two weeks later, it will answer the business question. When you have that question answered, then you can move on to the next 20 questions, 40 weeks later. Even worse, if your statistician has a vacation planned, then you will have to wait for his return. Statistical analysis lacks quick replication. A data warehouse, by design, should eliminate the time lag. The business people can define the reports they wish to see with an easy-to-use application. The reports will return the exact figures, with plus or minus *zero* margin of error. The response should be the same day, so that the next 20 questions can be answered in that same day. Persons with specialized statistical degrees are no longer needed for simple analyses. They can focus on the more complex algorithms, such as automatic replenishment analysis. When business people are given the flexibility to create their own reports, they will be able to get accurate answers, with no margin of error, to their questions so they can make better decisions faster.

We should apply what has been discussed so far to a retail situation. Just before a company decides to build a data warehouse, the situation in the information technology department is fairly typical. They have tons of data from various systems. They have thousands of paper reports, generated daily, weekly, and monthly. The most current information is usually maintained for only one to three months. It is accessible on-line via OLTP screens that require a key value to be input. Information beyond the current quarter is on tape. This can be extracted and formatted into a new report, but it takes about three weeks before the report will be finished. The data that is available is summarized data. For a retailer there is sales information, but it is summarized to department, store, and company level for this period compared to last period. It is still difficult to put data from different systems together on a single report. Usually, there are no article sales transactions by store or basket-level information. Most of the time, this is the situation that drives a retailer to begin construction of a data warehouse. This situation was no different at Wal-Mart.

By the way, for those of you who are not saving your data, particularly retailers, I have some advice. Save your data for at least 65 weeks back. This will give you a full quarter-to-quarter comparison, this year and last year for the same quarter. Saving it for two and a quarter years back is ideal. Particularly save your point-of-sales (POS) data. Tape backup is just fine; make two copies. I am often shocked that a retailer will discard this data, but it does happen. Retail companies are notorious for not keeping their data. For some reason, they don't realize the data will become very valuable. I am sure that other companies in other industries do not maintain historical data, either. Save the data! The tapes are cheap. The data is invaluable. It might add 2% of your total sales to your profit someday. Pay

**Save your data for at least 65 weeks back. Saving it for two and a quarter years back is ideal.**

the $1000 one-time cost for the tapes. You won't regret it when you begin to use the data.

During the construction of a data warehouse there are three main areas to concentrate on: the database maintenance, the user interface, and the supporting infrastructure. I will talk more in depth about these in later chapters (Chapters 6 and 7), but it is important that you understand the general concepts now. The database maintenance is the part of the process where the data elements are mapped and copied from the operational functional systems into the data warehouse system. The user interface is usually developed concurrently with the database maintenance process. Basically, it provides the access to the database, transformation of this data into information, and the presentation of that information. This user interface is what the end user will see and use. This may be a graphical user interface (GUI), or it may simply be a Web browser. Nowadays it certainly involves a PC. The last part is a very technical part, the technological infrastructure. This is everything you need to capture, move, and use data and processes of the data warehouse. For example, if you are using a Web browser as the data warehouse presentation tool, you will need an intranet infrastructure that can support it. Building strength in these three areas is very important for the successful implementation of a data warehouse. All of these processes are typically performed concurrently.

Most retailers start building a data warehouse by building a data mart. They usually focus on these subject areas: POS, orders, store receipts, and inventory. They take the data from the operational systems and bring that into another database, the data warehouse database (see

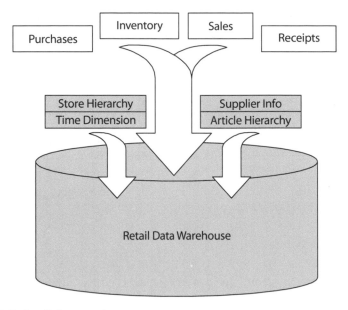

**Figure 1.7** Retail data warehouse.

Figure 1.7). They will maintain this data down to the store and article level. The time frame is usually down to a specific date, but it might be by week, depending on the retailer. Of course, some retailers go directly to the transaction log (TLOG) level of every cash register in every store. Usually, however, a single day is enough detail for the first implementation. They will have this data available in the data mart for either 65, 104, or 117 full weeks. There might be slightly more data, 69 instead of 65 weeks, to make full financial, merchandising, or marketing month-to-month comparisons. They will also bring copies of the supporting data structures into the database. These are typically hierarchies such as the article hierarchy, store or organizational hierarchy, supplier information, and the time dimensions. Determining the length of time to retain this data is a challenge for many companies because they have a tremendous amount of data. For Wal-Mart, Sam's Club had fewer stores but had more detailed information

**Determining the length of time to retain this data is a challenge for many companies. Regardless of the volume, it should all be maintained on tape.**

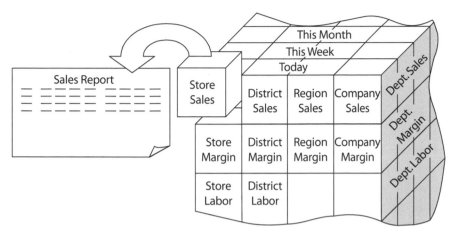

**Figure 1.8**  Data element selection.

than the Wal-Mart stores. They had a customer dimension that was not yet available to the Wal-Mart division. For example, because of their membership card, Sam's Club systems maintained records of every customer and what they purchased. Because of this, Sam's Club required almost as much disk space as Wal-Mart, even though they had fewer than one-quarter the number of Wal-Mart stores. If you then consider the information that is available on the Internet today, and the fact that every click can be recorded, the volume of data is staggering. Regardless of the volume, it should all be maintained on tape.

After the database for your data mart is built, you now have to provide access to that database. There are many ways a user can access the database, and this is where the different presentation tools come into play. Without going into much detail, the user is given access to the data, normally through a PC workstation. The user will be able to define a report by adding and removing data elements from a list. He will be able to graph the information, when practical. This should be a simple but effective application (see sample reports in Chapters 10 and 11). The functionality is like a Rubik's cube; users can change the analysis at will and turn it into a different analysis (Figure 1.8). They should be able to see and select multiple dimensions of the data and analyze those dimensions. It is difficult to show more than two dimensions on paper so the sample reports in Chapters 10 and 11 cannot easily show this type of flexibility. As mentioned earlier, the first groups of users are usually the "power users" because they are a bit more comfortable with the technology; then access is given to other users methodically. There are the usual training and technology issues that will be associated with any technology rollout.

What comes next? Many retailers will stop at this point and wait. Don't misunderstand, you can achieve a tremendous degree of success after implementing just this phase. But the benefits do not stop at the data mart. In fact, this is just the beginning. The more aggressive retailers will measure their success, exploit what they have already done, and continue to build the database. They will add new subject areas: marketing, store operations, merchandising, transportation, price management, seasonal analyses, and so forth. With each subject area added, a corresponding analysis becomes available for the users. When new subject areas are in place, they will have a data warehouse.

Aggressive retailers (like Wal-Mart) will not stop there; they will continue until all company data is available for analysis. They will build an enterprise data warehouse. They give all this information to their internal (buyers) and external users (suppliers) to exploit and demand measurable improvement. Today, very few companies have actually reached this point because it is difficult and costly. Many retailers will never reach this point because they will never measure their return on investment (ROI) and, therefore, cannot justify and obtain additional investments. I will discuss the importance of measuring ROI and the timing in Chapter 4.

Another important theme arises after the enterprise data warehouse is built: the data warehouse is actually used to feed the functional operational systems. A cyclical process between the data warehouse system and the functional operational systems begins. It usually starts with planning. For example, data is extracted from the data warehouse for planning purposes, and this data is processed and fed into the functional planning system. A retailer will be planning the basic articles for spring and will extract last year's actual figures, apply planned percentage increases on profit or sales, adjust inventory purchases for over- and understock situations, and then feed this data into the merchandise management planning system. Most of this is done by building on what already exists within the database and therefore requires small

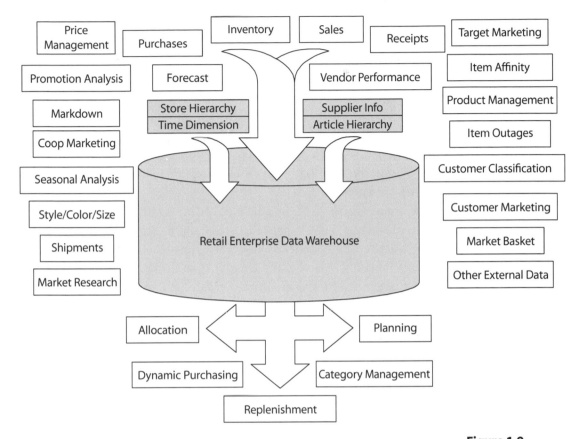

**Figure 1.9**
Retail enterprise
data warehouse.

steps with minor additional work. When all the data is available, the development cycle can be substantially reduced.

As you can see in Figure 1.9, there are many more ways to use and exploit the data in the enterprise data warehouse to improve the operation of existing systems. This concept of *data agility* is a huge benefit of having an enterprise data warehouse.

## BEYOND THE ENTERPRISE DATA WAREHOUSE

You can improve on the enterprise data warehouse concept still further when you integrate it into your functional operational systems. This means there would be no distinctive difference between your decision support system and your other functional systems. The various types of systems would effectively be merged into one unified system. I know of no terminology to describe this yet, but perhaps *unified data system* (UDS) is a good name for this concept. A UDS is a combination of an operational data store, an enterprise data warehouse, and functional operational systems. For this to be created, the database and processes must be designed as one system. This means that the real-time OLTP applications and historical DSS applications are intentionally designed and integrated to work together on the same logical system. The database (physically and logically) is also designed to closely reflect the business operations.

The challenge in creating a UDS is in integrating the current view and the historical view of data in the database. Both need to be maintained together. The historical view refers to data as it existed prior to an event (such as a customer's change of address), as opposed to data that is current as of a specified time or date. When these two views are integrated, it eliminates the need to pull data from the operational system and into another system (as in a data warehouse).

To integrate current views and historical views based on events, applications must be designed with an understanding of the potential changes to the data in the database. That is, a database record cannot simply be modified; the change must be documented. This means that instead of a simple update transaction, the old record must be marked as historical and a new active record must be created. To properly track changes, all database records need a timestamp, a transaction sequence code, a reason code, and the manipulator code. The timestamp obviously indicates the date and time of the change. The sequence code links all the changes together. The reason code defines why the record was changed. Finally, the manipulator code tells you who or what changed the record. These key fields in your design allow you to determine who changed what data element, when, and why. For the OLTP systems that need the most up-to-date record, the largest value for a transaction sequence code or the use of a null date value in the timestamp can identify the most current record. This should not be confused with *database recovery*. Database recovery is used to recover the database to a consistent and stable state. Although a UDS could be used to recover a single record to a specific point in time, its value lies in integration and future analysis of the data, not the recovery of data.

As an example, let us suppose an individual moves to another city and submits an address change. The address cannot be updated to the new address without regard for the old data in the database. Even though the old address is not important for most of the systems, which use only the current view, the old address must be retained for the historical view. The old record must be read from the database, but the data field should not be updated with the new address. When the address is changed, the old record must be updated with a new timestamp, transaction sequence code, reason code, and a manipulator code. Next, a new record, using the values in the old record and the new address, is inserted into the database. The new record has a null timestamp, a transaction sequence code equal to the previous transaction sequence code plus one, a reason code, and the manipulator code. This process may seem laborious, but it is the only way to tightly integrate both current and historical information into a UDS. Although your company may not need this event today, it could become very important to your company in the future (e.g., for a historical trend analysis of potential sales revenue that could be moving away!).

I have no intention of implying that you can get by with only one computer system. There will always be remote independent systems. Retailers will always need to have local computers in each store. The benefit of independent continuous operations is obvious. However, the data in these autonomous systems needs to be managed. The UDS can provide another benefit regarding remote data management. When you have integrated the messaging concept (which I describe in Chapter 7), current and historical transactions can be easily passed to, and tracked through, remote systems. Not only can the UDS push and pull the data, but the autonomous system can push and pull the data. The transaction sequence code, created from the source of the change, is essential to enable this type of synchronization. Both the UDS and autonomous systems can identify missing transactions and request one, all, or a range of transactions from the other systems. With a UDS and the messaging concept in place, moving and sharing data becomes less cumbersome and almost easy.

Let's look at how seamless data integration can work for a retailer. When a customer asks a clerk for a specific product (which may be out of stock, wrong color, wrong size, etc.), normally the clerk can check in the back or see if the product is on order, either physically or with a so-phisticated handheld radio-frequency scanner. With a UDS, the clerk would check the local system within the store to determine the inventory status for this article. If there was no inventory locally, she could access the central UDS to determine the closest store with the inventory (a neighborhood store, a warehouse, the supplier, a store in another city, a store in another state, and even a store in another country). Once that article was located, the clerk could do one of several things: sell the article to the customer and have it delivered directly to his home, add that article to the local assortment, order the article, or allocate that article for transportation to the store.

This concept requires that the different systems be unified and integrated seamlessly—a UDS. Today, I know of only a handful of companies that are even close to having this type of systems integration. The main reason companies do not integrate their current and historical systems is manageability and price/performance of the technology. As the technology gets faster, cheaper, and easier to use, there will be many more companies creating this totally integrated system in the future. I would encourage your company to have a similar vision for your data warehouse.

# 2

# Project Planning

At the beginning of a data warehouse project, companies are always asking for guidance. What should they expect? How should they proceed? How is it different? It is important to understand what will be happening in the data warehouse project and, where possible, to plan and allocate time for it. I have divided this chapter into two main sections, "Before You Start" and "Planning for the Project Life Cycle." The first section is dedicated to answering those "first-step" questions. The second part will highlight the process and the typical human resource requirement for the three phases of a data warehouse construction. I want to emphasize that you do not have to have every issue solved before you can begin. Each company will have its own hurdles to jump before it can begin building the data warehouse. This chapter is not designed to put hurdles in front of a data warehouse project that is currently being implemented. If you have started your implementation and have not completed all of these points, you should not stop the project.

## BEFORE YOU START

I have created a list of critical success factors. These are important for the long-term success of a data warehouse implementation. When you have all of these clearly defined, you should be in good shape to move into the construction phase. This is not an exhaustive list, but a practical list of points that need to be addressed prior to implementing a data warehouse. The critical points to consider before building a data warehouse are:

1. Clear focus on the business
2. Business sponsorship
3. Long-term vision
4. Short-term plan
5. Assigning a responsible leader
6. Effective communication
7. Providing something new
8. Partnership planning

These key planning points exist in every successful data warehouse implementation. You will notice that there are no technical requirements. The technical requirements will become much more important during the construction phase. Here, we are talking about having a successful launch of the data warehouse. You need no technology to have a successful launch. There must be a business need. The data warehouse project needs to be aligned with that business need.

### Clear Focus on the Business

Before you begin construction of a data warehouse, you need to align the data warehouse implementation with your business strategies. This is not a difficult concept to grasp, but it is very important. A business strategy might be to "improve the customer base by 10%." Therefore, the new data warehouse needs to be aligned with that strategy. This is the kind of strategy to which a data warehouse could make a substantial contribution. There are some business objectives, however, that a data warehouse will not impact in a substantial way. For example, a strategy of "99% article scanning at the cash register" might not fit in a data warehouse implementation although it may give the company an advantage over their competitors. In that case perhaps resources should be dedicated to delivering that instead of a data warehouse. However, you might just find that the strategy is complementary to a data warehouse concept. In the POS example, the data produced from scanning is very valuable, but the company must be ready to use this data. When you have aligned the data warehouse with a business strategy, the business users will be the driving force behind the successful implementation.

The more successful data warehouse will be constructed after business benefits have been illustrated and active corporate sponsorship has begun. A data warehouse implementation can stagnate because it lacks the support of the company. Such data warehouses tend not to grow or enhance the business like other implementations. I see this where the focus of the data warehouse is not aligned with the business but rather is based solely on a technical perspective—for example, where the technology department knew there was value, so they built it. Data warehouses can be built like this, but these implementations take much longer to become an integral part of the organization.

Misconceived alignments can also cause problems. Forcing the data warehouse to align with a company goal that does not really fit well can become an issue during implementation. Sometimes this misalignment causes the data warehouse to be used for functional business processing and not for providing information. Take, for example, a case where the data warehouse is tied to a functional process that initially had no response-time requirements; as the business comes to depend on the data warehouse, a subsecond response time becomes mandatory. As I mentioned in Chapter 1, the management of the functional systems will force the people that want information off of the system. So don't force a misfit application onto the data warehouse implementation. This is easy if you keep the first priority and align the data warehouse to provide only data analyses. Keep in mind that the data warehouse is a historical representation of the company's actions and, in most cases, data will be added but not updated. The point is that if you align the data warehouse with business strategies that require data analyses, you will be able to get involvement from the entire company. When the company goal is the same for everyone and the data warehouse complements the goal and aligns with the business, then the entire company will be charging in the same direction. The entire company will pull together to ensure the successful implementation of the data warehouse. This important point will guarantee a good start and will enable a successful implementation.

> **When the company goal is the same for everyone and the data warehouse complements the goal and aligns with the business, then the entire company will be charging in the same direction.**

Wal-Mart certainly focused on the business. They built a prototype system with a much smaller computer system than would be needed in the real implementation. After this was functioning, they built a business case based on the success of the prototype. Because the system would be extremely large and therefore more expensive, they also had to obtain business sponsorship. They obtained the sponsorship and the additional funding of the Wal-Mart board of directors using the prototype and the business case. For Wal-Mart, this ensured the data warehouse was clearly aligned with the business.

## Business Sponsorship

After you have determined there is an alignment between the data warehouse and the business strategy, you need to find one or more business sponsors. This person (or persons) will set the data warehouse objectives and confirm the acceptable delivery of those objectives. Normally, this does not come from the IT department but from another part of the business. If you have found the proper alignment of the data warehouse within your organization, then finding this sponsor should not be too difficult. Ideally, business sponsors will pay for all or part of the construction of the data warehouse project. This means that they will be very interested in the outcome of the implementation. This also means that they will be more willing to contribute the needed human resources. They will provide the feedback necessary to guide the data warehouse implementation through the initial construction and into the business. I can be so bold to say that if you have no business sponsor, you will have no data warehouse.

Sponsoring the data warehouse is an important undertaking for the business executive. He will need to be involved in the project every week, at a minimum. Team members of the business sponsor will be involved even more. An important characteristic of the business sponsor is skill in decision making. He will be involved in the decision-making process. He

> ## If you have no business sponsor, you will have no data warehouse.

must make decisions rapidly regarding the business rules. These business rules will be documented and applied to the data warehouse. In every implementation, there are times where something must be decided quickly. A good retail example is defining a formula such as percent increase in sales. This concept is relatively easy until you must decide the *exact* formula for all situations. For example, say you have received only a partial percentage of the sales data for an article in a particular week and you need to determine the weekly percent increase over last year. Do you calculate it using week-to-date, or leave spaces, or something else? These requirements could change the application substantially, causing additional work and even a delay in the project. This is an important part of the business sponsor's job. He needs to understand the problem and the impact, in terms of the project implementation, of the decisions he will make. He may know the answer immediately, he may need to call someone else, or he may never resolve the problem. In any case, a decision must be made so the development can continue at a rapid pace. Making no decision can cause huge delays in the project. Such delays will result in real costs. To minimize the project costs, the business sponsor will have to facilitate business issues and provide quick resolutions.

## Long-Term Vision

A 30,000-foot long-term vision is not required but it is very helpful. This is the 30,000-foot business view of the data warehousing initiative, not the technical viewpoint. You need not present a substantial amount of detail. The goal of the long-term vision is to communicate internally how the data warehouse initiative will provide value to the company in the future. It will describe what this data warehouse will mean for the company. Ideas on data availability, flexibility, and standardization need to be communicated to your company. This does not have to be explicit but can be very general—more like a world map than a road map. You will need only a few slides in a presentation. If you do not have this long-term vision, you may not be building something that aligns with the business. Even worse, you might not get the continued support from the business after the application is built. The short-term vision will need to be incorporated into this long-term vision.

> The goal of the long-term vision is to communicate internally how the data warehouse initiative will provide value to the company in the future.

I would suggest not having too much technology detailed in this long-term vision, although there can be some technology visions defined. This is a good place to integrate the information technology (IT) department's vision with the data warehouse concept. Knowing you are going to build an enterprise data warehouse as opposed to a data mart is a simple long-term technical vision. The technical department may be the driving force, so my advice to them is to avoid providing in-depth technical details of the data warehouse to the business people. They will want to know some details, but mostly they will want to know how long it will take to build so they can analyze their business situation and make faster decisions. Very often, the IT department will already know and understand the value of data integration, standardization, and the commonality that the data warehouse will provide to the business. They will understand the differences and similarities of the data within the various databases and even the data elements. The IT department may already have a technical conversion plan with new technology that needs to be implemented. The IT department should know the technology requirements of the entire company. Therefore, they may already know where to find several business sponsors that can benefit from the same data warehouse implementation. Defining and communicating how each will benefit should be part of this long-term planning.

## Short-Term Plan

The short-term plan is the first step in the construction of a data warehouse. This is where you will set delivery expectations. Highlights of this short-term plan are included in the presentation of the long-term vision. This is the data warehouse road map, a breakdown of the long-term vision. It outlines what will be implemented in the next 3 to 18 months. Implementations outside this 18-month plan should be identified as future implementations, so there will be no misunderstanding. It is very important that this plan identify and clearly show the business value of the first implementation of a data warehouse. If the short-term implementation is not a success, the data warehouse implementation may be terminated and considered a failure. A business case study may be needed to justify the short-term plan. I have dedicated Chapter 4 to building a business plan and will discuss additional details about a data warehouse business case study in that chapter.

You will need specific details in this plan. You will need a timeline, expected resources, sponsors, funding, and so on. This is more of a business plan with a vision and an implementation approach. It should include the major milestones that will be accomplished. I would not include exact dates but would use elapsed time or duration instead. If you give an exact date, like January 12, 2001, and the project starts later than expected, most likely that date will be remembered by the executives, not the fact that you started in March because of lack of funding. Therefore, the milestones should read something like "5 weeks after the project starts," or "20 weeks after the project starts." The most important milestone will be an identifiable conclusion of this project (e.g., "9 months after the project starts"). Cost for the first deliverable is another feature of this plan. The cost will vary depending on your company and the way you choose to implement. The cost should be broken down for the business areas that have sponsorship. If the deliverable is

> **The most important milestone will be an identifiable conclusion of this project.**

within a specific time frame and there is a business sponsor, then cost figures have already been discussed. The cost should not be a surprise to any of the business sponsors.

It is important to decide what your company needs from this short-term plan. Some companies will need lots of details, like a full-blown business plan, and others will need less. The short-term plan can be a paper document, a prototype, a proof of concept, or the first implementation of the data warehouse. This may include the results from a prototype that was built. The prototype or proof of concept may be needed to prove to the top-level business executives the value of the data warehouse. The costs of the prototype or the proof of concept need to be outlined. Additionally, the user community will still need to be involved. There may be third-party consultants that will be building the prototype. Their involvement and cost will need to be outlined, too. If you have a prototype or a proof of concept, be sure to propose a decision point milestone for the business. If the business executives are not able to make a decision at that time, then perhaps there is not enough value for your company at this time. Or you may simply need a more detailed business plan.

### Assigning a Responsible Leader

Companies sometimes forget to assign a single person to be responsible for the data warehouse. This person will have the power to make daily decisions. Only one person should be identified as the project leader for your company. That way there is no question as to who is the responsible (and 100% dedicated) project leader. This becomes more important when two or more groups in your organization need the data warehouse. Each group may have a very different viewpoint of what the data warehouse should become. Maintaining a short-term gain as well as the long-term focus is precisely why a single person needs to become responsible for the entire data warehouse project.

> Only one person should be identified as the project leader for your company. That way there is no question as to who is the responsible project leader.

This person will be responsible for prioritizing, communicating, and implementing the system based on the business needs. Facilitation of communication is a very important task of this leader. This person will need to drive the open issues to closure quickly. If there is more than one person, the result will be that each individual will build a database for one group and not the entire company. They will each make their own decisions independent of one another. It is almost certain that they will slow down the implementation. In the worst case, they will focus on their solutions independently and forget about the long-term focus. If you have this situation it will be difficult for your company to achieve an enterprise data warehouse. Someone has to be able to decide the small battles regarding the source and the accuracy of the data. One person is needed full-time and no more than one.

This leader is especially important when a third party is involved as he or she will be the main company contact. When there are issues to be resolved that are time-critical, this person must take responsibility to push for a quick decision from the business sponsors. This person will be responsible for resolving those issues that cross the business border, leaving the third party to concentrate on its deliverables. Another important task of this person is to control and contain the project scope. Constant expansion of the scope of the initial data warehouse dramatically increases the risk of failure, so keeping the scope in line with the original proposal is critical. The project leader will determine if a project is within the guidelines established in the short-term plan or the business case proposal.

## Effective Communication

Effective communication is very important during a data warehouse implementation. It becomes even more important toward the end of a project, when the users must acknowledge the success or failure of this new application. The application must meet their expectations, and the only way this can happen is if communication is flowing freely. Anything that inhibits communication must be resolved. A data warehouse cannot be created in a vacuum. Your successes (and failures) must be communicated to the business sponsors and the organization, at the minimum on a weekly basis. I am talking about more than just a weekly status meeting. When problems arise that will delay the project by even a day, that needs to be communicated. Monthly status meetings are inadequate. Too much time can pass before communicating the successes and problems. Most of the communication should come from the project leader. However, the participating team members should be an important part of the communication process, and they should have a direct link to the business sponsors' team members.

Some companies do not adopt an open type of communication. The consequence for them is that the project can lose focus or be delayed. If the communication is flowing freely, then the problems will be easily and quickly identified and the successes will be equally easily seen. I am not suggesting you overload the business sponsors with small mundane issues but that any clear escalation of problems that might jeopardize the project be communicated. I would suggest that the core team meet every morning for no longer than 15 minutes. The project leader and perhaps another member should meet with the business sponsors weekly for a similar duration. I would not enforce a strong hierarchy of communication procedures, as this will only complicate the project. In other words, everybody participating on the team should be able to speak to other team members without fear of retaliation. An open model of communication is a bit different from the classical development processes. However, this communication process is very practical when transforming data into information in a timely manner because the need for information is driving the entire system design. Open and effective communication will also promote team building when people work together to deliver the business solution.

> **A data warehouse cannot be created in a vacuum. Your successes (and failures) must be communicated to the business sponsors and the organization, at the minimum on a weekly basis.**

At Wal-Mart, the combination of responsible leadership and effective communication was the key for rapid development. The manager of the data warehouse project was definitely a hands-on person with high contact to the team. He held a status meeting every morning during the critical times and weekly afterward. This was one of the few planned meetings. Impromptu meetings were standard practice when a technical obstacle stopped development progress. When there was a technical obstacle, key players were brought together to openly discuss possible solutions. After reviewing the options, a decision was made then and there on

> **At Wal-Mart, the combination of responsible leadership and effective communication was the key for rapid development.**

what would happen next. The objective was set and expectations were very clear. Often these meetings would immediately change the work schedule and cause the entire team to focus on solving the immediate problem. It was not uncommon to have two people solve the problem at the same time using different methods. When this happened, we would objectively and quickly choose the best solution.

## Providing Something New

If you are going to develop an enterprise data warehouse, providing something new is a requirement. Replacing an existing system is a valid reason to build a data warehouse, but even then, there must be something new. This new functionality is why the business is providing the funding for the data warehouse. You must highlight this new functionality in your plans, and it should offer an obvious benefit to the business. Simply replacing a system is a waste of time and money if there is no new functionality. Can you allow more people access to the database? Or could there be a new analysis? Perhaps flexibility can be added to combine several analyses. If nothing new is to be provided to the business, your chances of success are slim. It is not adequate to simply rewrite an existing application and call it a data warehouse. You must decide the new value the data warehouse will bring to your company, something that will enhance the business. If you cannot provide something new to the business, then consider postponing the project until new value can be identified.

Providing something new is also important for measuring the return on investment (ROI). If you do not provide something new, it will be very difficult to calculate the ROI because the same work can be done with another computer system. Wal-Mart did provide something new. They had daily POS transactions for 65 weeks, and it was easily accessible to everyone in a tabular and graphical presentation. Also new was the requirement that to access this system, every user had to get a PC instead of a simple terminal. This new functionality was dramatic, and the ROI could be clearly measured and documented. Because this information was new, the user community could easily be asked, "What would you have done without this system?" Most of the responses would have been "I could not have identified this problem, therefore I could not have corrected it."

## Partnership Planning

Assuming you are not going to do all the work yourself, you will need to form partnerships with various other companies. These other companies might be internal divisions within your company, but the principle is the same. You will choose one or more professional services partners for human resources. You will choose one or more software partners. Finally, you will choose one or more hardware partners. You must be comfortable that each can deliver, and that they can all work together when necessary. This is very important because if you rely too heavily on the wrong supplier, your data warehouse project could fail. With almost every partnership you make, I would suggest a 50/50 partnership. Your company will take 50% of the responsibility, and the external company will take the other 50%. If a partner is 100% responsible, then you must have 100% confidence that they *can* deliver what they are supposed to deliver.

> If a partner is 100% responsible, then you must have 100% confidence that they can deliver what they are supposed to deliver.

The expectations from every service supplier should be clearly outlined, showing resources that will be needed and delivery time frames. If you outsource the entire project, which I do not recommend, you should still ensure that there is a responsible project leader who can make decisions daily. This project manager will "co-manage" with the project manager from the partners you choose. Therefore, you will always need that project manager. You have to decide which external resources will be needed (database analyst, software, hardware, etc.) and ensure that your partners can deliver the required resources. Business analysts are just as important as technical analysts. Their experience is very important from both perspectives.

## PLANNING FOR THE PROJECT LIFE CYCLE

Throughout the life cycle of building a data warehouse, the organizational structures will change. Fundamentally, there are three basic steps in the data warehouse life cycle that need specific consideration: the analytical phase, the construction phase, and the postproduction phase.

The human resource needs and deliverables are very different in each. In this section, I will describe the essential needs for each of these phases.

First, we need to talk about the project duration. The time frames will vary depending on the scope of the first data warehouse project. Starting small is very important for the success of the project. Normally, the first implementation of a data warehouse is relatively short, about six months. If the first implementation takes longer than a year, it may be that there is too much to do or the analysis phase is too long. If it is possible, you should plan deliverables in only one subject area. If there is more than one subject area being implemented (for example, a marketing subject area and a merchandising subject area), there is a danger of losing focus and delaying the project. This also has an impact on the number of people that will be needed throughout the project.

To decide how many people are needed and for how long, you need to know the size, scope, and time constraints of the project. For this discussion, let's assume the data warehouse project is nine months long. How much time should be allocated to each of the three phases? From my experience, I would allocate about two months for the analytical phase, five months for the construction phase, and about two months for the postproduction phase. These time proportions are usually about the same for shorter and longer projects. After the initial analysis is completed, a "time-boxed" approach is an excellent way to continue information delivery. For example, every two to four weeks, a new deliverable is produced. Over time this will slowly deliver more and more information, with each small increment improving the information provided to the business by the data warehouse.

One issue that can substantially extend the project is the data transformation and cleansing process. At the beginning of a data warehouse project, the most obvious data transformation and cleansing issues will be identified. Unfortunately, it is almost impossible to plan for all of the transformation and cleansing tasks that will be needed during the lifetime of the project. In fact, some of them will not be identified until the user community begins to analyze their data. Depending on the company culture, this could cause huge delays in the project. If the company culture is such that all the data must be perfect and flawless, then I would narrow the scope of the project to the bones and double the construction time estimates. I would also start applying terms like *alpha* and *beta* to the project, until *omega* was completed. A perfection-ist corporate mentality will extend the project, most likely well beyond a year. Most corporate cultures, however, will tolerate some minor data imperfec-tions, as long as they are in the process of being cor-rected. The point is to determine how your company will approach this issue and plan accordingly.

> If the company culture is such that all the data must be perfect and flawless, then I would narrow the scope of the project to the bones and double the construction time estimates.

We were constantly finding data integrity issues at Wal-Mart. Actually, the user community would find the problems in their data. In one instance, we were selling a $100 item for 1 cent. In other in-stances, we were selling twice as many articles as were being shipped. Some companies would have stopped the project until all these problems were re-solved. Wal-Mart, however, educated people on the data integrity situa-tion, developed a solution, and continued development. We learned, for example, that some stores in Louisiana were selling lawn tractors at half price, but they were selling twice as many as were shipped. Actually, the problem was that the POS system was not able to manage the special tax situation in Louisiana. In Louisiana, lawn tractors are considered farm equipment and are taxed at half the normal rate. The store managers, to quickly solve this problem, placed two bar codes at half the retail price on the mowers. One bar code was taxed at a full rate while the other was not taxed. This gave the consumer the proper tax rate of half the normal tax, quickly solving the customer problem, but it confused the calculations of accurate inventory figures at the home of-fice. Because every company has a different culture, your company would likely manage this differently. You will have to gauge what will be done when data integrity issues arise. How your company responds will determine how quickly your data warehouse can be built.

During the project, the one and only person involved in all phases is the project leader. This same person should be involved in all phases of the data warehouse implementation, not three different people. This is very important, particularly for the first data warehouse implementa-tion. If you use more than one project leader for the different phases, you can be sure there will be delays and redundancy will occur. This project leader should also be an employee of your company. When the project leader is a consultant from a partner or supplier, he or she may have a difficult time making business-oriented decisions. When this happens, the data warehouse project could be in danger of overanalysis or of becoming the never-ending, never-delivered project.

## Analytical Phase

The analytical phase of a data warehouse project is the most important phase. It is here that you will

> During the project, the one and only person involved in all phases is the project leader.

analyze everything from user needs and expectations to hardware selection. The project leader will become very important in setting expectations in this phase. It is the project leader's task to push for completion and documentation. It is in this phase that, without guidance, overanalysis turns into project delays. This is also where additional, often unessential requirements get included in the project. The project leader must communicate clearly and concisely about the delivery to keep the project focused. The key tasks in this phase are

1. gathering and documenting the business requirements, *PL & BA*
2. creating a logical design of the database and processes, *DBA*
3. determining the sources of the data, *DA*
4. determining technical readiness, *TRA*
5. selecting tools, and *TW*
6. creating an implementation timeline with required resources. *TRA*

Depending on the company, there may be some additional tasks to be explored, such as security administration. These should be added to this phase if your company demands this. Often, security is not a big part of a data warehouse because the normal access path is by internal networks only. This means that when the entire corporate network is secure, the data warehouse is secure. Most of the time, a simple user-ID and password is enough security for a data warehouse. (If you are building a database for the Central Intelligence Agency (CIA), however, security will have to be an important issue that needs to be clearly defined.) My approach is to disregard strong security in the first implementation. I believe you should find business value first and exploit that value, then implement security. If security is a factor in your company, these tasks can be developed simultaneously with the other tasks. They can also be addressed before the project begins or in the next implementation phase.

After you've gathered all of the information necessary, it should be compiled into one document. The analytical phase ends when the business sponsor approves the deliverables. The deliverables should be clearly documented and signed by the business sponsor.

The analytical team should be composed of the following members:

◆ project leader
◆ business analyst
◆ data analyst
◆ database analyst
◆ technical writer
◆ technical readiness analysts

### Gathering and Documenting the Business Requirements

This is probably the most important task of the entire data warehouse project. In fact, it is so important that I have dedicated an entire chapter (Chapter 3) to discussing it. It is a difficult task too because you must bring different people with different backgrounds into the same room to discuss what will be delivered in the data warehouse. Of course,

> **Gathering and documenting the business requirements is probably the most important task of the entire data warehouse project.**

they will all have different ideas of what they think should be built, but they must come together to decide what is best. Fortunately, there is a relatively simple way to help them come to a conclusion. This process is very nearly a joint application development (JAD) session, geared for data warehousing. Some companies call this *business exploration* or *business discovery* because you are trying to determine the information needs of the business people. This process does not actually take a lot of time to perform, usually only a few weeks. Sometimes it will take longer if you have to get the executives to coordinate and allocate time with few or no interruptions. Sometimes this must be done at a location away from the office. I will describe more about the business gathering processes that work well for me in Chapter 3.

During these business exploration sessions, the users will discuss their business needs and how technology can assist them. They will define the data dimensions and the metrics that they need to help them solve their business problems. They will define their existing (and future) data hierarchies and the exact data elements that are needed, including the formulas they use to calculate figures. Finally, they will name the data elements clearly. The easiest way for them to do this is to draw the analyses they want to see on a flip chart. The result is that the users themselves define the logical data model, the logical process model, and the data standards. The people that will be building the data warehouse simply facilitate and document their discussions and conclusions.

Another important challenge is the reality that some data will not exist. The business people may be requesting something that simply has not been created. If it can be created with the data warehouse project, then well and good. Providing something new is an important success factor that I have already discussed. The challenge comes when what they want is impossible to create, that is, when the users are demanding something that simply does not exist and cannot be created. The project leader and the business analyst will play a very important role when this happens. They have to set the expectations from the beginning. The business people need to clearly understand what will and will not exist in their data warehouse. If a data element cannot be created, then the analyses that use that data element may not function. There will be enough surprises with data integrity, so you should not ignore the obvious missing data elements. These obvious data shortcomings should be addressed and documented quickly.

## Creating a Logical Design of the Database and Processes

After working with the business users, you will very nearly have all you need to create a data warehouse. From the user session you should have been able to gather the data elements that are required and understand basically how those data elements will be presented. Creating a logical data model should be a relatively easy and quick process at this point. If the logical design takes more than a couple of weeks, then the scope of the project may be too large. Remember that the first implementation should be limited to only one subject area. Another piece that should be relatively easy to create, after the business discovery with the users, is the basic design of the front-end analyses and presentations.

At this point the logical model will have only the data elements that were discussed in the sessions with the business users. Typically, there are more data elements needed that were not discussed. Normally, the data elements that were not discussed turn out to be attributes to an entity that is already in the data model. Flags and codes are often forgotten, but this is not really a problem. As you proceed through the next steps, these can be added to your data model. Where you must be careful is in defining the entities. You want to be sure that all of the entities are documented. For example, a retailer that has a high return rate will want to analyze the returns separately from the sales. Therefore, there may need to be two entities, one for sales and one for returns. Attributes to those entities will be easily defined from the source systems.

The Wal-Mart executives initially did not appreciate the value of logical data modeling for the database. In fact, it was perceived as an unnecessary waste of time. A colleague and I convinced Wal-Mart management to allow us time to logically model the data before we created a physical model. We were given only one week. In this week, we created and proposed four new logical/physical designs. One of these designs added the daily data, in nearly the same size database. I will discuss more about this design later, but they were planning for weekly data. We were given another week to explore the possibility of maintaining daily data. We concluded, after a lot of analysis, that it was possible to implement daily sales history on the computer Wal-Mart had purchased. That database design was used, without being changed, for the next three years. Shortly after this success, Wal-Mart created the logical database design group.

**The Wal-Mart executives initially did not appreciate the value of logical data modeling for the database.**

The high-level presentation processes, or analyses, should be relatively complete after the business session. The basic diagrams should be documented, and the business people should be satisfied that they will be able to use this information to help solve their problems. They should also be comfortable with the general layout (graph, bar chart, scatter chart) of how it will be presented. This information will feed decisions regarding the presentation tools selection process. Finally, this should include the database backup and recovery strategies. In a data warehouse implementation, it is important to clearly define, document, and communicate the database recovery expectations. This is important because the volume of data is normally much larger in a data warehouse than in the individual OLTP systems. This higher data volume will naturally extend the backup and recovery processes. If possible, the backup and recovery processes should provide the same guarantees as the existing classical systems. If the volume of data is very high, as it was with Wal-Mart, you may need to explore the backup and recovery techniques more carefully. At Wal-Mart, we did not use the standard backup and recovery utilities at the beginning of the project. There was simply too much data. Recovery from a database failure using the standard utilities would have taken longer than reloading the entire database. Initially, it took three days to reload the database. We would have used the backup and recovery utilities—they were easier to create and use—but we didn't want to add more time to the recovery process. As described in Chapter 7, we used the built-in mirror function to duplicate the data in the database and relied on the source files to recover the database. Your company's database may not be that large and you may have a more powerful computer, but be sure to consider the larger data volumes. For most companies, the backup and recovery times will be dictated by the size of the computer system. The larger and more expensive computers will normally back up and recover faster, thereby narrowing the recovery window. For example, mirroring the data will require twice as much disk space as nonmirrored data. Even when your data is mirrored and a failure is much less likely, the recovery expectations need to be clearly documented and communicated.

> **Even when your data is mirrored and a failure is much less likely, the recovery expectations need to be clearly documented and communicated.**

## Determining the Sources of the Data

Using the previous data model and process model, you need to determine the true source of the data so you can capture the data into the data warehouse. This phase is simply the documentation of which data, which database, and which applications will be involved in the data warehouse. With every data source, there is a point at which a data record is in a consistent state, and this is the point at which the record is ready for the data warehouse. This point comes after the modifications, validations, and conversions of the data, just before updating the database. For example, there may be "work in progress" that puts a record in the database, but it may not become active until all of the fields are completely filled in. It is after this point that you want to capture the data, not before. This is what you are documenting here—the basic "health" of the data. You may need to create additional programs to "clean" the data. Verification and cleaning of the data is done before it can be placed in the database. You may have to create additional programs to merge, add, or eliminate records, too. Of course, this is not the time to create the programs, only to document what is needed for each piece of data.

Another benefit of determining the sources of the data is validating the logical model. As you are determining the sources of the data, more data elements will appear to be necessary. That is, you will discover there are new data elements that were not discussed earlier that you need. This is where a lot of value can be added by including these extra elements in the data model. Often these are merely extra codes that were overlooked in discussions with the business people. If these elements are attributes of an already documented entity in the logical design, it might just be a simple matter to change the logical design. However, you may find an entire new entity exists, and the logical model needs to be changed dramatically to reflect the newly found data relationship. You will need to be prepared to change the data model at the same time as you are searching and documenting the source data.

### Determining Technical Readiness

Determining technical readiness is the process of deciding whether the various aspects of system operations are ready for the data warehouse. This is a very technical process that may require the help of several people. For an average-sized company, this normally takes only a couple of weeks. Anything that can technically inhibit the construction of the data warehouse has to be evaluated. Details are very important. Some of the issues that need to be understood are network protocol compatibility, available network bandwidth, host computer capacity, and software compatibility. There are issues that can delay the development that are not so obvious, such as the electrical phasing and cooling requirements for the computer room. Speaking of the computer room, there may not be space available to put a new computer! The product of this analysis is a document detailing the technical limitations that exist with priorities that need to be addressed before the data warehouse can progress to the construction phase.

## Selecting Tools

The tool selection process can be a very important aspect of data warehousing for many companies. I think it is fairly obvious that the tools that will be used must be selected before the construction phase. The prototype or proof of concept should help narrow the tool selection process dramatically. If they were not already selected during the prototype or proof of concept, then they need to be selected now. Each company usually has its own tool evaluation process. If such a process exists, then it should be used. Otherwise, a new process will need to be adopted. The two major tool decisions for data warehousing are the front-end application (GUI) and the database. It is important that both can deliver what the business needs. (I discuss this selection process in more detail in Chapter 6.) The key consideration in the tool selection process is time. Be very careful not to spend too much time evaluating tools. If you spend longer than two months evaluating tools, then you probably have spent too much time. At Wal-Mart, we selected tools that worked without lengthy evaluations. As soon as a tool no longer worked, we used another one. We had to create most of the applications from scratch anyway because they did not exist. For the GUI and the database, there were not many choices. We quickly eliminated most of them by trial and error.

> **If you spend longer than two months evaluating tools, then you probably have spent too much time.**

Sometimes it is better to simply jump in, purchase the tools, and use them. In about two months of use, you will certainly find out the limitations and the compatibility of the various tools. If they work together nicely and solve the problem, you win. If they don't, you win again because you learned this without much investment in a relatively short period of time. Additionally, you have a licensed copy that can be inexpensively upgraded and reevaluated next year when you are expanding the data warehouse. I think you will find that your tools will require a considerable amount of customization, no matter which ones you select. The question is not if you will customize your data warehouse applications, but how much.

### Creating an Implementation Timeline and Resources Required

The human resources you will need will vary slightly for each data warehouse implementation. In this phase of the development, you must determine the general skills that will be required. For each skill set you should list the duration, in terms of elapsed time and actual time, needed on the project. You are simply trying to determine a reasonable estimate of the resources. For example, you will need a database specialist. If you have chosen a database platform, then you know exactly the skill set that is needed. For most data warehouse implementations, you will need a database specialist part-time in the analysis phase, then full-time at the beginning of the implementation until the project is in production. Finally, this same resource is needed part-time after the implementation. In this case, the database specialist will be needed for the duration of the project (perhaps nine months), and this person will be needed full-time for the four months in the middle of the project. You should document every skill needed and for how long. This will be used to secure the resources at the beginning of the construction phase. At this point, try to avoid names and just list the required skills.

An implementation timeline should be crafted so that everyone understands the time requirements. At this point, the timeline should be only one or two pages long and very simple. When you get into the construction phase, the timeline will be much more extensive. Until you begin the construction phase, the smaller timeline is better. I recommend that there be no specific dates, but only the duration of the main tasks involved. A duration-only timeline is important because you might not start at a specific date for some reason. Specific dates are appropriate only if you are guaranteed that you will be able to begin on that date. You may be delayed because the people are not allocated to the project yet, or perhaps because the technology resources have not been purchased. It could be that the business might not be ready to begin. They might not have considered the resources

> **Until you begin the construction phase, the small timeline is better. I recommend that there be no specific dates, but only the duration of the main tasks involved.**

required for implementation. I have known of situations in which one company purchases another company and delays the project. Therefore, if you have a duration timeline, then you can start your data warehouse project when the business is ready.

## Construction Phase

The construction phase will prove to be the most time consuming and will use the most human resources. After you have completed the analysis phase and you have the support of the business people with the supporting documentation, you are ready to begin the construction phase. The next step is to determine exactly which people have the skills to build and deliver your data warehouse. You should select the team members in this phase very carefully, as the people in this phase will develop, test, and install all of the applications. The skill level and professionalism of the team members will determine the success of this phase. There should be a core data warehouse team with extended data warehouse members and, perhaps, external temporary data warehouse members. The construction phase is finished when the applications for the newly developed data warehouse are running normally and are fully automated. They will produce everything that is commonly needed in any application development cycle for your company, such as documentation, process flow diagrams, operations guides, and backup and recovery procedures. For larger companies, this development team may need to gain acceptance from another group, the maintenance organization, before they are allowed to relinquish control of the day-to-day systems maintenance.

The skill level and professionalism of the team members will determine the success of the construction phase.

The core data warehouse team will consist of one or more of the following people:

- project leader
- database analyst
- graphical user interface (GUI) analyst
- data warehouse programmer
- "host" programmer.

As mentioned before, you will need one dedicated project leader. When there is a third party responsible for delivering the data warehouse, they will have a project leader too. The database analyst will need to be dedicated full-time in this phase, with another person acting as a substitute during vacation and illness. It may go without saying, but the database analyst will be responsible for the database design, implementation, performance and tuning, and backup and recovery on both the development system and the production system. You could need two to ten GUI analysts, depending on the scope of the project and the GUI tool that is selected. Obviously, if you plan to program the GUI with Visual Basic or C++, you will need more people than if you purchase a product that will not be developed from scratch. You will also need a "host" programmer and a data warehouse programmer who will be responsible for moving the data from the functional operational systems into the data warehouse. These people should be dedicated for the entire construction phase. You may need more than one of each, but that depends on the size, scope, and time constraints of the project. These programmers will spend most of their time writing the summarization routines, match-and-merge programs, verification routines, and load scripts/programs. Just as in a normal application development project, they will be responsible for the integration of the newly developed process flow. They will need to place the programs into the production process streams. For most companies, this requires standard documentation and working through the normal change control procedures for new application development. This is particularly important when linking the new data warehouse processes and data flow with the currently existing production processes and data flow. This group should develop and install the standard process failure, restart, and recovery procedures with accompanying operations documentation. These processes should be installed with data recovery procedures in place.

Of course, you could have many more people, but for most companies, more is not necessarily better. It is best if all of the people on the core data warehouse team are senior-level people with a breadth of experience in all areas. The junior people should be partnered with the senior people. The skills of the team should complement one another. Each member should be willing to assist in areas outside his or her own job title. For example, it could be that the database analyst would have to write a program or two. This may be because she has the skill to write a standard subroutine that will be used by all other applications. You may not have known that this standard routine was needed, and all other members of the team are in the critical path. The team members need to be flexible enough to realize their strengths and their team members' strengths, using this knowledge to strengthen the entire team. They should be working closely to facilitate problem solving. I would suggest that the team members move their offices near one another so their working relationships can be strengthened. If the core team is physically separated, they may not behave like a team. This could cause project delays because of communication problems. Flexibility and communication skills are certainly an important aspect of the data warehouse team.

> **The team members need to be flexible enough to realize their strengths and their team members' strengths, using this knowledge to strengthen the entire team.**

The extended data warehouse team members are very important too. These people will participate in the construction of the data warehouse but will not be committed to it full-time. These people are generally the technical support people and the functional business programmers/analysts. The technical support people are those who will manage the technical issues such as the communications network, the system hardware maintenance, and the system software maintenance. They are needed to set up the systems and to solve technical problems. This is why they will not be used full-time. They are definitely an important part of the implementation, but they are normally committed to the entire company and not to a single project.

The functional business programmers/analysts are a critical part of the data warehouse delivery. They are responsible for maintaining the existing functional systems, such as the purchase order entry system. They will determine and modify the programming code to "capture" the detail transactions in their respective systems. These people will be needed for about two weeks at the beginning of the construction phase. The number of such people needed depends on the number of entities you will have in the data warehouse. For example, a retailer would want to capture store sales, store receipts, and store orders into the data warehouse. In this case, you could expect that three people will be needed to make the necessary modifications in each functional area. This is the best, and most cost-effective, way to ensure that the data is captured properly and passed to the data warehouse system. Normally, it takes about two weeks to make the necessary modifications for each functional system. After these modifications, the data will begin to flow toward the data warehouse. The participation of the functional business programmer/analyst is important because these systems are needed in the day-to-day operation of the company. An analyst who is not familiar with the system may not capture the completed data records in a reasonable amount of time. Even worse, he could cause a system failure that shuts down that application function. You definitely do not want this type of visibility. The construction team should consist of the following personnel:

- **Core data warehouse team**

    project leader

    database analyst

    graphical user interface (GUI) analyst

    data warehouse programmer

    "host" programmer

- **Extended data warehouse members**

    technical support analysts

    functional business programmers/analysts

- **External temporary data warehouse members**

    partner project leader

    contract consultants

## Postproduction

At this point the applications have been developed, tested, and installed into the production environment. After the construction phase, there are still plenty of tasks to be completed. The postproduction phase basically consists of the field rollout of the application, the user acceptance and sign-off, and user training. Of course, the first step is to get agreement that the system satisfies expectations. The business sponsor needs to confirm that you have delivered. The user acceptance may be a very formal process with a signature requirement. Assuming that you have developed the application with the participation of the ultimate users and that the business sponsor has been involved, there should be no surprises and they should accept the system. If they do not accept the system, they were not involved in the design or the design changed without their knowledge. Setting expectations and managing scope changes are very important aspects of the project leader's job. Only after this acceptance can the postproduction phase really begin. In the construction phase, there may be several users who have been trained and already have access to the data warehouse. The remainder of the users will need to be given access to this application. Most companies have an automatic rollout procedure established within their information technology group. If there is no automatic process, then someone will have to install these applications. This is typical for smaller companies where there are only a handful of users. If there are hundreds of users, then a rollout process may need to be created. With today's Web-based intranet data warehousing, the rollout is much simpler than it used to be and may not be much of an issue. There will be some additional tasks that will need to be done, however. It might be necessary for one or two of the people from the construction team to return to fix some minor problems. Be sure to communicate that this could happen so you can obtain the needed resource for a week or two again. This phase should be about two months, using our theoretical nine-month project. The remainder of this phase is training. The postproduction team should consist of the following personnel:

**After the construction phase, there are still plenty of tasks to be completed.**

- project leader
- software installation process/person
- technical writer
- data warehouse trainer

The creation of the training material can begin before this phase, but the training itself should not begin until the software is available on the users' desks and functioning properly. The training can be done in several ways: classroom, books, or CD-ROM. However the training is done, the application should be simple enough that only one day of training is necessary. Simplicity is a very important aspect of a data warehouse. The data warehouse application should be very, very simple to use. The simpler the application, the faster this part of the project becomes. Unfortunately, simplicity normally means more investment into the application development, so there is a trade-off. Every attempt should be made to ensure that not much more than one day of training is needed before the business users can become productive with the application. I recommend a classroom-style lesson, so the users can learn together. This will put them in the "same boat," and they will know there is someone else that is learning about the technology just like them.

After completing the postproduction phase, the system is up and running. The user community is happy because you delivered exactly what they were expecting. The users have more information than they ever had before. They are asking for more and more information to be added to the data warehouse. The project is complete but there is still more work to be done. Typically, a new data warehouse project will begin again, and you can start the analysis phase and once again focus on solving the business needs. The techniques in the next chapter will help you define more critical business questions with the user community. This cycle is a normal process for most companies, but there is yet another important issue that needs to be addressed at this point. It is easy to overlook, since everyone is happy with the new application, but now is the time to plan for the ROI analysis. This should occur 6 to 12 months after the first data warehouse project is complete. This business-focused measurement process will require another small team of two or three people. Chapter 4 will assist you in developing and documenting the ROI, but now is the time to plan to complete the ROI documentation; otherwise, it will be forgotten.

# 3

# Business Exploration

Getting started building a data warehouse can be a challenge for many companies. The concept may be a good idea, but where do you begin? How should you proceed? This chapter is dedicated to creating that first data warehouse application and ensuring that it is aligned with the business direction and focus. Because the investment in a data warehouse is a substantial commitment, many companies will need to assure their management that they can successfully implement the data warehouse. Because the investment can be substantial, the first implementation needs to be clearly aligned with the business. Your company may require a business case study and/or a prototype (or proof of concept) to be built before implementing a full-sized data warehouse. The business exploration process will become the essential part of a prototype and a business case study. The concepts that I will discuss are not completely new, but there are some small variations for data warehousing. You can use these techniques to gather requirements, prioritize requirements, scope the project, deliver the prototype concept, and build a business case justification for the first data warehouse development. This process will ensure the support and backing of your company.

Before I begin describing the process of gathering business requirements, you really need to understand why this is important. In many data warehouse implementations, this step is overlooked. Most people know there is value in building a data warehouse, and they have a general idea of the data requirements and the process requirements. Even some of the analyses are understood clearly. However, it is rare to find documentation specifying the analyses that are wanted, much less the priority of each analysis. If you aren't clear about the priorities of the analyses, then how can you know which analyses should be built first? You need to gather these requirements before you begin the construction phase.

Fortunately, there are plenty of documented processes that are specially designed for gathering requirements. Joint application development (JAD) is probably one of the most well known of those processes. It seems that every company has its own process and techniques to obtain requirements, but these are usually designed for the functional process-oriented applications. I like to use the following process to define the first implementation of the data warehouse with the business people. I am not trying to define another process. I am not going to try to correlate what I do to some other process either. I am going to describe the ideal method that works for me. Some companies cannot or will not proceed with exactly what I put forward here, and therefore there may need to be customized minor deviations. In fact, I have never been able to re-create the exact process twice. There is always some minor deviation. This is okay. You should follow the processes that are familiar to your company. Most of the time these deviations are minor, and this is normally no problem.

Wal-Mart built a prototype based on the needs of the business, then they received support from the entire company. They worked closely with the merchandising group to create the prototype. When it was approved, they built the system. Therefore, they had a general idea of what was needed before they began, and then they invested their resources to build a prototype. Some companies will not be allowed to invest any resources into a prototype that is not clearly defined. This is simply a company culture difference. This process will help you create the scope and define the priorities, as defined by the business community.

To understand what is needed for your data warehouse, you have to speak with the business people. This is not an option; it is a requirement. These are the people that will benefit from the data warehouse. Often the people in the information technology department will say that they have already done the requirements research and they know what needs to be delivered in the data warehouse. That is fine and good if they can produce the documentation and prioritized analyses that they will deliver. If they have this already, they should be able to deliver it themselves. Sometimes the requirements are documented but not prioritized. The consequence of this could be that the first implementation is too large, an attempt to solve all business information needs in the first implementation. When the scope of the project is too large, the probability of success shrinks. If you do not get the required analyses with their corresponding priority at the same time, the business people will have no perspective of the scope, and everything will become the first priority. My point is to prioritize the business needs and deliver a small, but valuable piece of the data warehouse. This does not mean that all of the analyses will not be delivered. They will all be delivered, but they should be delivered in small steps based on the business priorities. The only way I know to do this effectively is to speak with the business people and ask them to determine the most important analyses. They will want everything, of course, but they should understand the concept of building a solid foundation. Therefore, together you should define and limit the scope of the project, deliver the analysis/project, and repeat. The next iteration will most likely be completely different from what was expected.

> To understand what is needed for your data warehouse, you have to speak with the business people. This is not an option; it is a requirement.

## THE BUSINESS EXPLORATION PROCESS

The goal of this process is to help you gather and document the information you need to align the data warehouse with the business. The information needs to be clearly documented so that the business people

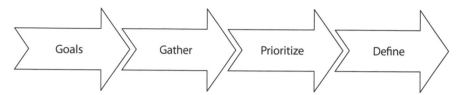

**Figure 3.1**  Gathering data warehouse business requirements.

understand the technical parts and the technical people understand the business parts. Sometimes this is not an easy task. The good news is that it can be done relatively quickly. This process should take about two weeks of work. The elapsed time is usually much longer, let's say two months. This is because it is difficult to coordinate the schedules of the key people to allocate the two or three days for the workshop. There are basically four main processes to accomplish before you will be ready to begin building a data warehouse (Figure 3.1). I will detail each of these processes further in this chapter. They are:

1. Define the goals
2. Gather the business questions
3. Prioritize the business questions
4. Define the business question

The goals will constitute the basic scope of the data warehouse. Then there will be questions that need to be answered to help achieve those goals. Those questions will need to be prioritized, so as to understand their relative importance. And finally, the answer to each question will need to be described. To accomplish this, I prefer a workshop approach. In each workshop I like to have only one group of business people in a two-day session per business group. For example, I would want to work with all of the marketing people in one two-day session and all of the merchandising people in another two-day session. This is mostly to keep the groups small and focused. The ideal number of business people in each session is five. Of course, there should be a facilitator and a scribe, for a total of seven peo-

> The ideal number of business people in each session is five. If there are more than this, some people do not participate. If there are fewer, you might lose the synergy of the conversation.

ple. If there are more than this, some people do not participate. If there are fewer, you might lose the synergy of the conversation.

Choosing the right mix of people is important too. I prefer to have all the participants at the same management level. When a manager and employees are in the same session, the employees can become intimidated. We want a healthy discussion. Sometimes a manager, with subordinates in the same session, will dominate the conversation and hinder open communications. This can create an uncooperative silence, hesitation, and indifference by the subordinate employees. The best way to avoid this is to exclude the manager when she has subordinates in this session. This is difficult or impossible if the manager is the business sponsor. Most managers will understand that they will be included, but just not at this time. Each participant and his or her job function should be selected carefully and discussed prior to the workshop. Therefore, the right mix of participants needs to be determined.

## Defining the Goals

There is one more issue that may need to be resolved before getting into the details of a workshop session: defining the basic scope or goal of the session. If the general scope has not been defined, it may be important to allocate time to do this. If the project is particularly difficult to define, this may push the workshop into a third day. Often, this is already defined and the goal is clear. This goal will become the scope, theme, or mission statement of this work session. A sample goal might be, "Utilize the existing data in our systems to provide information that can reduce advertising costs by 1%."

This statement needs to be defined before beginning the session. It will become the moderator's responsibility to stay focused on that, and only that, goal. Conversations will move in and out of this topic, and that is fine for short related discussions. The moderator will need to constantly remind the participants of the goal. When the moderator or a participant does not see the correlation between a business question and the goal, the question "What does this have to do with the work session goal?" must be asked. I encourage participants to ask this question often, as this will keep the session focused on the goal. This creates a healthy discussion where either the relationship to the goal is identified or the issue is determined to be outside the scope of this workshop. Therefore, the goal is a constant reminder to stay focused throughout the entire session.

In the first implementation of a data warehouse, there should be only one goal. This is an important point because you will want to keep the project small. Having more than one goal makes it difficult to focus on delivering the different goals, which in turn means that the project will become larger and more difficult to deliver. It will also take longer to build. Sometimes there must be two goals. Having only two goals or objectives is really not so bad, as long as they can be managed. If you have more than two goals, you face a real danger of never finishing the project. If you have only one goal, then all of the team members can clearly understand the goal and focus to deliver that goal.

> **In the first implementation of a data warehouse, there should be only one goal.**

## Gathering the Business Questions

A data warehouse essentially provides information that will answer a business question. I have found that the easiest way for the business people to communicate their information needs is to ask a question. I ask the participants to ask a question that the data warehouse should answer. A question can be very complex or very simple. A question for a retailer might be, "What is the gross sales of an article in each country?" The questions should be written down on a paper (I use a flip chart), each one numbered uniquely. As the paper is filled with questions, it should be posted onto the wall so that all the people in this session can see them (Figure 3.2). This part of the session goes really fast at the beginning and much slower toward the end. Believe it or not, there are a finite number of questions that will be asked, although it may not appear that way in the beginning because the questions come very quickly.

How long should this take? For a group of five business people, this process should take from three to six hours. There should be a planned break in the middle of this session, so participants can consider more questions in a less stressful situation. It gets more difficult for the participants as the list of questions increases. This is also why it begins to

1. What are the gross sales for an article in each region?
2. What is the cost of an article by region?
3. What is the sales-per-square-meter of an article?
4. What is the sales-per-square-meter of a category?
5. What is . . .

**Figure 3.2** Documenting the business questions.

slow down at the end. They will be reviewing all the documented questions to ensure their question is not a duplicate. The number of questions you should expect from this group is around 50, although there could be well over 100 questions, depending on the scope. As a general guideline you will basically be able to document about 40 questions in two days. But don't worry too much if you have 60 or 70 questions because the prioritization in the later steps will allow you to focus on the most important questions. I would be very concerned about the scope of the project if the number of questions were much higher than about 130.

You can stop this phase of the workshop when there are long pauses between new questions. This is an indication that the participants have nearly exhausted their list of questions. Most likely, the most important questions are documented. It is not a problem to add more questions later. This will happen throughout the workshop. The questions need to be documented as clearly as is reasonable to be sure there is no confusion about what is being asked. Confusion typically arises when two people read a single question, think it is unique, but each expects a different kind of result. This discussion is an important part of the workshop. Be careful not to define the analyses, as this will be done later, but the questions need to be clearly defined. It could be that no names have been defined for the different analyses or the participants were using their terms incorrectly. Either way, they must discuss and define the differences and define a unique question for each. At some relatively planned point, you will have to stop this part of the session and proceed to the prioritizing phase. It is difficult to define this stopping point exactly. One indication that this phase of the work session is over is when questions stop flowing freely. Before proceeding to the prioritization phase of the workshop, a break is required. The questions need to remain on the wall throughout the prioritization phase of this workshop.

## Prioritizing the Business Questions

The process of prioritizing the business questions can be difficult for the participants. There are several ways to foster the prioritization process. If there are not many questions (fewer than 30), then you might be able to prioritize the question directly with the participants on a white board or flip chart. Normally, there are more than 30 questions,

> **All of the business questions need to be consolidated into a single handout. I call this handout a prioritization worksheet.**

and most groups of people will not be able to quickly prioritize so many questions. Therefore, there is work that must be done by the moderator and the scribe before the participants return to the workshop. All of the questions need to be consolidated into a single handout. I call this handout a *prioritization worksheet*. The prioritization worksheet that I use is a grid with four columns. Across the top will be the four column headings: Goal, Group, Priority, and Question. On the first handout, all columns in the grid are empty except for the Question column. The Question column lists every unique question number and the corresponding question identified. For validation, the questions are still hanging on the walls. The prioritization worksheet looks something like Figure 3.3.

In this phase, the worksheet is sorted by the unique question number. Each participant will be provided with one copy of the prioritization worksheet, which lists all of the questions. The aim of the group is to rank each question based on importance, the most important question being ranked 1. This is difficult to do when there are more than 30 questions. If there are more than 30 questions, rather than prioritizing

| Goal | Group | Priority | Question |
|------|-------|----------|----------|
|      |       |          | 1. What are the gross sales for an article in each region? |
|      |       |          | 2. What is the cost of an article by region? |
|      |       |          | 3. What is the sales-per-square-meter of an article? |
|      |       |          | 4. What is the sales-per-square-meter of a category? |
|      |       |          | 5. What is . . . |

**Figure 3.3**
Prioritization worksheet.

all questions, participants should be asked first to group the questions into five groups. Using the space under the Group column, they should give each question a value of 1 through 5, 1 being the most important and 5 indicating the least important. At the same time they are grouping each question, they should ask one additional question: "Does this question assist in achieving the goal that was defined at the beginning of the session?" They will put $Y$ or $N$ in the empty space under the Goal heading for every question. This should take between 15 and 20 minutes to do. To help them maintain a pace, the halfway point should be announced. The announcement of the halfway point will allow them to determine if they are falling behind or are ahead based on the total number of questions on the prioritization worksheet. I always give them an additional five minutes after the time has expired, so they can wrap it up. It is important that they are not given too much time to do this. They often want to overanalyze each question. This is not important right now because they will discuss their groupings and priorities together. Therefore, don't let them take their forms home to study. Additionally, don't be concerned if one person was not able to complete the form in the small amount of time given because the ensuing discussions are more important.

After this is complete, they must discuss their answers. Starting with question 1, the moderator will ask: "Does it fit the goal?" and "What group is it in?" For the first question, "Does it fit the goal?" it is very important to find the No answers. If a question does not fit within the goal, it is not a part of this data warehouse implementation and will be given the lowest priority. If even one person in the group says the question does not fit within the goal, this needs to be discussed by the group. The group must decide if the question fits within the goal or not.

For the second question, "What group is it in?" they must agree on the group number. The passionate part comes when one person classifies a question as a 5 and another as a 1. They need to explain their choices and decide together what the proper grouping should be. Once again,

> A side benefit of such discussions is that they normally lead to a better understanding of the business and themselves.

they each may have a different interpretation of the question. Perhaps there are really two separate questions. They have to discuss this and come to a conclusion themselves. This is sometimes difficult and it will take time. A side benefit of such discussions is that they normally lead to a better understanding of the business and the people involved. It is not unusual to find that some people want to put some questions in an intermediary group between two other groups, such as group 1.5. This implies that the questions are not as important as the first group but are more important than the second group so they belong in a 1.5 group. This is good and very typical. If the participants all agree, a 1.5 group can be added. This will actually help them in the next step. The grouping should take approximately two hours. The agreed-upon group number will be assigned to each question. The group number should be written next to the unique question number on the prioritization worksheet and written next to the questions that are still hanging on the wall.

There is another value to the grouping process. This is a great way to identify and define the scope of the project. There is no reason to discuss this with the participants during the workshop, but as you can imagine, the first, second, and perhaps the third groups of questions can become the entire scope of the data warehouse. They are the most important to the company and to the success of the data warehouse project. The other questions may need to be implemented later. Normally, there will be very few questions in the fifth group, and most questions will be in the second, and third groups. This is important to understand when you begin to define the technical scope of the project. Most likely, questions in the fifth group can be discarded. By the time the system is built and the users have answers to the first, second, and third group questions, the priority of the fourth group of questions will change too. If you have to contain the scope of the project, the data warehouse

| Goal | Group | Priority | Question |
|------|-------|----------|----------|
| Y | 1 | | 9. What percent of profit does an article contribute to the category profit? |
| Y | 1 | | 12. What was the profit of a category before and after an article was introduced into that category? |
| Y | 1 | | 13. Which stores showed the largest profit improvement when a new article was introduced? |
| Y | 1 | | 29. Which geographic area showed the largest profit improvement when a new article was introduced into the category? |
| Y | 2 | | 3. What is the sales-per-square-meter of an article? |
| Y | 2 | | 4. What is the sales-per-square-meter of a category? |
| Y | 2 | | 34. What are the daily sales of an article? |
| ⋮ | ⋮ | | ⋮ |
| N | 5 | | 45. What are the departmental sales for a store? |
| N | 5 | | 18. How large should a new store be? |
| N | 5 | | 64. What is the best new store location? |

**Figure 3.4**
Prioritization worksheet sorted by group.

should provide only the first group and part of the second group of questions. At the end of the workshop, the participants will clearly see the value of the ranking and should support the project scope containment that may be needed.

After all of the questions are grouped, the participants will definitely need a break. The moderator and the scribe must prepare for the next prioritization process while the participants take their break. The same prioritization worksheet should be used, but this time the questions are sorted by Goal, Group, and Question number. The questions with a No in the Goal column should be on the bottom. The other questions should be grouped into their respective groups, starting with the first group at the top. Upon the return of the participants, they will be given a copy of the new worksheet. The new worksheet should look something like Figure 3.4.

Once again, participants will be asked to prioritize the questions within each group. Based on the time limitations, it may be necessary to prioritize only the first, second, and third groups. Either way, it is important to repeat the same process as in the last step. Interestingly, this should go faster than the previous session because some of the major points in the ranking have already been discussed. Because of the

| Goal | Group | Priority | Question |
|------|-------|----------|----------|
| Y | 1 | 1 | 29. Which geographic area showed the largest profit improvement when a new article was introduced into the category? |
| Y | 1 | 2 | 13. Which stores showed the largest profit improvement when a new article was introduced? |
| Y | 1 | 3 | 9. What percent of profit does an article contribute to the category profit? |
| Y | 1 | 4 | 12. What was the profit of a category before and after an article was introduced into that category? |
| Y | 2 | 1 | 4. What is the sales-per-square-meter of a category? |
| Y | 2 | 2 | 3. What is the sales-per-square-meter of an article? |

**Figure 3.5**
Prioritization
worksheet sorted
by priority.

groupings, there are fewer questions to evaluate, making it easier. It is important every question be ranked and that no two questions have the same rank. Naturally, questions with similar ranking values will be placed next to each other, but they still must be given a unique priority. Another positive by-product of this process (which should be documented) is discovering the relationships among the questions. Some questions will be similar or will be "follow-on" questions. Document these relationships as you go along because this understanding will help scope the project later. The rankings of each question should be written clearly next to each question still hanging on the wall. Once again, the reason these questions remain on the walls is so participants can see the documentation and their work as the workshop continues.

> It is important every question be ranked and that no two questions have the same rank.

After all the questions have been ranked, the attendees should be thanked and dismissed for the day. The next part of defining the business questions is difficult to start and should not be attempted in the same day, even if you finish early. The participants need to rest up and start fresh. After they are dismissed, the moderator and the scribe should prepare the handouts for the next phase: defining the business questions. In Figurre 3.5, you can see a sample of the handout that will be used for the next session. It is the same prioritization worksheet filled in completely and sorted by priority.

## Defining the Business Questions

The purpose of this next session is to clearly define the data elements that will be needed to answer every business question. Specifically, you want to be able to define, understand, and document the data hierarchies that exist, the data metrics that the hierarchies will use, and the analysis that will provide the desired information. A data hierarchy is just like an organizational hierarchy, and it will look something like an organizational chart except that it is used for documenting data elements. A metric is a figure they wish to analyze, such as gross sales, profit, and costs. These can be a formula based on other metrics too, such as percent increase over last month or stock-to-sales ratio. Once you have the hierarchies and metrics related to each business question, you will need to define the analyses. The analyses simply describe a relationship between the hierarchies and the metrics. After these are documented, you should be able to begin construction of a data warehouse that is tightly tied to the business.

You still need only a flip chart, markers, and tape. Essentially, there are three different types of formats that I use on flip-chart paper: a glossary chart, a hierarchy chart, and an analyses chart (Figure 3.6). It would be nice to use three flip charts, but one is enough. There is no need for the business people to understand the three types of flip charts; their purpose is solely to organize the sessions and keep everything documented. As in other sessions, after a flip-chart paper is full or complete, it should be taped to the wall. You can start defining the questions using any or all of the types of charts. What I have learned is that they will all progress together. As you define the analysis for the first business question, you will likewise define the hierarchy and the metrics. With the second business question, the group will use some of what was already defined and add more hierarchies and metrics. As this proceeds, they will begin to group the metrics into categories such as "article performance metrics" and "store performance metrics." This should be documented as part of the glossary. At another question they may say, "the analysis is the same as question 4, but we need the store performance metrics and the store hierarchy." As the work session proceeds, it will get easier and easier. In fact, by the time the analysis for

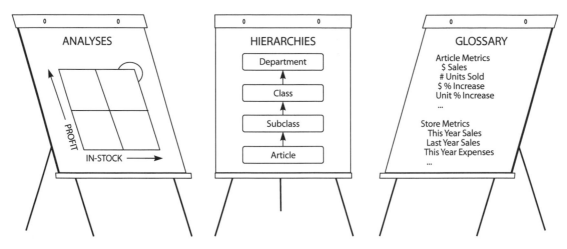

**Figure 3.6**
Analyses, hierarchy, and glossary charts.

the fourth question is defined, you may have defined several other analyses for different questions.

The most difficult part of this session is defining the hierarchies. While this may sound easy, most business people do not think in these terms, and very few of them will be able to clearly define the hierarchies. Business people are usually very good at defining the metrics that they want, which is why I start with the glossary chart. Many times, completely different hierarchies are called by the same name in different business organizations. This can be difficult. Therefore, instead of asking them to define these hierarchies, I ask them to define what they want to see in an analysis first. I have a few rules when they are defining their analysis. The most important rule is: If you don't see it, you won't get it. Therefore, they need to define what they want to see from the data warehouse implementation. The second rule is that they must define their requests in two dimensions. Even though there are 3D-capable applications and tools, the majority of the information we use every day has only two dimensions. This does not mean that they will not be able to see the information on their computers in 3D. In fact, several analyses may be needed to clearly answer each business question. It means that we are not going to add a third dimension to this analysis definition, or to the analyses chart. It adds too much complexity. The final

> # The most difficult part of this session is defining the hierarchies.

rule is: If we have defined a hierarchy, the metrics will apply to all levels of that hierarchy. If this is not true, then perhaps the hierarchies are not clearly defined, or it is not a hierarchy.

How do I start? I start by reading the first question. This is the question with the highest priority to the business. Then I ask, "What data elements do you need to see that will answer this question?" I write the unique question number on the top right-hand corner of the blank sheet of flip-chart paper. For every flip-chart paper that is used, the unique question number should be on the top for later documentation. Typically, participants begin to say what they need faster than I am able to write it down. In the beginning, most of these elements will go on the glossary chart. It is important to get the exact meaning of every data element. In the beginning, they will have to slow down with all the definitions so each one can be documented. They may need to obtain a sample report to remind them which data elements they normally use. Clarification is a very important part of the moderator's job now. For example, someone may say they need "the percent increase." It is the moderator's job to ask for clarification, "What does *percent increase* mean?" This can mean very different things to different people. From a retail perspective, for example, does "the percent increase" mean percent increase of gross sales or the percent increase of number of units? Is this for an article hierarchy or a store hierarchy? Is this percent increase from last year, last month, last week, year-to-date, or month-to-date? This must be clearly defined. This is where the hierarchies will begin to be identified and defined. The hierarchies should be drawn on a separate piece of paper—the hierarchy chart. They also belong on the glossary chart too. The important issues are to define, document, and facilitate conversations.

As you can imagine, defining the first question is the most difficult and will take a long time. After about 15 minutes, participants will have mentioned many of the data elements they think they need. They will have identified the beginning of several hierarchies. Additionally, they will have discussed the time dimension, which is unique to itself. The list will look big and, frankly, a bit of a mess. This is essentially the beginning of a glossary that you are building in your documentation. When they slow down

**The important issues are to define, document, and facilitate conversations.**

giving all of the data elements needed to answer the first question, you will have time to refocus their thoughts. It is okay to skip between each of the three types of charts while defining the information needs of each question. As you find a new hierarchy, you should create a new hierarchy chart and name the hierarchy. At some point it will be time for clarifying the analysis. Clarification means determining if the question can be answered with this analysis. When the group agrees that the analysis or analyses will answer the question, you are ready to define the next question.

You may have noticed that *time* is a special data element. It can be defined as a hierarchy (fiscal years) and a metric (duration). It does not fall clearly into any of the three types of charts I have described. It needs to be defined clearly too. An important issue that needs to be resolved regarding time is defining an accounting time period versus other time periods. For example, when someone wants to know the percent increase of an article from last year to this year, what week are they talking about? When does it begin and end? A retailer, for example, typically has three calendars for the weeks: an accounting week, a merchandising week, and a marketing week. An accounting week begins and ends based on the financial calendar; sometimes this starts on February 1. A merchandising week may run from Sunday through Saturday. Finally, a marketing week might begin on a Wednesday and go through Tuesday. Then, there are quarters. Where do they begin and end? These are the types of issues that need to be documented when you are defining the time dimension. It is important to communicate and document which time periods will be used with each analysis. Normally, you will be dealing with one group of people such as the marketing group, and the time period will be consistent for all analyses, but not always. From a technical standpoint, when these different time periods are known, they are relatively easy to manage within the data warehouse application.

The analyses charts will normally have only two axes to represent the two dimensions of the analyses. On each axis will be either a hierarchy or an attribute. In the middle will be the metrics. Basically, they must decide which data elements they need to see. First they will decide which values should be on each axis, then they draw up a list of the metrics that will be in the middle. This can be a challenge because two business people can have different ideas of what the analysis should comprise. When this happens, another analysis chart should be drawn. There can be many analyses charts to answer a single business question. The participants should be allowed to get up and draw their own ideas on the flip charts too. This is good, because they may be thinking of something completely different. It could be a new and different question that causes the business question to be split into two questions. It could be that they are trying to solve two questions that are on the list, but at a lower priority. This type of interaction should be encouraged, if only for clarification. Visualization of the business questions, via the analysis charts, will clarify the different perceptions and thoughts of how that question is supposed to be answered. Regardless of how many analysis charts are drawn, there will be a finite number that will answer the first and most important business question. Participants will have to agree that the business question can be answered with these specific analyses charts (with the metrics) and the hierarchy charts. If they agree, you can continue to the next highest priority question.

**Visualization of the business questions, via the analysis charts, will clarify the different perceptions and thoughts of how that question is supposed to be answered.**

Fortunately, each succeeding question goes much faster than the last because many of the metrics, hierarchies, and analyses will already be defined with previous questions. The goal is to finish the remaining questions as thoroughly and quickly as possible. After several questions have been answered, and you begin to hear statements like "It is the same as question 11; the same analysis will solve this question too," it may be time to review all of the questions that can be answered with the analyses that have been defined so far.

It is interesting to find that many questions will be answered after others are answered. This is good. This is another reason to focus on the business needs because it illustrates that the priority of current and future business questions will change substantially as the business people learn more about their company. This fact should illustrate the importance of building a data warehouse that is flexible and scalable enough to answer more business questions in the future.

The remainder of the session should be dedicated to defining the remaining business questions, based on their priority. You may have to stop because you run out of time. You will have to decide if an extension of this session is needed or not. Even if you did not finish defining all of the business questions, you definitely have a very good start for your first implementation.

After this session is completed, the work is not finished. The entire session will need to be documented. This should take another couple of days. You will want to create additional documentation (such as a data model, data sizing, and perhaps even data warehouse conceptual models) and create a *business analysis* document. You have reached a milestone after that documentation is distributed to the participants (and perhaps to their management). This is when you are ready to determine the estimated costs of the implementation. From this point, your company has to decide to build a business case study, a prototype, or the data warehouse. If you need a business case study, these results will be a component of this study or justification. If you build a prototype, part or all of this documentation will become the prototype. If you directly build the data warehouse, this documentation will be used as the basis for the technical specifications. Assuming you can implement the data warehouse before the business needs change, the data warehouse will be aligned with the business. Whatever you choose as the next step, you are off to a very good start.

# 4

# Business Case Study and ROI Analysis

This chapter is about building a business case study and a return-on-investment (ROI) analysis. I put these two together because, with few exceptions, they are nearly identical. A business case study is usually created in the beginning phases of the data warehouse. It is needed when management is not sure of the benefits of building a data warehouse. The ROI analysis, on the other hand, is created approximately one year after the data warehouse is built. I discuss these together because of their similarity, but there are some differences between an ROI analysis and a business case study. Most of these differences are minor. For example, an ROI analysis will not have an implementation timeline. While I could outline every minor detail that you could possibly think of putting into a data warehouse business case study or ROI analysis, that would require another book to be written. I prefer to keep it simple so that it is easy to understand and therefore can be constructed by normal business people. Therefore, I will focus this chapter on only the key sections that are needed in each.

The key sections of a business case study are the following:

1. Business user visions
2. One-to-one discussions
3. Business user profiles
4. Potential payback
5. Accumulated potential payback summary
6. Projected investment costs with ROI forecast
7. Resource plan

The ROI analysis will need to highlight the following points:

1. Data warehouse background
2. One-to-one discussions
3. Business user profiles
4. Actual payback
5. Actual accumulated and projected payback summary
6. Investment costs with ROI conclusion
7. Next-step implementation plan

Other than the first point, the difference between the business case study and the ROI analysis is a matter of past and future tense: that is, projected payback versus actual payback. Their structures are similar but the content will be substantially different. As you might expect with the ROI analysis, there will be more concrete examples detailing who, when, and how a specific analysis was used to improve the business. A business case study might only have sample applications and theoretical payback figures. You might have very concrete examples in the business case study if you have built it after building a prototype. Obviously, it is better to have an ROI analysis as opposed to a business case study, but an ROI analysis implies that the application is functioning and the value of the investment has been quantified.

> **The difference between the business case study and the ROI analysis is a matter of past and future tense: that is, projected payback versus actual payback.**

Which one should you do? Some companies will never do either. Many companies cannot proceed with the investment needed for a prototype without the business case study. You might have to build two business case studies, one to obtain the sponsorship to build a prototype and another to show the result of the prototype. It essentially depends on the company, the company culture, and the sponsor's credibility as to what justification is needed and how detailed that justification must be.

## BUSINESS CASE STUDY

The business case study is a selling document for the data warehouse. If you have funding to build a data warehouse, you don't need to create this document. It is possible to go directly into the construction phase. This does not preclude you from aligning the data warehouse with the key business drivers. However, you can use the information and documentation from the business exploration sessions I described in Chapter 3 to build a project plan. If you have business sponsorship and funding, then starting without a business case study should be no problem. The main reason companies build a business case study is because they are not yet convinced of the value of information and therefore need it to be demonstrated and clearly documented.

Wal-Mart did build a business case study, but it was based on the prototype, which was built with the merchandising group. This business case study contained the business user vision, the potential payback, the projected investment costs, and a resource plan. About a year later they also built a business case study for Sam's Club, another division within Wal-Mart, with almost all of these points. The Sam's Club data warehouse was not built for some time afterward.

> Wal-Mart did build a business case study, but it was based on the prototype, which was built with the merchandising group.

### Business User Visions

The vision of the business user can be broken into two main sections: the vision of a group of people, and a vision that an individual believes he can obtain. The remainder is simple supporting material. The group vision basically comprises the documentation from the business exploration sessions. The first short description of this vision in the business case study highlights the theme of the data warehouse. In terms of supporting material, this is a good place to identify and list the business sponsors of the data warehouse. The sponsors are the people that have and will continue to commit their time and their people's time to this project. After the first page listing the business sponsors and their function, more detailed visions—the overall business vision and individual business visions—should follow. The overall vision is simply the goal of the data warehouse implementation. This goal was determined earlier, perhaps in the business exploration session. This must be written with a business perspective. Using the example from Chapter 3, the goal might be, "Utilize the existing data in our systems to provide information that can reduce advertising costs by 1%." You should definitely refrain from using technical terms and should focus entirely on the business benefit.

> **You should definitely refrain from using technical terms and should focus entirely on the business benefit.**

The individual visions will follow, and these should be more concrete. Once again, these visions should be very business focused and unique for that business unit. A sample vision might read something like, "I want to reduce my research time from 80% of my time to 20% of my time." This vision statement is very individualized and quantifiable, particularly when you understand the job function of this person. You can present many such statements from individuals throughout the company. During the project, statements like these are often verbalized. It is important to capture them on paper. With every vision statement, there needs to be an accompanying business user profile of the person who made that statement. The user profile is simply the person's name, department, and job function. This is important for several reasons. First, you will want to measure the individuals' results after the data warehouse implementation and use them in the ROI analysis. Second, you will want to be able to identify who these people are within your organization. This is very important in larger organizations because it is difficult to know everyone within the company. Next, it will provide proof that the business people are supportive of using the technology to improve their business. Finally, it will be used as a selling document to the top executives in the company to help them understand the benefits of constructing a data warehouse.

Another important part in this section of the business case study is the results from the business exploration sessions. This will provide the executives with details of the short-term road map of the construction of the data warehouse. This is where you can communicate the needs of the business and explain how the data warehouse will be aligned to solve the most important business issues. You know the needs of the business because the documentation from the business exploration process indicates the highest priority analyses, the relationship of applying technology to the business, and the scope of the initial project. This information should follow directly after the vision statements.

## One-to-One Discussions

Not all of the information vital to building a data warehouse will be covered in a workshop. Some one-to-one discussions will be necessary to obtain information of value for constructing a business case study. The one-to-one sessions can be formal interviews conducted with the highest management or less formal discussions. Management's visions and expectations on how this data will be turned into information is very valuable and should be presented with a strong business orientation, with limited technical jargon. Essentially, this should comprise a detailed account of the individuals, their job functions, their expectations, and the processes and analyses they use, or would like to use, to improve their business. You should have at least one page per person, although in most cases there will be more

> Management's visions and expectations on how data will be turned into information is very valuable.

than that. The analyses described can be anything the individuals do to get information. Often, they are analyses that an individual has perfected using a PC and a spreadsheet. Their most successful processes can be documented to become easy-to-use, "best-of-breed" analyses of the data warehouse. A "best-of-breed" analysis is one that was created

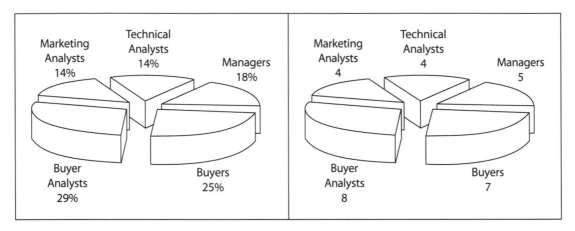

**Figure 4.1**
Profile of business users.

by one person and is clearly better than the analyses done by others with a similar function. I will discuss this further in Chapter 5. Some of this information may need to be included in the vision section of this study, but you will have to determine where it should go.

## Business User Profiles

Management executives will want to know the mixture of participants within the business that this business case was based on. To show this, you should prepare a simple one-page chart depicting the organization and how many people from the different areas of the company participated (Figure 4.1). The point is to present the key beneficiaries of the initial data warehouse implementation. If all the participants are from a single organization, then perhaps a further breakdown is necessary to show the different job functions within that organization. For example, if the subject area is based only on the merchandising group of a retailer, the job functions might be buyer, buying assistant, purchaser, and planning analyst. To that you should add the number of people that participated from each job function. This is also a good thing to do before the business exploration to ensure that you will get quality results with a broader scope. If you have such a chart, perhaps it will be obvious if there is an absence of a particular relevant organization that should be participating in this development.

## Potential Payback

Compiling projections of the potential payback can be a difficult task. This is particularly true for the business people because they think they might be held responsible for the figures that they put forward. Therefore, they can be very reluctant to provide financial figures freely. The safest way to obtain your projections of the potential payback is to build a prototype with the data from only one organization. This allows you to show these improvements, from which you can then project improvements for the remainder of the organization. For a retailer, it is possible to build a small prototype for only one department and then measure the results. With that as a starting point, the potential payback can be determined by computing the benefit of adding additional departments. The potential payback should be calculated very conservatively. This is the way that I recommend going about this process. With a prototype, you will be able to quantify other things besides cost reductions, such as purchasing extra merchandise because of higher-than-expected demand. The prototype will actually prove that the company can earn money from this system! This is what you want in the ROI study too—definite proof of improvement.

> Compiling projections of the potential payback can be a difficult task. This is particularly true for the business people because they think they might be held responsible for the figures that they put forward.

Unfortunately, not every company is afforded the opportunity to build a prototype before the justification as there are costs involved in building a solid prototype system. The simplest and least expensive way to obtain the potential payback without building a prototype is to apply some simple math to the vision statements you drafted. For example, a vision statement may be: "I want to reduce my research time from 80% of my time to 20% of my time." From here it is very easy to calculate the time that will be saved. If that person is spending 80% of the time researching, that comes to 32 hours a week based on a 40-hour workweek. For a conservative estimate, perhaps that time can actually be cut from 80% to 40%—that is, to 16 hours a week. Therefore, the potential payback is 16 hours (32 − 16 = 16). If you calculate that this person will work 48 weeks, the savings in time is 768 hours per year. When you multiply these hours by the person's yearly salary, it comes to a big annual payback. If there are other people doing the same job, the saving of time would easily pay for the system. This does not even consider the fact that their time can be spent in a more productive manner.

## Accumulated Potential Payback Summary

This next section of your case study should present an accumulation of all of the payback opportunities that a data warehouse will provide. Because the details were described in the previous section, this section should not be very long. Basically, you should list each unique payback that you identified and summarize these into a single total. This estimate needs to be very, very conservative. You want everyone to be successful, including the data warehouse implementation. If you are not able to achieve this potential payback number, you may not be ready to build a data warehouse and may need to continue searching or find another approach to finding the payback. Building a prototype is something that can help find more tangible payback figures. The payback projections need to be defined in order for the data warehouse to be successful. If this figure is not achieved, there will be no way to take the data warehouse further after the first implementation. It will be very difficult to build an enterprise data warehouse. The first implementation is very important for later success, so these figures should be conservative.

## Projected Investment Costs with ROI Forecast

In this section you will describe all of the costs that will be involved in the construction of the data warehouse. These costs should focus on delivering the potential payback. Each company will have its own process to calculate this. Some companies will go into great detail to calculate human resources, operation costs, network cost, and the like, while others will need only the hardware and software costs. However your company measures the costs, this is what you need to present here. After you have the cost figures, they need to be compared with the potential payback. There are two dimensions to this: the short-term gain and the long-term gain. The short-term gain is the gain that will be achieved after the first implementation (or the first year). The long-term gain is a forecast beyond the first implementation. For example, the first implementation may be for only one department (short-term), but there may be 16 departments that will eventually be brought in (long-term). Simple graphs are very effective. This section should be only one or two pages long.

## Resource Plan

Finally, you need to outline the resources that are required to implement this data warehouse and to state how long it will take to build. Thus there are two key parts to the resource plan: an implementation resource chart and an implementation timeline. The resource chart is a simple list of the resources that will be needed for the implementation. This should be classified into several areas, such as human resources, computer resources, and project resources. Since you have already mentioned the costs of the project in another section of this business plan, here you should focus more on the required physical resources of the project. For example, you will need a full-time project manager for the duration of the project (nine months). This is a human resource requirement. A computer resource that you will need, other than the computer, is a location to install and maintain the computer. Eventually, you will need two computers: a test computer and a production computer. You will need a couple of trained computer operators. There are many more resources that will be needed for the data warehouse project. This section must outline those resources, other than money, that will be needed to complete this project. At the minimum, this will comprise a physical resource chart and a human resource chart (organizational chart). These are resources you need to complete the project on time and within budget. The details that should be included in this section will depend greatly on the needs of your company.

The very last page of this section should be an implementation timeline. This is a simple one- or

> If there is a completion date in the business case study, I can guarantee that it will be a point of discussion if you start three months later than expected.

two-page chart showing the duration needed to complete each of the major milestones. There should not be so much detail at this point. Additionally, there should be no dates, only tasks and their duration. The reason for using duration has been mentioned earlier: sometimes the project does not start on time. The business plan should state that the project will come to completion nine months after it begins, assuming that all the resources that are needed have been obtained. If there is a completion date in the business case study, I can guarantee that it will be a point of discussion if you start three months later than expected.

## ROI ANALYSIS

After you have built your data warehouse, or a prototype, you need to confirm that the return on investment was achieved. The ROI is a very important part of a data warehouse implementation and should be an integrated part of the project. An ROI study is not an option; it is a necessity. If used properly, it can ensure the future success of the data warehouse implementation as it can enable you to continue investing in the construction of an enterprise data warehouse. Without the ROI analysis, there will be no substantial additional investment. Many companies publicly mention that the data warehouse was a "fantastic investment," but they do not quantify the ROI. I believe such pronouncements indicate that either (1) they don't know the ROI because they did not measure it, or (2) they know the ROI and are not talking about it. In the latter case, they are obviously viewing their investment as a strategic advantage over their competitors. Interestingly, many companies never do an ROI on their data warehouse. Sometimes the technology department will get a favorable response from the business people and see no reason to determine the ROI. They are simply happy that the business people are happy and no longer yelling at them. This is a shame, because determining the ROI is very important for long-term success. Unfortunately, I have been involved with many companies that have never done an ROI after they implemented a data warehouse or data mart. Of course, they have since had a very difficult time proceeding to the enterprise data warehouse implementation because they could not justify the additional investment. If the ROI is not done, the information systems department is not seen as a peer-to-peer partner in the company but remains a cost center. Therefore, you should plan on building an ROI after you begin to see success with your data warehouse.

Wal-Mart did measure the ROI and determined it was over $12,000 per query, and they were performing over 1000 queries a day! By simply extending the ROI across the entire company, that comes to $12 million a day! I will discuss more about how they calculated this in Chapter 9. Interestingly, I don't recall a Sam's Club ROI document, but they had already proven the value of technology with Wal-Mart stores.

The ROI analysis should be prepared approximately one year after implementation of the data warehouse. Building the ROI is an important timing issue. It needs to be built at the right time because the people that benefit from the data warehouse will quickly forget about the older and cumbersome processes they had to use before to obtain the same information. They will think that this information has always been available, so the opportunity for measuring the ROI will fade. The best way to develop your information is to ask the business people what they did with the system. All of these sessions will be one-to-one sessions. No group sessions are needed. You don't have to ask all of the users, just a sample. You will be searching for actions that were taken specifically because of the new information that the data warehouse provided. Here are some good lead-in questions for starting a conversation about ROI: "What did you do with this system this week?" "Did you take any action because of this?" "Did it save or earn money for the company?" Finally, "Could you have done this without this system?" These are critical questions that will drive you down the ROI path. As you get some positive answers, ask for their analyses. In other words, "How did you do that?" Then you listen, document, and gather their results as documentation, including the ROI for the company. You want to be able to compare the before and after situations, with examples. Continue searching for these successes until you have identified enough money to cover the costs of the investment. After these figures are gathered and the accumulated ROI is calculated, it can be expanded for other areas of the company, showing the projected ROI for the year.

> **The ROI analysis should be prepared approximately one year after implementation of the data warehouse.**

There are other benefits to performing the ROI analysis as well. You will be able to determine some "best-of-breed" applications that can be implemented more broadly. You will also learn about the improvements and modifications that are necessary to improve the data warehouse. The most important point is that the individual successes are the companies' successes. The ways in which the business people were able to use the information to make better decisions need to be clearly documented. The ROI can be a reduction in costs, but it also can be an increase in sales and profits. Hopefully, it will equate to a substantial improvement in the total operation. This is where the information technology department should position itself—improving the total company operation. An ROI analysis is the selling document, proving that investing in technology was good. This in turn can change the company's perception of the technology department as a "cost center" to that of a "solution center." To become known as a solution center, the IT department needs to tout the ROI, get it talked about and distributed among the executives of the company.

The remainder of this chapter will discuss the variations from the business case study that are needed to define the key components of an ROI analysis.

## Data Warehouse Background

The first part of the ROI needs to present some of the history of the data warehouse. This information can be taken from the business case study. It should outline the original business sponsors, the first implementation, the basic implementation timeline and resources, improvements over the original design, and so on. This section will set the stage and expectation level of the past; it should not be much longer than three pages.

## One-to-One Discussions

This section contains the details from the one-to-one sessions conducted with the business people. Like the analyses in the business case study, this section presents the results achieved with this system that could not have been achieved before; however, there are ROI figures with each analysis. This section constitutes the majority of the ROI analysis. There should be several pages, including a summary ROI, for each person. A single person can offer more than one analysis that provided a substantial ROI. A personal profile of the individual should accompany every example. This should include their job function, area of responsibility, what they achieved, and the value to the company. A substantial amount of documentation should be included in this section. Specifically, the charts and graphs that were used for each analysis should be included. The ROI figures for each individual will be summarized in the later sections.

## Business User Profiles

This section is identical to the similar section in the business case study, described earlier in this chapter. It should be a simple chart showing the organization and how many people from the different areas of the company participated in the ROI study. A pie chart like Figure 4.1 is good, but be sure to include the ROI for each business area, too. This will illustrate exactly who benefited from the data warehouse and will likewise imply which groups will benefit in the future.

## Actual Payback

Here is the place you list the actual ROI detailed previously for each person that showed a payback. Their names should be listed with their organization and the amount of money they were able to earn or save. If possible, you should categorize each type of payback. You can choose your own categories, but three likely choices are cost reductions, sales increases, and operational improvements. These categories will become important when you want to understand where and how technology can be applied to improve the business. These figures will be used in the next section of your ROI, the Actual Accumulated and Projected Payback Summary.

## Actual Accumulated and Projected Payback Summary

This one- or two-page summary is the meat of the ROI study and may need to be placed in the front of the ROI document. It contains a compilation of the actual payback and the projected payback. These are the two key figures. The absolute or actual payback figure is based on the one-to-one sessions, and the projected figure is based on a reasonable assumption, namely, that other business people using the system will have a similar ROI. The projected payback is very important when the data warehouse is not fully implemented or not being used to its full capacity. The remainder of this section should show the breakdown of the ROI among the different parts of the organization, similar to what is in the same section of the business case study.

## Investment Costs with ROI Conclusion

This section is identical to its counterpart in the business case study, showing the actual cost versus the profit of the data warehouse implementation. It is a simple cost analysis and should be one page long. I would use the estimated payback against the actual cost in this section. What you include in the cost comparison is based on how your company measures costs. You must decide which cost figures are needed based on experience with your company and your company's culture.

## Next-Step Implementation Plan

This last step is often overlooked. When you are successful, you should have a "next-step" proposal. Many companies stop after building only a data mart so the advantages of an enterprise data warehouse are never realized. I would suggest that, since the investment in this data warehouse was profitable, the project should continue. A new vision should be identified here and the access to information should be broadened. Of course, the expectations should be broadened, too. For example, a retailer that successfully created a data mart using the sales data to focus on logistics might want to expand the data mart into a data warehouse by including another subject area, such as supplier performance or promotion effectiveness. This is where you can communicate and document the next steps that are needed. I would hope (for the benefit of your company) that the plan for your company would be to fully integrate the data warehouse into the enterprise so that an even more substantial ROI can be realized.

# 5

# Organizational Integration

The hunger of business people to obtain information is the driving force behind the development of the data warehouse concept. The ability to obtain information easily is often hindered by a lack of support from the technology department. The technology departments of most companies are not accustomed to providing support and training for taking data and turning it into information that can be applied to making better decisions. Therefore, after a data warehouse is implemented, an organizational change usually must occur, to ensure that the business executives can effectively use their data. This change can be substantial for many organizations because such jobs may not have existed before the data warehouse was implemented. This chapter will outline the typical organizational supports needed when moving from earlier information systems into a data warehouse.

Human integration is a very important part of the data warehouse implementation. If you intend to build an enterprise data warehouse, then you will integrate information from all parts of your company into every aspect of decision making. To continually improve the data warehouse applications, you will also need to integrate the various business people with the technology people. With classical application development, the project was finished when the user could access the list of data on a green computer screen. When the user accepted that this green-screen application was built as planned, the technology department could build the next green-screen application. Typically, there was very little training and support after the green-screen application was functioning properly and in production. A data warehouse implementation should not be handled in this manner.

With data warehousing, you can never really walk away and think that you have finished the job. For every analysis that is completed, another better analysis will be needed. There will always be a better "best-of-breed" analysis that needs to be built. As mentioned earlier, a best-of-breed analysis is a process that a business user has created, or pieced together, that provides a far superior analysis than a previous one. Usually, its creator has used this best-of-breed analysis to substantially improve his or her business function. When other people performing the same function can improve their own jobs using this analysis, it is a best-of-breed analysis. These best-of-breed analyses normally need to be automated, made simpler to use, documented, and made available for other people with the same job. Identifying these applications is very important to expedite and improve business decisions. In fact, these are the very analyses that will provide your company with a strategic technological advantage over your competitors. Finding the best-of-breed analyses will not be possible if the business people and technology people are strictly separated. Essentially, both groups need to undergo a learning process, spending more time with each other and learning to work together to apply technology to solve business problems.

> **With data warehousing, you can never really walk away and think that you have finished the job.**

Providing people to support a new information infrastructure is an evolutionary process. Evolution may not be the perfect word to describe the formation of different organizational structures because the older organizations may still remain. However, the organizational structures within a company will go through an adaptive process to the new technology. Look at the evolution of the telephone. The telephones of the 1930s are essentially the same as we use today. However, we now have a larger selection of home telephones. In addition to a huge selection of colors and styles, we have a choice of wireless home phones, mobile phones, and even satellite phones. All of these phones and systems provide the same basic service as that available in the 1930s. The supporting technology, on the other hand, is completely different. This new technology allows people to talk on the phone anywhere in the world. From a business perspective, the mobile phone enables more effective communications and faster decisions. These new technology structures have allowed us to adopt an entirely new method of communication. As with any new technology, there are new issues that arise: for example, how many times have you heard a mobile phone ring in a meeting? (We have even advanced that ringing technology. Now the mobile phones can ring with songs from Beethoven!) The point is that there are completely new organizations that support this new technology as well as the classic technology. Data warehousing requires adaptation. It should integrate into your business gradually, easily, and painlessly—without loss of other services.

In Chapter 1, I talked about executive information systems as being one of the earliest types of decision support systems. The same people who built the OLTP systems built these systems. To their credit, they were very reliable systems. Yet they were very structured and had very little support. The EIS systems were not given the same level of support that the functionally oriented applications received. If, for example, the purchase order entry application had an incorrect value in a field, it would be fixed as soon as possible. If the EIS system had a wrong value, it would be fixed as soon as practical. This was not wrong. Truly, the other applications needed the higher level of support. And this level of support for the functionally oriented applications will remain very high. What happens over time after a data warehouse implementation is that information becomes more critical for the day-to-day decision making and, therefore, information delivery becomes more important. As a

> **Data warehousing requires adaptation. It should integrate into your business gradually, easily, and painlessly—without loss of other services.**

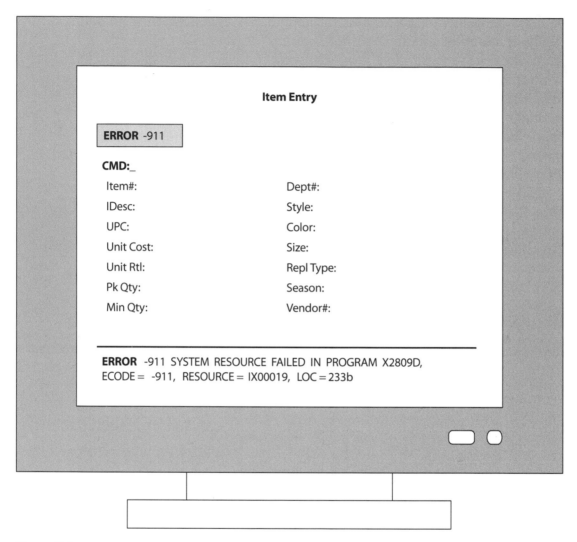

**Item Entry**

ERROR -911

CMD:_

| | |
|---|---|
| Item#: | Dept#: |
| IDesc: | Style: |
| UPC: | Color: |
| Unit Cost: | Size: |
| Unit Rtl: | Repl Type: |
| Pk Qty: | Season: |
| Min Qty: | Vendor#: |

**ERROR** -911 SYSTEM RESOURCE FAILED IN PROGRAM X2809D,
ECODE= -911, RESOURCE = IX00019, LOC = 233b

**Figure 5.1**
Typical technology
error message.

result, the support structure for the data warehouse becomes more and more critical as the company begins to rely on that information. The higher level of support will become mandatory, particularly as you begin to build an enterprise data warehouse. When information delivery is not essential, the people in the technology department will remain focused on solving errors such as "-911 SYSTEM RESOURCE FAILED IN PROGRAM X2809D, ECODE=-911, RESOURCE=IX00019, LOC=233b" (Figure 5.1).

This type of problem resolution is important, of course, but different problems will arise with a data warehouse that are equally important. Someone might ask, "Why is the year-to-date unit percent increase positive when fewer units were sold this year?" A problem like this could indicate a substantial problem with the data, the analysis, or even the source system. It could be that the source system is not functioning properly after a software upgrade. This illustrates another benefit of the data warehouse: it will often identify problems in the legacy systems. When many people are using the data to make decisions, they will find the anomalies that exist in the data from the older legacy systems as analyses show strange deviations. With this heightened awareness, there will need to be additional support for both the data warehouse and the legacy systems. The functional operationally dependent applications will always have a higher priority than information-only applications. The organizational structure to support them will remain too. But the level of support needed to maintain information dissemination should be much higher after a data warehouse is built. Therefore, you should plan to build an organizational supporting infrastructure for the data warehouse.

> Another benefit of the data warehouse is that it will often identify problems in the legacy systems.

After the EIS applications were built, companies began to separate the two types of applications. They also separated the support organizations. Larger companies, at one time or another, created something called an *information center*. The information center was a place where people could call, or come to, to ask for help on the informational systems. The purpose of the information center was to understand the business situation and provide the needed information as quickly as possible. Realistically, the people at the center called other people and translated the business question into something a programmer could understand. After developing some experience with repetitive business questions, they would be able to direct the business user to an existing report that might be of help. If he was lucky, he might get his report the next day. The information center people might even create an entirely new report for that user. An important benefit of such a center to the business was they could show the business people how to retrieve information from the functional operational systems. Of course, they could provide other information too. They knew where all of the "on-demand" reports were located and how they could be run. They might even run those reports for the business users.

Information centers still exist today, and they will continue to evolve. As information becomes more valuable to a company, more people will be dedicated to its support and dissemination. A big improvement for information centers came when a new technology was implemented, structured query language (SQL). With SQL and some formatting applications, reports could be provided more quickly. The people in the information center began to set up some dynamic SQL scripts that the users could run themselves. Soon the business users began modifying these scripts. They learned enough about SQL and technology that they could get the required results without the help of the information center. The technology people also claim, "They learned enough to be dangerous." In fact, their dangerous appetite for information has caused problems with the functional operational systems. Ironically, these people were often viewed as pests by the technology department because only a few people in the company had this monstrous appetite for information. The technology department definitely did not need pests; they already had enough bugs in their code. Consequently, not much time was dedicated to helping these people learn better techniques of information retrieval. Most computer departments were even a bit concerned that if the business users learned more, those users would simply gorge themselves with the technology department's precious computer resources. Some people in the technology department were even afraid they would lose their jobs if the users could do some of the work themselves! The information center was there to help and provided a substantial amount of flexibility for the user community. Unfortunately, these small impromptu applications were not seen as a production system, even though they were valuable to the company, so the support structure was still not there.

As companies adapted to the information center concept, more resources were put in place to support this group, especially in regard to the business aspect of the company. Sometimes business people who had learned the technology better than others were brought into the information center group to narrow the business knowledge gap between the business people and the technology people. Wal-Mart brought people from the business area into the technology department after they had built the data warehouse, and this certainly created an appreciation of individual strengths by both parties. They also went one step further and created an information help desk in the merchandising department. This created a substantially different type of information center, representing the first step toward changing the focus from technology to business. Additionally, this substantially improved the interchange of information between these very different disciplines. Business people could ask for a report with the confidence that the business concept was understood. But they still had to wait for their reports, and the applications that were built from this organization were still not perceived as business-critical applications.

> **Wal-Mart brought people from the business area into the technology department after they had built the data warehouse, and this certainly created an appreciation of individual strengths by both parties.**

At the same time, a new technology was being utilized, the personal computer (PC). When PCs began appearing in businesses, the technology department viewed them as pests too, because they created a whole new set of problems. Yes, they were very good at spreadsheets and graphing. The technology department had to maintain these machines, but the business users essentially had complete control of their PCs. The business people could download data to their PC, load it into a spreadsheet, and perform some analysis. They could do this analysis away from the production systems. The point of contention was that they still had to obtain the data from the production systems and download it into their PC.

The data warehouse became a concept to eliminate that contention. The data was copied to another database so the PC business users would not have to contend with the production systems. Additionally, they would not have to wait for a report to print. From the technology department's perspective, removing the pest off the production systems was a good thing. Reluctantly, the technology department allowed the information center to have a duplicate copy of the production database. The users with and without PCs could access the database without interfering with the "real" database. Normally, the copy was updated nightly. This really made everyone happy. The business people were not knocked off the system because they ran a query for eight hours. The technology department was happy because they did not *have* to knock them off the production system. Their requests did not create contention with the functionally operational database. More importantly, the information center began to maintain the PCs and the read-only applications. When this happened, there was more information than ever being consumed and the support level increased slightly. There was still not enough support, however.

Many companies are in this exact situation today. They don't develop further because they do not fully understand the value of infor-

> **Many companies don't develop further because they do not fully understand the value of information to their company.**

mation to their company. There are still many more opportunities to provide value to the business with information. The key to raising the level of support is to integrate these two different types of applications, the decision support application and the functionally operational applications. The data in the data warehouse can be used for analyses and the results can be fed into other applications. This process is not difficult; it is quite natural, if it is allowed to proceed. What is the process? The data warehouse is used to

build information, or create data from data, through an interactive process. Once the data reflects the desired results, it is posted into the functional process. This is one element of an enterprise data warehouse and an operational data store.

Let's look at a retail example: allocation for a new product that will be introduced into the stores. First let's discuss the classic process of creating the first purchase order. Before the data warehouse was created, the allocation of a new article was an educated guess. For most retailers, the process of determining the proper store allocation required calculating a percentage of units to be shipped based on 10 size groups. The largest store would get the largest percentage of units, while the smallest store would get the smallest percentage of units. The buyer would plan this out on paper, then key the quantities and percentages into the purchase order entry application. Some retailers allowed the buyer the option to adjust the amount per store, but this process remained less than ideal. With a data warehouse, by contrast, the buyer could use the sales history data from a similar article as the basis for the new product allocation. Using the other article's sales trend, the data warehouse analysis could subtract overstocked inventory and add the out-of-stock inventory to create a better allocation for this new article. This could be created for each store location and would be more accurate, and quicker, than in the past. Using this process, the buyer is able to manually override any allocation suggested by the data warehouse application before the data is automatically fed into the purchase order entry system. The buyer can work with the suggested allocation figures until she is comfortable with the allocation. When the buyer is ready, she can press a single confirmation and all of the information will be automatically moved into the purchase order system. The allocation suggestions of this analysis tend to be far superior to the most experienced guesses of the past. A far more accurate allocation will be produced from all buyers. An often unexpected by-product of a process like this is that the level of support becomes very high. At this point, the analysis is just as important as the functional operations systems. The business will demand a much higher level of support, and it will have to be provided.

This retail example illustrates the best-of-breed approach to a data warehouse (Figure 5.2). A best-of-breed application builds upon the business and technology foundation together. Finding the best-of-breed applications requires that the company be actively searching for better processes to apply this technology to the business. Companies must want to improve their business with the technology. The level of support must be high. Companies must be able to identify the people that are performing better because of the technological processes they use. They must identify, document, and build these unique processes. This takes time. It has nothing to do with added complexity but is more of a management process. If you have all the data from all areas within your company in a single database, applications such as these can be created relatively fast. To get to this level, development of the data warehouse must be in the more mature phases. Implementing

> **Finding the best-of-breed applications requires that the company be actively searching for better processes to apply this technology to business.**

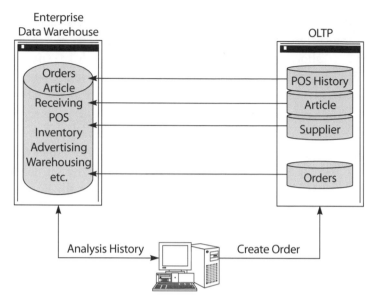

**Figure 5.2**  Best-of-breed new article allocation data flow.

these best-of-breed applications will become more important approximately one year after the data warehouse is built. When you get to this point, you have enabled business executives to make better, faster decisions, but you also have enabled them to easily take action based on the information. This type of integration takes you beyond the typical data warehouse implementation into an enterprise data warehouse.

The business will learn that it cannot manage without these applications and that the level of support must increase. The users of this application are not experimenting, they are outperforming their colleagues. These are no longer "pesky" users "playing" with data, but are business people providing real business value. As more of these types of applications are delivered to the business people, the desire for information will continue to be supported by the business. The more the business learns about its information, the more it learns about the business itself, and the more information will be needed. As the information needs increase, the company will view its ability to utilize this information as a com-

> **The more the business learns about its information, the more it learns about the business itself, and the more information will be needed.**

petitive advantage. The priority given to the previously neglected information center, as well as to the technology department, will increase. The business will provide more support to the technology department. When the company is supporting the technology department's business initiatives (to apply technology to improve the business), then the cost-center perception of the technology department will change. Companies must learn how their technology departments can do more than reduce cost. They can increase sales. When this cost-center perception changes, technology departments will be viewed more as partners. When they become a business partner, then they will no longer be viewed as a "necessary evil" but as more of a strategic business advantage. Wal-Mart believes the technology they have is a strategic advantage over their competitors. The company shows its support of that technology by investing more in technology as opposed to investing that money in something else, such as inventory. When other companies share this viewpoint, it will be easier for them to invest more in their technology department too.

> **Wal-Mart believes the technology they have is a strategic advantage over their competitors. The company shows their support of that technology by investing more in it.**

How does this apply to the organizational structure? Hopefully, it will change the function of the information center. As it evolves to be able to suggest and document the needs of the business users, its function will become more like that of a business information analyst than that of a clerk. This is a new job that did not exist before the data warehouse. The center will become the main interface for the new development of many information-related applications. A major advantage for both the technology department and the business department is that the information center will learn and teach more about the daily functions of the business people to enable better, faster, information-related application development.

Of course, it is a partnership in development. The business people will need to allow information center people to become part of their organizations, and vice versa. Essentially, this means that the technology people will need to move, physically, into the business offices. I see this as the only way to learn what the business people do on a daily basis. It must be a long-term commitment too, not just a day or two. Working together, both parties will be focused on delivering the day-to-day business information needs of the company. To move the technology beyond a data warehouse, they must merge together. The easiest first step is to move the entire information center into the offices of the business executives. This will quickly remove the physical barriers of communication. This is a natural fit because the people in the information center already know a lot about the business needs and how to apply the technology to those needs. The challenge is to bring the other people from the technology department to the business community. The opposite is difficult as well—bringing the business people to the technology community. This is how companies can foster new application development with a business focus. Certainly, the entire organization cannot mix effectively. In the technology department, there are some people that are not allowed out of their box! ☺ Some people will mix like oil and water, but many will mix nicely. When they mix well, communication will improve and the depth of business knowledge will grow.

This concept goes completely against the classic definition of an information center. For many companies that build a data warehouse, access is restricted to only a few people. These people, perhaps only people from the information center, deliver the reporting needs of the company. These people take requests, build the reports, and deliver the results as soon as possible—not uncommonly a week later. While this is an improvement over a three- or four-week wait, this is not adequate because there will be a second request. The business people will return to ask another question as soon as the report is completed. If this is happening in your company, there are probably countless latent business questions waiting to be answered after other questions are resolved. The only way to get to these questions is to freely give the information to the business people. There is no need for an information checkpoint guardhouse. Give information freely. Knowledge will grow as you give

**There is no need for an information checkpoint guardhouse.**

information away freely. You must plan on building your data warehouse so that these decision makers have the information they need to make better decisions faster. This means they must learn more about technology and the technology people must learn more about the business. They have to integrate.

Of course, the important aspect of this integration is the human aspect. The interaction and understanding of the two different disciplines will foster better information-related application development. This is a partnership where both parties benefit. The technology people will learn more about the business. The business people will learn more about the technology. Together they will build more effective applications. A side benefit is that understanding brings patience from both. Hopefully, your company's culture will adopt this, and it will bring a new partnership between very different business units that will have a common focus to improve the business.

# 6

# Technology

There are so many new technologies that can be applied to building a data warehouse that you could spend years learning about them all. The front-end tool is what the business people will see, touch, and understand as their data warehouse. The database will determine the flexibility, speed, and growth capabilities of the data warehouse. I believe these two are the most strategic pieces of technology that will be chosen. Many companies become obsessed with evaluating the new technology. By the time the evaluation period is over, a new product crops up that needs to be evaluated. This cycle can continue endlessly. I do not like this endless evaluation game. I have a more practical approach to the technology: if it helps solve the business problem, then it should be purchased and used as soon as possible. If you are building a data warehouse where the technology will substantially improve the operation of your company, then buy the technology that works. You must ask yourself, "How much money will be lost in the technology evaluation period?" Make a decision and go with it! Practically, you will have to evaluate some technology, but my point is not to spend so much time doing that. There is a business that needs a solution to earn more money, and it is often the case that the worst technology implementation can enable a better decision.

There are two key pieces of technology that need serious consideration when building the data warehouse, the front-end tool and the database. If you get these two right the first time, then you have made 80% of the technology decisions. There will always be technical implementation issues, no matter how long you evaluate the tools. You could create a list of functional requirements, such as ANSI SQL, ODBC compliant, drill-down, drill-up, drill-across, OLAP, MOLAP, efficient filtering, DDE and OLE support, ad hoc capabilities, Alert function, batch reporting, and trigger support. Then you could rank the importance of each one and determine the average score based on group participation. This can be done if the business has time to wait or, might I say, waste. How much time should you spend evaluating technology? The maximum I would allow is three months. Even this might be too long. Perhaps the evaluation should be combined with the prototype application. If you combine it into the prototype, you will understand exactly what the technical issues are and you will have a system built from this effort. The technology pieces have to fit and function together, so constructing the prototype is an excellent way to evaluate the tools. When all the pieces of technology function nicely together, it is time to move the application into a production environment. A better way to evaluate the tool is to determine if it solves the business problem, yes or no. If yes, the next question is, What does it cost? After you know the cost, then the business people can make a decision on whether to invest their money or not. This chapter will discuss what I believe are the important issues in selecting a front-end tool and the database for the data warehouse.

> There are two pieces of technology that need serious consideration when building the data warehouse, the front-end tool and the database.

> The technology pieces have to fit and function together, so constructing the prototype is an excellent way to evaluate the tools.

## THE FRONT-END TOOL

The front-end tool is the application that will be seen by the business people. Normally, it will reside on their desktop PCs. Of course, if you are building an enterprise data warehouse, there will be many, many front-end interfaces to the data warehouse database. Some examples of the front-end tool are the desktop PCs, portable PCs, radio-frequency (RF) devices, older CRT screens, Web sites, and standard reports. The selection of the front-end tool in the first development of the data warehouse implementation seems to be the most difficult choice for many companies, mainly because there are so many choices. There are so many choices, in fact, that I will not list any of them in this book. If I were to list them, their product names would change, the company would be bought, and five new companies would provide very competitive products—all of this before the ink is dry on this book. With all the new and improved technology popping up every day, it is even more difficult to make a decision on the proper front-end tools.

The most important decision regarding the front-end application is the choice of strategic implementation. Do you build a customized front-end application or buy it off the shelf? There are pros and cons to both. The off-the-shelf application is the simplest to implement, while the customized application is the most powerful for a specific solution. Each has its place in the life cycle of the data warehouse. It is reasonable to assume that you will need to do both. In the beginning it might be best to purchase an off-the-shelf product. Later, as you begin to develop very complex, repetitive, or best-of-breed applications, the self-built customized application will be best. If you are building an enterprise data warehouse, you will definitely

> **The most important decision regarding the front-end application is the choice of strategic implementation.**

have both. Wal-Mart used a combination of both. They purchased what they could and built the remainder. Most of their systems are customized because they focus on delivering what the business needs.

Most definitely, the off-the-shelf front-end tool will be the fastest to implement, but it certainly will not solve all your problems. There are two flavors of off-the-shelf products: multipurpose and single-purpose.

The multipurpose tools provide a great deal of flexibility with their analyses, as they are designed for all industries. Because of the flexibility, however, the user interface is normally more difficult to learn and use. These are very good for those power users with the undying thirst for information and a very broad scope of the company. The single-purpose tools, on the other hand, have perfected a specific task. They are usually very industry specific. Because of the special functionality, the interface is usually easier to use for that task. These tools are excellent for enabling power users to perfect their specific job functions. So both of these types of off-the-shelf applications are directed toward the power users that understand either the broad use of information or the very narrow functional focus. Some developers of off-the-shelf tools try to cross over these boundaries; some are successful, too, but it is difficult to become a perfectionist at both multipurpose and single-purpose tasks.

The crossover is where customized applications can become very powerful. They can be designed to perform both multipurpose and single-purpose tasks. They can be whatever you make them to be. Frankly, a customized application is the best way to go. Of all of the DSS applications that I have been involved in, the customized applications have provided the most value to the business. They are also the easiest to use and, when developed properly, require little training. The best-of-breed applications can be developed to enable the normal user to perform the very complex analyses that previously only the power user could perform. They can be integrated into other existing applications to provide those applications with detailed information that was not available previously. The drawback is the cost: developing your own application in the first implementation can be higher than purchasing an off-the-shelf tool. You can build a combination of off-the-shelf applications and a customized application with some tools. Some data warehouse tool providers allow you to use their analysis engine while you build the front-end application. This is a great middle-of-the-road solution. It takes some of the complexity out of the database retrieval in the development phase and can speed development while providing a simple, easy-to-use interface. Of course, when you integrate the data warehouse into all facets of the business, customized application development is the only way to do this properly. You cannot possibly integrate the information into every applicable job task with an off-the-shelf application; customization is required.

To illustrate the limited capabilities of an off-the-shelf application, let me give you a practical retail example while comparing an off-the-shelf product versus a custom application. The example is again allocation of a new article. Keeping it as simple as possible, a retailer has already decided to introduce a new article into its stores but has not decided how much of this product each store will receive. Of course, this is a big retailer with over a thousand stores. Today, the buyer creates the initial purchase

**When you integrate the data warehouse into all facets of the business, customized application development is the only way to do this properly.**

order using the purchase order entry (POE) system of old. First, he puts in a total quantity of this new product to purchase. This fancy POE system automatically calculates a distribution for each class of the different sizes of stores. This retailer has 10 size classes. Of course, the buyer has the ability to modify each of the volumes of every size class. After the buyer is satisfied with the figures, he presses the Create Order button, and the order is entered into the PO system. When this fancy POE system was implemented, well over a decade ago, it was fantastic. Now, however, a more precise method of determining the allocation is needed. The buyer wants to use the actual sales of a similar product to determine the allocation of new articles. Sounds like a good application for a data warehouse, right?

As you can imagine, we will need to have the same functionality as the old PO entry system plus the ability to analyze historic information. After working carefully with the buying organization, we determine the steps needed to improve on this function (Figure 6.1). Here are the steps:

1. The buyer wants the ability to review the sales, inventory, and out-of-stock of various similar articles.
2. He wants the system to calculate a suggested allocation for the new article based on the sales, inventory, and out-of-stock situation of the existing article.
3. He wants to be able to review the suggested allocation by the 10 size classes as well as by each store.

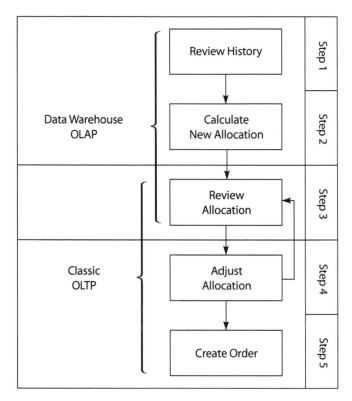

**Figure 6.1** New order entry steps.

4. He wants to be able to override each figure manually or dynamically by changing dependent figures such as the total purchase amount.

5. Finally, he wants to be able to create a purchase order for each store.

This advanced application requires both the data warehousing (OLAP) resources and the functional (OLTP) processing. Both a customized application and an off-the-shelf application will be able to perform steps 1 through 3, as this is a typical data warehousing application. At step 4, there will be many off-the-shelf applications that will not be able to perform. At step 5, there are very few that will even claim to have this capability. Those that do claim the ability to do it require a tremendous amount of customization. As you can see, or will find out for yourself, it is quite a challenge for the off-the-shelf application to perform a full-task cycle of this new function. Step 4 is the point at which the off-the-shelf data warehouse applications have a difficult time delivering. Another challenge is integration. Many off-the-shelf applications cannot integrate into the older applications either. Therefore, they cannot be customized to enable this type of new functionality. This leaves your company with only one option, a customized application.

As you can see, these technology choices can be difficult. The choices become much easier as you tie the data warehouse implementation to the business. This is why I have advised focusing on one, maybe two at the maximum, business areas. Deliver that first area, but constantly design for the entire business operation. Enable other applications to easily connect to your data warehouse. Decide on the front-end application for that first project and buy only what you need. I can guarantee it will not be needed for all other business information requirements. You will need to select another off-the-shelf application or build another customized application to solve new problems. The important point is to focus on the business and finish that single project, then move to the next application that will improve the business substantially.

From a financial perspective, there is the cost of software licenses. If you create your own application, there will be fewer ongoing licensing costs. Even if you buy the software, you do not have to buy licenses for the entire company, only for the people that will be using it this year. If your first project is the prototype, then buy only what you need for the prototype. As the implementation continues, the data warehouse will begin to resemble your entire company, and the needed software will be clearly understood.

> **Decide on the front-end application for that first project and buy only what you need.**

## THE DATABASE TOOL

The other equally important tool is the database. This is something that the business people will feel, in response time and flexibility, but they will not directly see. Making the selection can become a very technical process but need not be. There are essentially three main concepts that need to be understood: compatibility, maintenance, and linear growth. The mix of these three concepts will allow you to choose the appropriate database for your data warehouse. Once again, you could create a list of required functionality, such as ANSI SQL, ODBC compliant, efficient SQL parsing, outer-join capability, binary joins, efficient filtering, ad hoc capabilities, full-file scan time, trigger support, mixed workload management, and optical-fiber connections. Then you could rank the importance of each one and determine the average score based on group participation. I think you know my viewpoint on that already. If you can quantify the compatibility, maintenance needs, and linear growth needs of your data warehouse, then all other issues are less important and can be resolved in due time.

When Wal-Mart was deciding on the database, Teradata (now NCR) was the only practical choice. Their database was specifically designed for queries. They were the only company that could easily manage that large volume of data for the purpose of ad hoc querying. They were not the only MPP (massively parallel processor) hardware provider, but Compaq's (former Tandem's) Himalaya was at this time a pure OLTP system. There was no MPP platform available from IBM. Certainly, the merchant databases, such as Oracle, Informix, and Sybase, were not in the MPP business. Today there are many more choices. Most would agree that managing 650 gigabytes is no longer an impossible task for most database vendors. For this size of a database, you now have a choice that Wal-Mart did not. Of course, it would be a huge undertaking for Wal-Mart to change databases now.

## Database Compatibility

The main reason to discuss database compatibility is so that the database is not chosen blindly. What I mean by compatibility is that the database will work with the front-end application, and the data can be transferred from the older systems. Nothing else should really matter. I am not really concerned about other types of compatibility. The main issue is data flow. The computers need to be compatible enough that data can flow from the classical operational system all the way through to the user, with relative ease. If the front-end application has been chosen and only runs on a specific machine, there is no need to discuss another option. Your choice is made, and you have to live with the database that the application runs on. Otherwise, you need to ensure that the database and the computer on which it will run can connect to both the front-end application and the back-end applications (source systems).

I am really not too concerned about technical things such as ODBC standard and other interfaces. These types of standards are important but they are also confining. It is always interesting for me to hear the phrase *open computer system.* Technology people want to develop an "open" system. This implies that the system will run on any database on any computer system. Then they select a database that is "open" and immediately use the database extensions that are not considered open. I have never had a business executive with a business problem limit himself to a solution that requires an "open" system. He wants a solution to the problem. All too often the technology people bind themselves with minor compatibility issues that they themselves created. It is amusing to me that there are people who think Microsoft Windows is an "open" system. Microsoft Windows is a "cheap" operating system. If you develop an application on Windows, it will run on Windows. You do have a choice of Windows: Windows 3.1, Windows 95, Windows 98, Windows NT! If applications are truly open, they will run on other operating systems such as Unix, MVS, Linux, and Macintosh. Therefore, in the technological world, "standard" and "open" software really means "cheap" software. This is how standards are set. This is why the Internet has become so popular. It is easy and cheap. The Internet is currently the cheapest so it will continue to be a driving force. Anyway, the technology compatibility issues typically follow the money chain. If you have a huge list of compatibility issues, it will almost certainly doom your data warehouse implementation to failure.

> ## I have never had a business executive with a business problem limit himself to a solution that requires an "open" system.

There are some legitimate issues that need to be explored when selecting compatible database technology. Economy is a key consideration. One such economic issue may be that your company already has some resources that are not being used. If a computer is not being fully utilized and has a database on it, use it, if it is practical. Even if it is not going to be the final database, perhaps it can become the prototype or proof-of-concept data warehouse. If the database or computer is not strong enough, it will be easier to quantify the resources that will be needed. This database will need to be compatible with the front-end application. However, very few companies have computers lying around not being used.

## Database Maintenance

Database maintenance is a very important aspect of a data warehouse, particularly when the data volume becomes very large. When I say *database maintenance,* I really mean several things. From a practical point of view, it means managing the flow of data. Data will be flowing in and out of the data warehouse: in from the functional systems and out to the front-end tools. For enterprise data warehousing, it will also flow in from the front-end tools. The database, and the computer it will run on, must be able to manage this flow of data easily. If the flow of data becomes a difficult task to manage, then you can be certain that the technical people will focus on making the technology function instead of finding solutions for the business. Therefore, the data warehouse database must be able to manage this basic flow of data efficiently and effectively.

There are four major technological manageability points to consider when selecting your data warehouse database: reliability, minimal indexing, dynamic reorganization, and linear growth. I will discuss these four in more depth, but let me give you an overview of how they work together. If you are in the technology department, you know that every database supplier claims to have all of these qualities in its database, but realistically they do not. These four points all work together to substantially simplify manageability. When the manageability is simplified, the work needed to manage the database is eliminated and labor costs are reduced accordingly. Reliability is exactly that: the software and hardware must be reliable. What I mean by minimal indexing is *not* allocating space for the primary index. If you do not have to allocate space for the primary index, you eliminate the associated storage costs as well as maintenance complexity. If you do not have so many indexes, you do not have to perform so many database reorganizations. If the database can remain on-line while it is being reorganized, then you have eliminated a huge amount of the scheduled nightly processing window. Finally, if your database is truly a linear database, then you can guarantee a performance level as the system grows. Linear databases allow you to scale to thousands of CPUs and disks. When your application is designed for linear growth, performance is a matter of purchasing additional hardware and installing it, not redesigning the entire application. Once again, the three technology elements that will allow unbridled growth are minimal indexing, dynamic reorganization, and linear growth. You want a database that does not require space to be allocated for the primary index. You need a database that can be reorganized anytime even as other processes continue. Finally, you want to be able to grow your system linearly so you can guarantee the same response times no matter how large the database grows. When you have these, you have made a very solid database choice for a very large data warehouse implementation.

In the remainder of this chapter I make reference to "large databases." I think I need to clarify "large" so you will understand my perspective. If your database will be over 400 gigabytes, that is a large database: 400 gigabytes is 400,000,000,000 characters. I am referring to raw data, not disk drive space. Depending on the database you select, you will require a system to have anywhere between 550 gigabytes to 1.5 terabytes of disk drive space. The problems of managing the big databases are the indexing, sorting, reorganization, and growth. I will discuss all of these but sorting. There is not much you can do about sorting because this is normally integrated into the database you will select. Of course, there are databases that perform sorts better than others. The massively parallel databases are particularly good at sorting. They are also very scalable because of the inherent architecture.

## Reliability

Reliability is so fundamental in my thinking that I almost forgot to include it in this book. The data warehouse needs to be available when basic problems, such as disk failures, occur. I can guarantee that a disk drive will fail. When that disk fails, will your hardware, software, and application continue to run? The same goes for the CPU and other hardware components. Reliability means that you do not have to be concerned with the database becoming corrupt, or even going off-line, because of a common system failure. This usually means that you need duplication, minimally at the database level. Ideally, the duplication runs throughout the system and down to the hardware level.

> I can guarantee that a disk drive will fail. When that disk fails, will your hardware, software, and application continue to run?

From a project perspective, this means that something as simple as a disk failure does not slow down development. The bad disk is taken off-line, replaced, and brought back on-line all while the data warehouse application continues to run unaffected. Sometimes, a disk failure is not noticed until the serviceman is waiting at the door. This is the type of redundancy that is needed for a large-scale data warehouse application. The drawback is that extra money must be invested in the redundant hardware and sometimes in the application design. The investment cost of redundancy is difficult for some companies. They do not want to spend the extra money. The extra cost is usually associated with the extra disk space needed to mirror the database. If you are building a small data mart that is dependent on a data warehouse, then redundancy may not be an issue because you can reload your data in a matter of minutes. If you are building a multiterabyte data warehouse, redundancy is a must because the data may take days to reload. If the data warehouse is not reliable, you will spend all of your development time recovering from failures rather than developing business solutions. The extra investment in reliable technology will certainly pay off in the development and maintenance of the data warehouse project.

### Minimal Indexing

All databases require that an index be created so that you can quickly access the data records. An index is simply a method to gain quicker access to the detailed records in the database. It is a lot like a card catalog in a library. If you are searching for a book in a library, you can find it by searching through every shelf in the library or you can use the index cards. In a library, as the selection of books grows, the librarians will insert more index cards into a single drawer. When the drawer gets full, they must split the drawer into two drawers. They need to keep the alphabetical sequence, so they must move all other drawers over so the new drawer can become part of the entire file. If you want to find a book, it is relatively easy and quick when you use the card catalog. This is nearly identical to a database index. If you want to find a database record, using the index will be much faster than searching the entire database. A book is never placed on the shelf until the index card is created. As in the library, the index of a record is created at the same time the record is placed in the database. One of the problems of both the library and a database is to maintain the indexes.

To complicate things, you may need more than one index. What do you do then? A library usually has three sets of index cards: title cards, author cards, and subject cards. As you can see, this indexing concept is good but it gets more and more complicated and more difficult to maintain. There are some databases that can eliminate the primary indexes, as well as the reorganization associated with them. How do they do that? We should take the library example again. One of the indexes could be eliminated if all the books were maintained in a specific order on the shelf, by author or by title or by subject. If the books were sorted by author on the shelf and you knew the author, then you would understand exactly where to go, directly to the shelf. However, if you only knew the title, you would still need to use the author or subject index catalog. Like this example, some databases do not allocate any space for the index because they maintain their records in a specific key order. This is a substantial benefit for companies that are going to build a very large database. This not only eliminates a tremendous amount of disk space but it eliminates the management of those indexes and their associated space. By eliminating the primary indexes, the computer system size can be reduced by one-half. This helps manageability, too. There are two proven databases that do not allocate space for the primary index: the Compaq NonStop SQL database and the NCR Teradata database. Not surprisingly, they are used to maintain the world's largest databases. The point is that the majority of the index maintenance can be completely eliminated. Of course, that means that the database does not need to maintain the index and will not need to reorganize it. It does not alleviate the need for storing your records (or books) properly. You must still do this, but it does eliminate the maintenance process of one index. Most tables in a database will have only one index, so this can eliminate a tremendous amount of work and free the people to focus on delivering the business solution.

### Dynamic Reorganization

It is a relatively easy process to get the data into the database. Once the data is in the database, you have to be able to maintain the data. This is where you will learn whether or not your database is easy to manage. As the database gets larger and larger, many databases will not be able to manage the volume effectively. Because of their inherent architecture, some databases will begin to slow down the flow of data as they age. This is because the database becomes fragmented. To improve the performance of the database, it needs to be reorganized for performance. All databases need reorganization. The difference is in how each one does it. Many databases require that the flow of data be halted during this operation. This is not necessarily bad until the reorganization process bleeds over into the workweek, that is, from 8 A.M. to 6 P.M., Monday through Friday. Then this is a huge problem. If the volume is large enough, it can become an unmanageable problem. If the business comes to rely on the data warehouse and the database cannot manage the data, this can cause a huge technical problem—as well as a career-changing problem for the technology director! Other databases allow this reorganization to occur while the flow of data continues to be 100% available. These databases can even maintain the responsiveness of the database during the reorganization process, thereby providing the exact same response times to the business people's queries. Most of the data volume problems occur over time, as the system grows. Since most data warehouses start small and grow, this manageability problem is sometimes difficult to identify.

> **If the business comes to rely on the data warehouse and the database cannot manage the data, this can cause a huge technical problem.**

Using the library example, keeping the card catalog up-to-date and in good shape is a necessary function for the library. Just as in the library, maintaining the index in the appropriate order is an important function of the database. To maintain the indexes, as well as the base records, every database has a reorganization process. If the librarian needs to reorganize the card catalogs and does not allow anyone to access them during that time, you will have trouble finding your book. If the library is really large, the only practical way to find the book is via the card catalog, and therefore you will wait until she is finished. The same applies to a database. If the database does not allow access to the index, in essence you will not be able to access that record. In a decision support environment, this is unthinkable. I believe that a data warehouse must provide unlimited access to the data. This is even more important as companies grow and establish operations in all parts of the world. For example, when a company's business-to-business (B2B) interface is on the Internet, it will need access to the data warehouse around the clock. Therefore, it is my conclusion that the database must be able to perform these functions as the records are placed in the database, not in the nightly processing window.

## Database Linear Growth

Linear growth is particularly important for fast-growing companies. As I mentioned earlier, this has a lot in common with parallel processing. What is linear growth? From a database perspective, linear growth is the ability to maintain a database with the same performance requirements as the database grows. In other words, if the volume of data doubles, the database can still maintain the same responsiveness as when it was smaller. It is easier to see this in a graph than to imagine it, so review the included graphics as you read. Using parallel processing techniques, as the flow of data increases, the response times can be managed by adding new hardware, not by changing the database or the application.

Three types of computers are typically used in data warehouse implementations: uniprocessor computers, symmetrical multiprocessor (SMP) computers, and massively parallel processor (MPP) computers. The uniprocessor computers are personal computers. Most PCs have only one CPU with one or more hard disk drives, and this one CPU has control of everything. With a PC, you don't have much ability to perform multiple tasks effectively. PCs are normally used on the office desktop and as small network servers. They are usually individualized and not shared.

I will discuss the SMP and MPP architecture in more detail because

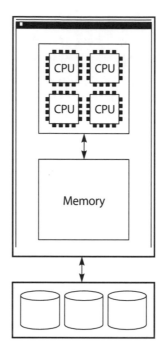

**Figure 6.2**  SMP architecture.

they can easily perform multiple tasks at the same time. Deciding between these two types is the major database decision for most companies building a data warehouse. SMP computers have more than one CPU. They can have two to hundreds of CPUs, although they are most commonly configured with 2, 4, 8, or 16. There are very few SMP machines that can upgrade beyond 16 processors, physically. Of the machines that can upgrade beyond 16, there are few that can provide the performance increase that you would expect when you get beyond 8 CPUs. With this architecture, the CPUs usually share everything: memory, disk drives, and software (Figure 6.2). They divide up the work, usually by determining which CPU is the least busy. To get beyond this limitation, they normally implement something called *clustering*. Clustering can be used in a couple of ways, as a combination of SMP boxes into an MPP architecture (described next) or as MPP nodes. A discussion on various ways to implement hardware clustering is beyond the scope of this book.

MPP computers can have two to thousands of CPUs also. The main difference is that each CPU operates independently; they share no re-

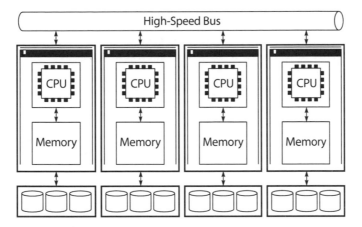

**Figure 6.3**  MPP architecture.

sources. Each CPU has its own memory, disk drives, and software. They communicate with the other CPUs by passing messages to each other via a high-speed bus (Figure 6.3). You can imagine MPP architecture by thinking of multiple PCs connected together with a very high-speed network. The difference is that MPP databases are managed as a single computer. One advantage of MPP computers is that the data from a single file can be spread across the entire system, allowing each CPU to analyze a smaller subset of the data simultaneously. Each CPU searches only a small set, sorts the results, and they all return the data to the user. With the SMP architecture, normally one CPU is assigned the entire task. The MPP system does this in parallel, with smaller sets of data. The result is faster response times for the queries.

How do these all fit into a data warehouse implementation? What you really need to know is which type you should choose for your data warehouse. If your data warehouse will be large, you will be choosing between the SMP and the MPP computers. You might even have both for different functions. I am talking here only about the data warehouse database that will hold all of the detail records. Of course, these computers can be used in several places in the overall data warehouse infrastructure. They are not normally used as desktop computers, but they are used everywhere else. SMP computers can be very powerful, but they do have their limitations. The main limitations of SMP machines are two: they are not linear, and they have a finite upgrade path. If the

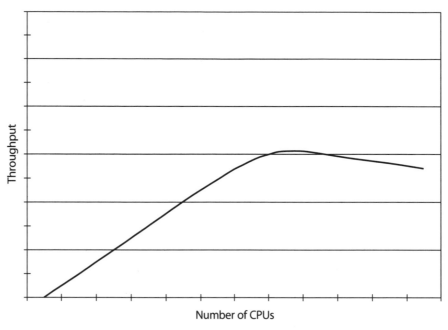

**Figure 6.4**  SMP performance curve.

volume of data or the number of users will be large, then you may run into a database management problem. Essentially, you will not be able to grow the capacity of the system because all SMP machines have a limitation, as shown in the performance curve in Figure 6.4. There are no figures on this curve because each SMP machine reaches its peak at different points. Adding CPUs will not help because of the shared resources. When you have reached this peak, adding CPUs will actually degrade performance because the CPUs must spend all of their time communicating to each other about the resources that they share. In other words, they spend a lot of time asking the other CPUs, "Is this resource free? Can I use this?" If your data warehouse is small and is not going to grow substantially, then you will never reach this threshold. The upgrade paths of SMP machines are, from a practical viewpoint, limited to eight CPUs. This is because they cannot grow outside their system (see Figure 6.5). If you will ever

**If you will ever need more power than eight CPUs, then you should be learning about MPP technology.**

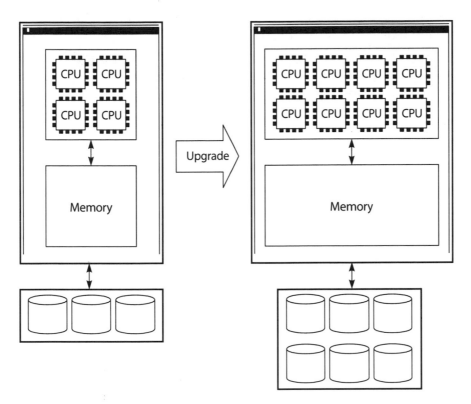

**Figure 6.5** SMP upgrade.

need more power than about eight CPUs, then you should be learning about MPP technology.

With an MPP machine, the CPUs do not share resources and therefore will not have the same performance problem when adding CPUs (Figure 6.6). In fact, you will always have a very nearly linear, scalable performance if you design your applications properly. As you add CPUs the performance is exactly as you would expect. If you double the number of CPUs, you will double the performance. There is no curve in the performance chart because it is linear (Figure 6.7).

There is also a special way to manage the data on MPP computers. With a linear scalable database, you spread the database across the disk drive, and each processor works to retrieve the information for you. If you want a faster response, you buy more CPUs and spread the data more thinly across the disk drives. As your data volume increases or

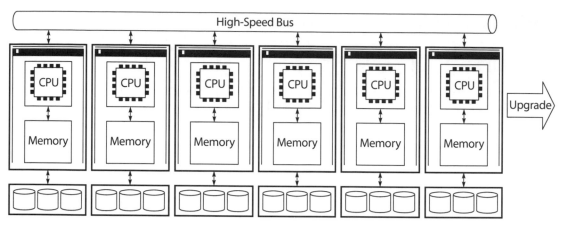

**Figure 6.6**
MPP upgrade.

you need more performance, you simply upgrade the hardware. No major upgrade change is necessary. No additional work is necessary. There is no performance degradation so long as the proper ratio of data to CPU/disk is maintained. It is linear. This type of computer architecture is called *shared nothing* massively parallel computer (MPP) architecture because the CPUs essentially do not communicate to each other until they must.

Building linear scalable applications is another issue that must be considered. Most application developers will design their applications serially, for SMP machines, and they will have to learn how to think and design linearly for MPP machines. This is not more expensive, simply different. The messaging concept (explained in Chapter 7) is another concept that will enable the linear growth of applications. But if your database is small and it will remain small, then you will not have to worry about linear scalable architecture and parallel processing because an SMP computer will be sufficient. Otherwise, you will need a database that can manage the increasing volume.

The benefits from the MPP architecture come in the management side of the database. The system is designed to look and feel like one computer and one database. Non-MPP database suppliers will suggest that you "break" your database into much smaller, more manageable pieces. For the very large database, such suppliers are essentially asking you to manage the shared database for them. They want you to simulate the MPP architecture by modifying your database and your front-end application. Speaking from experience, this will become a night-

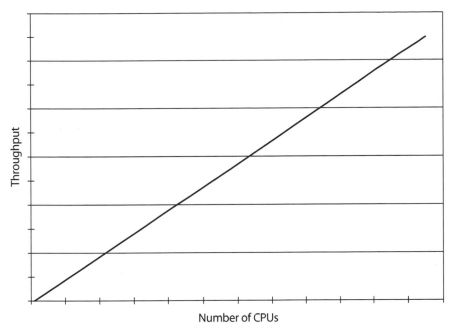

**Figure 6.7** MPP performance curve.

mare of never-ending problems. The data warehouse should be designed and built with one logical view and one physical view. Anything else would be a compromise that I would not want to manage. I don't think you should either. If you are a growing company, linear scalable MPP database architecture is an absolute must. If your database is in the large size range or the number of users is substantial, then an MPP database will be your key to a successful implementation. With the very large databases, you will not be able to sustain the insatiable consumption of information if you use the typical database architecture while building (or growing) the data warehouse without a linear scalable database. Additionally, you will be spending a tremendous amount of time and money to maintain that database. If the database for your data warehouse will be small, then your database selection is greatly simplified. You will be able to choose almost any database.

> **The data warehouse should be designed and built with one logical view and one physical view.**

# 7

# Database Maintenance

One of the major differences between a classical OLTP system and a data warehouse is the maintenance process. A person using on-line screens normally maintains the data in an OLTP system. When these users create or change the data, they demand a very quick response time for each transaction. There may be several hundred people each creating an individual OLTP transaction that must be processed at any one point in time. There will be peak processing times that the system must be tuned to handle. By contrast, load processes maintain a data warehouse. All the OLTP transactions that were processed during the day are essentially reprocessed. The data warehouse must process the very high volume of data that arrives at the same time, usually at night. Those same couple of hundred OLTP transactions will turn into tens of millions of transactions that need to be applied to the data warehouse database. This means that the load processes will be a very important part of a data warehouse. This chapter will discuss these loading processes, but more importantly will offer some tips that you may be able to use to reduce the development time of your first data warehouse. Finally, I am going to discuss a more advanced technique that can be used to smooth the database maintenance workload over a day for continuous 24-hour data maintenance.

I am going to discuss some techniques you can use to speed up the maintenance of your data warehouse implementation. However, all of these techniques will not work well with every database. It is important that you understand the limitations and functionality of your database. Some databases will have an easy solution for one problem, while another will have no easy solution and you must write your own program. Customized programs are not bad, but if you can reduce the development time of a task from four weeks to one day, then there is tremendous value, even if the process is a bit out of the ordinary. Out-of-the-ordinary processing does not mean that the quality of the data in the database should be sacrificed. In fact, data integrity is the most important aspect of the data warehouse. But there are ways to save time in the implementation without sacrificing data integrity. Reading these techniques may help you determine which database you wish to use.

> **Out-of-the-ordinary processing does not mean that the quality of the data in the database should be sacrificed.**

## CAPTURING, EXTRACTING, AND TRANSFERRING THE SOURCE DATA

Capturing the data is the most human-intensive part of building the data warehouse, but it is not the longest task. Most of this work should be completed in just two or three weeks. This is where the functional operational systems need to be modified to create the initial extract and capture the daily changes. There are tools that can assist in the capture of data records. These tools normally read the audit records and generate transactions for the data warehouse. Unfortunately, most of my customers believe that these are very expensive and have a difficult time justifying the expense. Therefore, most companies choose to do this work themselves. Of course, the data movement tool providers will say you should not do that. Even some professional people will tell you that you *must* use a data extraction tool. My view is that they are nice to have, but you do not need to purchase these tools. The difficult part is identifying exactly what transactions must be copied by every system. This is something that requires a person who understands the system. I suggest that you have one person for every source system to make these required modifications. This means that you will be using a lot of people for a short period of time at the beginning of the implementation. Another point about the extract and load tools is that they are slow. They are rarely designed for high-speed performance, and therefore they may run slower than what is needed on a daily basis.

The people capturing the data will deliver two essential data warehouse processes: the initial load extract process and the ongoing data flow changes process. The initial load extract process is very important in the early stages of development because this process will read the database of the functional systems and create a data file that will be used to load the data warehouse. You will run the initial load process several times before your system is ready for production as you correct, perfect, and tune your daily processing. If the data volume of a functional system is very small, this may be the only process that is needed to obtain the source data. If this volume is very small, it can be run daily to extract all of the records from the source system. This initial load process might become part of the backup and recovery strategy too, and I will discuss this later. After the initial load process is created, and depending on the daily volume of data, the daily changes to the source system will need to be captured. The challenge in capturing the daily changes is in finding the point in the process at which the data record is in a consistent and committed state. This usually requires someone who is familiar with your source application. Often these data records are already written to a file and simply need to be transformed to a form that the data warehouse can accept. Normally, there is not much work that needs to be done. Most of the time, only a small modification to the application is required, perhaps two or three lines; then the file needs to be transferred out of the operational system flow and into the data warehouse system flow, one more small change.

An important aspect of this process is standardization. You will need to describe exactly what must be done in these processes. Normally, the people doing this work are not part of the core team and are a limited resource. Therefore, you must effectively communicate exactly what you need, with examples. This means that you will need to have clearly documented standards for them. The standards can be anything from data type definitions (e.g., the format of a timestamp) to file formats,

> The first implementation of the data warehouse can be greatly simplified if you can plan for the database load in advance.

file sizes, and types of files. The records within each file must be standardized (i.e., header records, control records, and data records) for integrity reasons. I will clarify some standards that you might want to have in place throughout this chapter. The first implementation of the data warehouse can be greatly simplified if you can plan for the database load in advance. Hopefully, you can build a complete load cycle for the different types of loads to ensure the plan you have created will function properly with all of the new technologies. This is even more important if the source computer systems are different from the data warehouse computer system.

One very important example of a standardization issue that must be understood and clearly documented concerns the way different computer systems represent and store characters internally—that is, how the alphabet and numbers are stored inside a computer. This will impact how you create the file transfer process. For example, most Unix computers use an ASCII standard, whereas an IBM mainframe stores data in EBCDIC format. A simple explanation is needed for those of you who have not spent a lot of your life communicating with a computer. A computer does not understand anything but numbers. In order to display the letter A, the computer will use a unique number to identify that letter, such as 65 (see Table 7.1). The letter B is then normally the next number, 66, and so on. This is called the *binary representation* of a letter. The combination of these numbers represents a word. There are several problems that can occur when you are moving data between different computers. One problem is being able to differentiate the number 65—which could be the age of someone—from the letter A, represented by 65. If the source computer and the data warehouse computer are the same kind, there will be no problem. The problem comes when the two differ, because there are several standards. In some computers, like Compaq's, the letter A is represented by 65, while in others,

**Table 7.1    Decimal representation of the alphabet.**

| Letter | ASCII | EBCDIC |
|--------|-------|--------|
| A | 65 | 193 |
| B | 66 | 194 |
| C | 67 | 195 |
| D | 68 | 196 |
| E | 69 | 197 |
| F | 70 | 198 |
| G | 71 | 199 |
| H | 72 | 200 |
| I | 73 | 201 |
| J | 74 | 209 |
| K | 75 | 210 |
| L | 76 | 211 |
| M | 77 | 212 |
| N | 78 | 213 |
| O | 79 | 214 |
| P | 80 | 215 |
| Q | 81 | 216 |
| R | 82 | 217 |
| S | 83 | 226 |
| T | 84 | 227 |
| U | 85 | 228 |
| V | 86 | 229 |
| W | 87 | 230 |
| X | 88 | 231 |
| Y | 89 | 232 |
| Z | 90 | 233 |

like IBM's, the letter A is represented by 193. The technology people normally know about this situation, but occasionally it can cause a delay in the project if it is not identified early.

Another common problem in working with different computers concerns the way they store data on the hard disk. Some computers store their numbers with the digits reversed. For example, the number 71 could be stored on the computer as 17. This is just like the German way of saying 71: the number is read "1 and 70." Some computers do this too. This means that you cannot simply copy a file from one system to another because all of the numbers may be backward on the other computer. Then there are the carriage return, line feed, and end-of-file issues that vary with different computers. If you have one computer that stores these elements one way and another that stores them a different way, and this is not identified early in the project, there could be project delays. Wal-Mart has faced this issue because the store systems are from NCR and HP, while the home office and distribution center computers are from IBM, HP, and NCR (among others). Other companies I have worked with around the world have also dealt with this exact issue. There is a resolution to this problem, but it needs to be understood and documented for your specific situation.

The incompatibility problem among different computers must be addressed when you transfer a file from one system to the next. There are options that enable such conversions to be processed normally, but sometimes they are difficult and time consuming to create. I have a relatively simple solution to these incompatibility problems: do not transfer any data in the raw binary format unless you are using binary compatible computers; use only displayable characters in the files. The unloading, transfer, and loading will take a little bit more time, maybe a couple of seconds, but the rework savings (particularly when you are working with a new computer supplier) will more than make up for that. Some people might think this concept will waste disk space. However, disk space is comparatively cheap (computer labor is much more expensive), and these should be transient files that are being passed between systems, so the extra disk space should be minimal. I could get into the gory details of the differences between loading data into an IBM MVS database and loading into a Compaq Unix database, but the point is that you will need to understand the differences between your computers.

**I have created a standard that works well for transferring data between different systems, and it should work with your systems.**

I have created a standard that works well for transferring data between different systems, and it should work with your systems. All the data records are displayable characters, not raw binary data. This means that every field can be seen with a simple text editor. In particular you should be able to read numbers, dates, and times. This ensures that numbers are not "packed" into a smaller binary number, but each digit is displayed. Each of these records is of a predetermined fixed length for each data file. A unique displayable character separates each field. This character is one that is not often used, such as the squiggle character (~). You should avoid the variable-length records. They can cause a huge problem, depending on the compatibility of the computers, particularly when you want to use standard database utilities that are included with your database. If you must have header records, ensure that they are in the first so many number of lines (perhaps the first three records are header records) in every data file. Most database load utilities can start loading at a specific record (e.g., the fourth record) with no problems. The header records should be consistent for all files and should conform to the same file format across all applications. It is helpful to include the file name in the headers, along with other controlling numbers such as the number of records and the number of fields in the file. If there are decimal points, as with money, make them implied decimal points (e.g., $12.95 would be 00001295). Finally, define a standard format for time (e.g., YYYYMMDD.HHMMSS) that is compatible across all systems. If you define standards such as these, the initial loading process will become much easier.

Here is a sample of a standardized POS file for a retailer:

```
POS~080199~POS0002.DAT~009089112~63~8~
00001~1001008~092~012~19990108.112403~000003~00001295~00003885~
00001~1001012~092~012~19990108.112819~000001~00000499~00000499~
00001~1001029~092~012~19990108.113222~000002~00002199~00004398~
00001~1001112~092~012~19990108.120000~000001~00000195~00000195~
```

Creating a standard like this is helpful because it is readable. The first record is the header record. This record describes the contents of the file. "POS" is a three-digit unique file type identifier. "080199" is the date the file was created. "POS0002.DAT" is the name of the file. "009089112" represents the number of records in the file. "63" is the length of the file data records. "8" is the number of fields in this file. These header records are a fantastic way to ensure that everything is consistent and compatible. The data record I created for this example consists of store number, article number, selling clerk, selling department, selling date/time, quantity sold, selling price, and expanded selling price. This clearly defined file is a format that is consistent between two different systems. It will allow you to use most standard unloading and loading utilities to transfer the data between the different systems. If the machines are different, you will have to address this sometime in the project, and earlier is better. Even if they are the same manufacturer, this format can still be very helpful.

There are a couple of side benefits to this type of standardized file definition. One benefit is that you can dynamically create the initial load and the daily maintenance load processes. If you will be loading hundreds of files, you can use this file and the corresponding table data definition (DDL) to dynamically create the load scripts. You will need to create a program that reads both of these files and produces the proper load script. Once this program is created, you can change the load processes for the entire data warehouse in a matter of minutes. I have done this for my customers, and it is very effective. It makes minor file changes easier to manage. You may not be able to do this for all of the load scripts, but you should be able to do it for many of them because they are simple processes that reload the entire file. Another benefit is that you can use the header records to monitor the status of the load processes. This requires that you add two more steps to every load process. The first process is run before the load, and the second is run after the load. In the first process, you read the header record and insert that data into a "status" table along with the current date and time and a status of "running." After the load process completes successfully, the last step is to update this record with a date and time and a status of "complete." This simple status table will become invaluable for diagnosing load problems in the beginning as well as during ongoing daily monitoring of the loads.

## UPDATE FREQUENCY

I have been asked over and over how often the database should be updated. Weekly? Daily? Hourly? This depends on your company and how critical that information is to the business. My advice is to update your data warehouse as often as is practical. If your company can afford to invest in the technology, I would suggest you maintain your data warehouse instantaneously. "Instantaneous" means that the database is maintained in "real time" as the data changes in the operational system. After an instant update process is completely built and implemented, what will your people do after the database is maintained instantaneous? When you get to this point, you must focus your resources on something else, such as building new applications instead of increasing the update frequency. If you develop an update process that runs monthly, the resource utilization will be like a breaking dam every month. All users will be waiting until that database is updated, then they will issue their thousands of queries. This is bad because the business processes and decisions will begin to focus around the update time. This causes the business people to focus on the technology instead of the needs of the business. In other words, they will delay decisions until they can see last month's trend. Even worse, they will make decisions as they did before, without any information. If your data warehouse is updated daily, the business will have no self-imposed bottleneck on the flow of information. Users can make informed decisions immediately. This is why I would update more frequently than monthly, if at all possible. Weekly updates can cause the same problem as monthly updates, but to a less severe degree. Therefore, I recommend that updates to the data warehouse be made daily for most companies just now getting started. If the database is updated daily, you will see a data usage curve something like the graph in Figure 7.1. This graph illustrates that the data used most often is the most current and that from a year ago at this time. So, daily is frequent enough to clearly see trends happening and, more importantly, will not cause the postponement of decisions.

> If your data warehouse is updated daily, the business will have no self-imposed bottleneck on the flow of information.

There are some valid business reasons to update even more frequently than daily. In a retail operation, for instance, slow-selling, high-priced articles can be replenished more quickly. If you can determine which expensive articles will sell only once a week, then you can reduce the inventory needed by placing an order more quickly. For

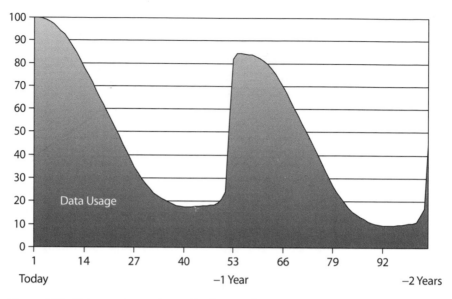

**Figure 7.1**  Data warehouse data utilization graph.

instance, a $3000 lawn tractor will sell, on average, one per week. Using the history data in your data warehouse, you have decided on a safety stock of two tractors per store. The risk of being out of stock on this article is an issue of timing and replenishment. The faster you know when one sells, the faster the order can be placed to maintain that safety stock. If you replenish your stores more than once a day, which is common with retailers that have a distribution warehouse, then the order can be placed multiple times a day. This can become very critical to increase the inventory turns and reduce the shelf space allocation. But is this a data warehouse application? If a trigger can be identified using data from the data warehouse database, and this creates a transaction based on specific criteria requiring an analysis, then this is a data warehouse application. The data warehouse can feed the other systems instantaneously when the analytical criterion is met. Rules-based processing and messaging are key to a quick business response. Whether you call this a data warehouse, an enterprise data warehouse, or an operational data store doesn't really matter. It is providing a very valuable solution using information to make better, faster decisions.

Wal-Mart updates their database continuously. They had reached a growth point where there was not enough time to process all of the records daily. This was happening with the POS application as well as with the replenishment process. Their normal processing required that they wait until all stores had closed for the day, and only then did nightly processing begin. This was effective, even during periods of growth, so long as all the stores were in the same time zones. But when they expanded into California, the entire processing had to wait another hour before nightly processing

## Wal-Mart updates its database continuously.

could begin. This meant that the processing for the East Coast stores did not start until the California stores closed, three hours later. At the time, most of the stores were on the east side of America. They had to change the way they processed their data. Of course, the first change was to process by time zone at the end of the day. This was finally driven to the lowest level, which was to process by store during the day, at a variable time. This way, when the store closed, there would be minimal processing for that store. Now they can process stores in groups so that a group of stores (e.g., all the stores in Florida) will complete the nightly processing first. The messaging concept I will discuss later along with the MPP application design mentality enables them to do this in parallel. It cannot be done sequentially.

## LOADING THE DATA WAREHOUSE

I have found that with few exceptions there are essentially four types of data warehouse maintenance processes. These are the initial load processes, the append load processes, the update processes, and the delete processes. The initial load process is needed for every table in the database because it loads into an empty table, and every table will be empty at the beginning. The append load process adds records to a table that already has data. The update process updates records that are in a table. Finally, the delete process deletes records out of the database. As much as possible, you want to be able to use the database utilities to perform these processes because the utilities are quicker and easier to implement than a customized program. A program will normally take from two to four weeks to develop. By contrast, you can often do the same task with a utility that will take only one to three days to develop. This can make a substantial difference in the development time of a data warehouse. The capabilities of the database utilities are something that must be understood completely. Sometimes a database utility will not provide some functions, or it may run much too slowly. If this is the case, you will have to write special programs. It is important to understand your database and its limitations. This section will help you evaluate the work that will need to be done for loading so you can better determine how much additional programming will be necessary. I will discuss each of these processes in detail starting with the simplest process, initial load, driving through to the more complex processes.

## Initial Load Processes

Every table in your data warehouse will have an initial load process. For some tables you will use this process daily, while for others it will be used only for the initial load. Normally, this process loads data from a file and puts the data in a table of your database. This is the simplest process of all. It is a one-directional load. It is typically the fastest because it loads into an empty table (Figure 7.2).

Initial load can also be used for the daily or weekly maintenance process. In fact, for the majority of the tables in the data warehouse, this load is the only one needed. Your load process could simply delete all the records in the table and then reload the new records in that table. This is okay until there is a failure in the load process. Let's say that the data file becomes corrupt. You might not know this until the load begins and after the records have been deleted. However, you can maintain the availability in the daily maintenance by using a three-step process. The first step is to create a temporary table. Secondly, load the temporary table. Finally, rename the two tables. This process works nicely on most databases. It causes only a short delay in accessing the table, during the renaming process. Of course, every database is different, and you may not be able to do this. Access authorization may need to be regranted, depending on the database that was used. You can also use views to help in this process. A view is a logical table that "masks" one or more tables. Perhaps instead of renaming the table, the view can

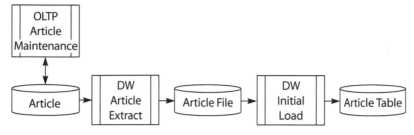

**Figure 7.2** Initial load process for articles.

be regenerated to point to the new table. This is very database dependent but can be an effective way to maintain high availability during the load process.

Initial load is the only process needed for those tables with a relatively small number of records. For a retailer, the store description file is a good example. Most retailers have only 500 records in this file. Why would you want to build a process to capture only the changes to the records in the file? You can just reload the entire table every night. This simplified load will save a tremendous amount of time in the development phase if this process can be used often. Exactly how much of this simple processing can be done with your company will depend on your volume of data and the power of your data warehouse computer and the associated interconnecting networks. Some companies can reload 10 million records nightly with no problem, while others will only be able to load 10,000 in a reasonable amount of time. You want to use as many initial load processes as possible. If you have some file standardization, as described in the previous section, then you can write a simple program to dynamically generate all of the initial load processes, as well as some of the other load processes. Because there is an identifiable character (e.g., the squiggly ~ character) in the data file, this process should be able to read the data file and match each data field to the corresponding column in the database table. After finding the matching columns, it can generate the required load scripts. Once

> After the data warehouse is implemented, adding some more data or changing the data structure is not a laborious task if you have a program that can dynamically re-create the initial load scripts.

you have created this program, the initial loads become very easy to create. After the data warehouse is implemented, adding some more data or changing the data structure is not a laborious task if you have a program that can dynamically re-create the initial load scripts.

## Append Load Processes

The append load process is specifically for the larger tables that will accumulate history over time. These tables accumulate more and more information as time proceeds, but they have no updates. A perfect example of this, for a retailer, is the POS data (Figure 7.3). Every day articles are sold. This becomes a hard fact that will not be changed or adjusted. Of course, customers can return articles, but that generates another POS record. Therefore, the process is nearly identical to the initial load process. Only new records are constantly added to the table.

Most database utilities can manage the workload of this type of load. The only exception is when the volume is extremely large. Sometimes a high volume is generated after a week-ending or month-ending process. Weekly and monthly summary tables might be more difficult to manage with this process. Normally, such larger volume month-end processes can be scheduled during the weekend.

Depending on the capabilities of the database, the append load process can be a substantially different process from the initial load. Some databases allow the loading of a single part of the table, or a partition of a table. This means that a new partition is created, loaded, and made available usually without any interruption to the normal database processes (see Figure 7.5). For example, a retailer may have a POS table with store number, item number, and date as the primary key. When the table is created, it can be partitioned on the date field. For the database, this may mean that a separate logical file is maintained for every date in the table. If you have two years' worth of data, then there would be 730 smaller files that make up the larger files. You do not want 730 tables, but one logical table with 730 physical sections within it. When new records for a day are ready to be added to the table, this process would create a new empty partition, load the records, and attach (so to speak) the partition to the table. There are several advantages to this

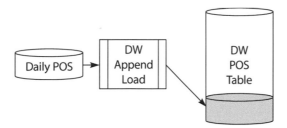

**Figure 7.3** The append load process.

type of processing. First, it is usually very, very fast to load the records. Next, the original table and the processes associated with it have no interruption during the loading process. Normally, this process can be developed with only a simple database load script, so it does not take long to implement. Finally, from the user perspective, all of the data for that date appears instantly. This strategy of using partitions can also be used with the delete process, which I will discuss later in this chapter.

There is one more effective way to perform an append load process, particularly with MPP databases such as Compaq NonStop SQL and NCR Teradata. Of course, you can use the special LOAD APPEND commands. If that is not a good option, you can create or maintain a temporary table that is identical to the table you will be loading. Then you can load the data records into a temporary table using the standard load utilities. Because it is an empty table, the load is normally very, very fast. After the load completes, you issue a single SQL statement called an INSERT/SELECT statement. The SQL statement would look something like this:

```
INSERT INTO Big_Table (SELECT * FROM Temp_Big_Table).
```

This INSERT/SELECT statement selects rows from the temporary table, Temp_Big_Table, and inserts the records into the other table, Big_Table. You should delete the temporary table when this process completes. The reason that this is so effective on an MPP computer is that every CPU (or node) is processing its data locally. Because the initial load is generally faster using an empty table, the new data in the temporary table is allocated to the same node as the larger table. All of the CPUs work at the same time in parallel, and no data is redistributed to other nodes. The number of records that must be processed will be an important consideration before implementing this process. Basically, if the number of records that need to be inserted is substantially smaller than the number of records in the big table, this will probably be a good way to process them. The success of this process will depend heavily on the database and the ability of the database to process in parallel. This process is strictly MPP database dependent. The good point about this process is that it is very simple to create and maintain.

## Update Processes

The update processes are the most difficult to build. Updates are required for tables that are too large to reload nightly. If the table is small enough to reload nightly, you should just reload it. Sometimes, however, it is just too big to reload and the figures must be updated. For a retailer, there are several application areas that will need to be updated. The purchase order (PO) system is a good example. A purchase order has a life cycle that can be quite long. First a PO is created, then it is approved, then it is sent to the supplier, then it can be partially or fully filled, then an invoice is matched to it, and finally the invoice is paid and the PO is no longer active (assuming it wasn't canceled). The status of an order will affect other applications, such as the open-to-buy figures. For most retailers, the open and active orders are the most important figures. This means that the current status of the PO is crucial and will need to be updated. Because retailers issue a lot of POs, you can see from this example that a special update process is needed for the PO system.

Of course, you can write a custom application to perform the needed updates. For the data warehouses that I have implemented, there were always one or two programs that had to be written because there was no other simple way. If you must review data in the database before adjusting a record, then you will probably need a customized update program. If you have summary information, and you must maintain perfect synchronization between the detail records and the summary records, you will need to write an application. Sometimes history in summary tables must be rewritten when hierarchies change. Retailers do this a lot. They move an article from one department to another in a process called *article reclassification*. To make comparisons with last year, all of the history of the article must be moved to the new department. If you have no summary tables, but only the detail records, this process is greatly simplified because the change is normally limited to the hierarchy reference tables and not the bigger fact table. If this is the situation with your applications, you will need to plan time to write a program. Such programs can take from two to four weeks to design, write, test, and implement. However, sometimes you can use the utilities that are provided with the database, and this may take only one or two days. Below I discuss some of the simpler ways to reduce the implementation time of these types of update processes using standard utilities.

Basically, you need to define the update process and how you will deal with it. You will need to determine which update process works best with your database. I suggest that you try the following process to simplify the standard update processes. First, separate the records based on their function. The records that will update go in one file, and the records that need to be inserted go into another file. Then you will have an insert file and an update file. You also might have a delete file. Next, transfer the files to the data warehouse processes and load them into tables. Create two processes, a delete process and an insert process. One process will delete the database records that need to be updated, and the other process will insert an entirely new "updated" record into the database (Figure 7.4). This will keep the processes very simple, thereby making it much easier to maintain with basic database utilities. This process may not be the fastest process, but it is very simple. If the data volume is very large and this process is not fast enough, there are still more options that are easier than writing a customized update program.

For many update processes, you need to understand the performance impact of your process more precisely. To understand which process is most efficient for your database, I suggest you carefully review your database logging procedures. If your database writes a log record for every update in the database, not just the action that occurred, then some of these options will not be optimal for your

**To understand which process is most efficient for your database, I suggest you carefully review your database logging procedures.**

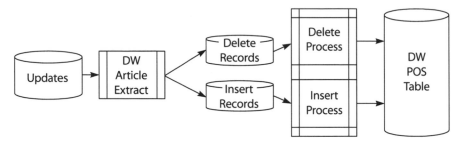

**Figure 7.4**  Update process using database utilities.

database. If you do not review the database logging and implement one of these processes, it could cause you big problems if you have a failure. If there is record-level logging, the logging issues will become painfully obvious if the process fails midway. With record-level logging in a failure, every record will be un-updated very, very slowly. This could cause lots of problems or just waste time. This logging is entirely dependent on the database that you have. Even if you do have record-level logging, and the volume of updates is relatively small, I would try to use the utilities before writing a program. It is also important to know the percentage of records that will be inserted, updated, or deleted. If you know that 90% will be inserted into the database, you will build the standard update process differently than if 90% are updates.

For ultimate flexibility with the update processes, I suggest that you pass the entire updated record to the data warehouse, as opposed to sending only the fields that have changed. While passing only the changed field is the fastest, and reduces the data volume, it is much more complex to implement. If you have the entire record, you can be more flexible in how you create and fine-tune the update process. If you have the entire record, then you have the option to create different processes over time—perhaps eight months later. If you send only the changed fields from the source system to the data warehouse, and you determine later that there is a better way to process these records, it could require the source application to be modified again. That would add more development

> As a standard, I think it is best to pass the entire record to the data warehouse, even when only one field has changed.

time. If you already have the entire record, then there is no rework for the source system processes when you want to change the data warehouse update process. As a standard, I think it is best to pass the entire record to the data warehouse, even when only one field has changed.

When you do not know whether the record should be updated or inserted into the database, there may be another simple process that you can use. First, load the records into an empty table that is identical to the table that will be updated. Second, issue a delete statement using the unique key in the temporary table to remove all of the records in the main table. The SQL statement looks something like this:

```
DELETE FROM big_table WHERE key_field IN (SELECT
    temp_key_field FROM temp_table)
```

Finally, insert all of the records from the temporary table into the main table with an INSERT/SELECT statement. The effect is an update. Sometimes this is called an UPSERT, a combination of updating and inserting. Basically, you want to try to update the existing record first and if it does not exist, then insert the record. Some database utilities do this exact function for you. If your database has this utility, you should use it.

A common problem with this procedure arises when the unique identifier is a compound key, such as store number and article number for inventory figures. Will this work when you have a compound key? Yes, there are ways to manage a compound key. Compound keys can be combined into a single key. By using an update statement, you can create a unique key. Using our retail example, the POS table might have a compound key of store number, article number, and week number. The store number is 4 digits long, the article number is 6 digits long, and the week number is 4 digits. All you have to do is concatenate these keys into a single unique 14-digit number. Then you have a unique identifier for the record. This field can be added to the database to simplify all of the update and delete processes. Once again, you will need to experiment on your database to determine what is best and most effective for you. The important thing is to keep the database maintenance processes as simple as practical.

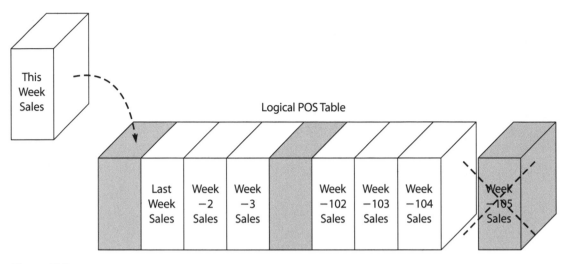

**Figure 7.5**
Partitioned inserts
and deletes.

## Delete Processes

In the previous paragraphs I explained one way to do the deletes. Just use the keys and issue a delete statement. Once again, this is fine if the quantity of deletes is small. But what if there are millions? You can create a delete program, or your database may have a utility to do this easily. There is one very powerful method that might be overlooked: the use of partitions. If you are using a database that allows for partitioning of the data, you can partition the data using your delete key. Then you can delete the entire partition. In the POS example (Figure 7.5), if your data is partitioned by week number, there will be 104 partitions for two years of data. Your database load processes will create a new partition for the new week's data and then simply delete the partition with the old data. This delete process normally takes about one second—super fast. This same process will also work for massive inserts. For large database maintenance, functionality such as this will become a very important factor when you want to lower your maintenance costs. And this type of simplification is an important aspect when you choose your data warehouse database.

> If you are using a database that allows for partitioning of the data, you can partition the data using your delete key. Then you can delete the entire partition.

## BACKUP/RECOVERY

Backup and recovery always generates a passionate discussion in the technology departments of the world. Some people would halt a project if the backup and recovery plan was not implemented in the way that other systems are implemented. If you have the time in your nightly window, you can always use the exact method of backup and recovery as the other processes. The standard database utilities can be used to back up and recover the database. This is the most practical way of performing a backup and recovery. However, there is a chance that you may not need to do any backup of your data warehouse. Some of the technology people do not realize that they already have a backup of this system, in the operational side of the system. If the operational systems do not back up the history data, there still may be an easy way to do this. At one point in time, you will create the initial load of the data warehouse. You can maintain that initial load process so that it can be run as the recovery process in the event of a failure. If you cannot do that, usually because of special processing that is needed, then there is another simple way too. You can maintain the daily maintenance records. Copy these records to tape during or after the daily data warehouse loads. Normally, this is the simplest anyway. Wal-Mart did this and probably still performs this process. We did not use the backup/recovery utilities for years because the process took too long. We did back up the catalog tables, but not the large data. It was faster to reload the entire database. Fortunately, because the data was mirrored, we never needed to reload the database because of a system failure. The exception to this concept is the update processes, but perhaps a similar process—like the initial load processes—can be used for them instead. This would alleviate the need to perform a backup using the database backup and recovery utilities. A performance benefit of this process is that you might be able to remove the corresponding database logging. If there is no logging, data is loaded faster. Saving the data, as a backup, before it is loaded is unique to building a data warehouse. In the longer term, the database backup and recovery procedures will need to function similarly to the OLTP systems of old,

**Copy daily maintenance records to tape during or after the daily data warehouse loads.**

particularly when you begin to integrate the data warehouse with the OLTP systems.

## MESSAGING

At the beginning of this chapter I told you I would describe a method that will allow you to update your data warehouse database continuously, 24 hours a day. Unlike the other sections in this chapter, where I have focused on reducing implementation times, this topic is about increasing throughput without sacrificing performance. This effort will have to be carefully planned and will require time to develop and perfect. Typically, the update processes of a data warehouse run in the evening, while the users query the database during the day. This is normally fine for many companies. The problem comes when the nightly processing time is not long enough to process the records. This is a common problem for companies with operations that span multiple time zones. The loading process is generally a very resource-intensive task and will affect the response time of the queries if the normal loading process is run at the same time. Running these two very different types of processes simultaneously is called *mixed workload.*

Managing the mixed workload can be accomplished by a concept called *messaging.* (This has nothing to do with email, but don't let that stop you from sending a nice message to your friends.☺) MPP databases use messaging to communicate between CPUs. You can use a similar process to manage the mixed workload of your data warehouse. Instead of processing a file of updates sequentially, you break up the file into smaller units of work. Each unit of work will be processed individually, as a *message.* Instead of being processed sequentially, each message is put in a queue to be processed in parallel. When the update process completes processing one message, it processes the next message. However, you will have multiple update processes running simultaneously, which is where the power of this method becomes apparent. Each update process will be pulling messages from the queue and processing them. The secret to updating continuously is queuing and managing the number of update processes that run simultaneously. In the evening, when the computer is relatively inactive, more of these processes can run. When the computer is very active, the processing of messages slows down or stops. When you dynamically change the number of update processes by reviewing key computer and database performance statistics, you can create a *data throughput throttle.* This means that the update process increases update throughput when the machine is not being utilized fully and decreases throughput when it is fully utilized. The architectural concept of what I have described is very similar to that of the OLTP architecture. It is, in fact, the inverse of OLTP. An OLTP system must be designed for the peak processing times, whereas this data warehouse messaging concept is designed to exploit the off-peak processing times.

> **The secret to updating continuously is queuing and managing the number of update processes that run simultaneously.**

We should discuss a practical retail example. Let's consider the POS processing of a company with 400 stores. Everyday each store sells 15,000 unique articles. This creates 6 million records that must be loaded into the data warehouse daily. The stores are evenly distributed across five time zones and close daily at 9 P.M. This means that 80 stores will close first, then one hour later another 80 stores close, then two hours later another 80 stores close, and so on. First, with messaging you do not have to wait until all 400 stores close before beginning the data processing. Second, you want to break the transactions up into messages. Each message in my example will be one store of 15,000 records. Therefore, you do not have to wait for the 80 stores in the first time zone to begin processing. You can begin processing when you get the data from only one store, or one message. The data for each store will be queued for processing. If there are sufficient computer resources, processing should begin immediately. The effect of this type of processing is that the available computer resources are used to the maximum (Figure 7.6), and there is no rigid nightly processing window. From a retail business perspective, each store is processed individually and, therefore, can be replenished individually. Additionally, if there is a problem, say, with two stores, the process can still continue without delaying the processing of the other 398 stores. From another perspective, 99.5% of the company can continue to be processed.

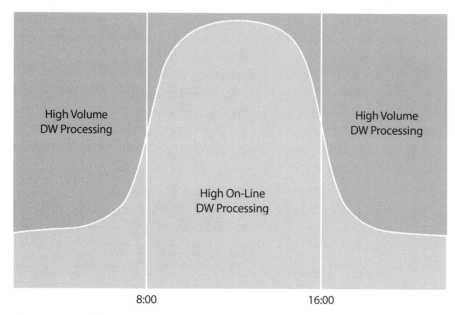

**Figure 7.6**  Daily processing resource usage.

This type of processing is complex, and MPP computers will be able to manage this type of processing better than other types. A common misconception in developing a messaging system, and MPP architecture, is that it is very expensive. The reason MPP technology is perceived as expensive is because the value-add of mirroring the data is expensive. If you mirror the data, which I recommend, the system will be twice as large, right? This is not entirely true because some MPP machines do not use as much space, particularly for indexing, in the database. There is also an intrinsic technological value simply because of the nature of MPP technology, such as high availability. But there is no higher cost when using the messaging concept; this is just another way to develop applications. The development times will be the same, perhaps less than traditional development once the messaging architecture is fully functional. The problem is getting started; the technology is new and requires a different development mentality. As with any new technology, there is a learning curve. The long-term benefits come when the applications are developed for linear growth. They do not need to be redesigned when the processing volumes double. The application is simply expanded with additional hardware, allowing the development team to focus on new development, not maintenance. Companies spend a lot of money and time redesigning applications to manage the unanticipated increase in processing and data volumes. The combination of MPP technology and messaging can eliminate this type of maintenance.

**The long-term benefits come when the applications are developed for linear growth.**

When you get to the point of discussing this type of processing, your data warehouse is probably in the process of turning into an enterprise data warehouse. For a retailer, this means that processing the POS records is also an integral part of other processes such as automatic replenishment. If the automatic replenishment can be processed in a similar manner, then 99.5% of the stores would be replenished using the most current data. The remaining 0.5%, or two stores, would be replenished using the previous day's data. This means that this concept is more than a technical implementation: it's a solution for the business.

# 8

# Technical Construction of the Wal-Mart Data Warehouse

I have been truly amazed at the tremendous interest in the Wal-Mart data warehouse implementation. People worldwide have asked me to explain what Wal-Mart does with their database and how it was built. It is a matter of public record that Wal-Mart has invested over $4 billion supporting this technology over the years. It is difficult for people to understand the value of investing such a huge amount of money into this technology. The reason they continue to invest in this technology is simple: they were able to show a marked improvement in their operation. In this chapter, I will discuss the chain of events that drove Wal-Mart to create their huge data warehouse database. I will describe the teams we had, as well as some technical issues that we had to solve. Along the way, I hope to give you an idea of the Wal-Mart culture.

After working with many other retailers, I am positive that their culture is a unique driving force behind the continuous construction of this database.

## PRECONSTRUCTION

Even before the data warehouse was ever discussed, Wal-Mart was definitely not a typical retailer. Of course, they were and still are growing faster than any other retailer. But it is their very special culture that makes them different. Before anyone is hired, they make certain the prospective employee understands their culture as best as they can describe, but it does not really prepare you for it. It is more than long workdays and working on Saturday. It is the compulsive obsession to improve, rethink, and improve again that is difficult to describe to people. Wal-Mart people will try a new idea, change it several times, and adopt it or throw it out before other retailers begin the planning phase. They do this in every area of the company, including the information systems division (ISD). I do know that they are behaving more like a large company today. Strategies such as longer-term planning (beyond a year) are much more important today. I am sure, however, that the Wal-Mart culture will continue to be a key differentiation in the retail industry for a long time to come. At Wal-Mart there is a "just do it" attitude throughout the entire company. This means that the employees take individual responsibility and action to resolve daily issues. They have rules such as "the sundown rule," meaning you must respond to the people who have contacted you by the end of the day. This does not mean you have a solution, but it does mean there is a plan of action to resolve the problem. They are fiercely competitive, constantly watching the competition and aggressively copying the good parts and improving them. In fact, Sam Walton even mentions in his book, *Sam Walton: Made in America,* that he essentially copied all his ideas from his competitors and improved on them.[1]

> At Wal-Mart there is a "just do it" attitude throughout the entire company.

---

1. Sam Walton with John Huey. *Sam Walton: Made in America.* Doubleday Publishing, 1992 (page 36).

The data warehouse that we built was no exception to this. Wal-Mart was not the first to have the idea of building a data warehouse. They never had the goal of building the world's largest commercial database, either. They were using the leading-edge (or "bleeding-edge" as it is sometimes called) technology because they had a business problem that they wanted to solve. This solution was essentially a matter of timing, competition, and leadership initiatives. The timing was right because there were tremendous limitations on the ability to access to information from the existing systems. Kmart, a fierce competitor at the time, had just a few months earlier announced they were building a merchandising database with historic data down to the store-item-level information. Finally, the managers leading the information technology group sponsored and commissioned the development of a business case study and a prototype application. These were the driving events that spawned the construction of the Wal-Mart data warehouse project.

From a technology perspective, Wal-Mart has always adopted technology quickly when it could improve the business. For a centralized organization with an enormous size, they have a very impressive record of technology implementation. When they began building the data warehouse in 1990, they were in a very similar situation as other companies. Today I still see companies in the same predicament that Wal-Mart was then in. Perhaps you can find similarities within your company too. They had a tremendous amount of data throughout the organization. Most of the data was from the functional operational systems—the warehouse systems, purchase order systems, and the like. They had installed scanning capabilities in every store and were retrieving the POS information from these stores. Most of the POS data was maintained on tape, but the most recent POS was maintained as a company summary on-line. Very little data was maintained beyond the current quarter. Most of the comparison data was maintained at a quarterly level from the previous year. They had paper reports that ran daily, weekly, and monthly. These were used as the basis for many other individual analyses. That is, people would key the figures from the paper printouts into a personal spreadsheet every week for later analysis. There were lots of people, like the buyers responsible for specific articles, reentering this identical data into spreadsheets. Data reentry was a tremendous waste of time. They had many "on-demand" reports that could be requested to run against some specific data. The requester had to supply specific parameters, and in a couple of days the report would be finished. Basically, the majority of the data was available on some media somewhere, usually on tape. Employees just did not have easy access to it.

Having the data is a very important point. Did you know that, even today, some companies do not save their historic data? That is truly amazing to me. If your company is like this, please take some advice from me now. Save your data! The cost of saving your data will pay off.

> ## Save your data! The cost of saving your data will pay off.

There is more value in using that data later than the $1000 it will cost you over time to buy the tapes to keep them. Budget $100 per month into the monthly spending allowance and save the data. Make two copies of every tape and store one copy off-site. There is a reasonable time retention period after which the value of the data begins to be less important. Every company must decide how long they will retain the data. For a retailer, I suggest a minimum of two and one-quarter years so you can make quarter-to-quarter comparisons for the past two years. This is just a minimum to save the data on tape. When your company becomes ready to build a data warehouse, if you have the data, you will be able to show a return on investment in the first year. If you do not have the data, the return on investment will take much longer to achieve, as you will have to wait for the historic data to accumulate.

Wal-Mart did have some good data available. In fact, they were improving it daily. They also had a decent management information system (MIS)—their name for an executive information system (EIS) discussed in a previous chapter—which the executives used daily. This was mostly oriented toward the operation side: store sales, labor costs, gross profit, and the like. This information was available daily, weekly, and monthly, viewable in a very structured set of screens. The system was flexible because you could drill down from the company level, to the region level, to the district level, to the store level, and even into the department level. You also had the ability to scroll to the right on your screen to view more information, so you had a lot of information available. This was a fantastic improvement over the previous applications that required you to enter a specific store, district, or region number. This worked well for store operations, but there was still not enough information for the merchandising side of Wal-Mart.

The merchandising people faced a challenge because they wanted to see the article sales by store for every week. However, the volume of data was so large it was just too difficult to manage with the technology that we were using. It was even more difficult to manage because the volume of data was growing as fast as the company was growing—faster, if you consider Wal-Mart did not maintain the detail data yet. A couple of major technology improvements were under way: scanning and replenishment. The POS registers were scanning almost all of the articles, and the data was being sent back and placed on tape. The automated replenishment system was also being developed, and this required that the inventory be maintained at the store and article level. The store managers would receive an order review sheet, and they were required to fill in the form and send it back to the home office. This paper process would finally find its way into the computer systems in the home office. (I will discuss this process in more detail in Chapter 9.) Essentially, it was a very functionally oriented application, but the information that had to be maintained was beginning to be used by the merchandising people. In particular, the merchandising people responsible for the basic articles in the stores were very, very interested in this information. The challenge facing Wal-Mart was how to allow them access to this data at the same time the automatic replenishment system was running. Only a few people were allowed access to this information, and they were restricted to querying the database only outside the replenishment process. The replenishment process was normally running at night, so it was okay to access the data during the day. However, sometimes it ran into the morning, and this was a problem because the merchandising users often interfered with the replenishment process. As I mentioned earlier, these users were considered "pests," people who had learned enough to be "dangerous." Their queries were always being canceled because they interfered with the nightly replenishment processes. Fortunately, they were learning how to use the technology to improve the business operation, but this took a long time. Their access to the data was severely limited. The analyses that they used were customized for them exclusively so they had a very narrow focus.

What happened next was that the data was moved from the operational replenishment system to another computer system where these few users could query this information. The information center was doing this on behalf of the merchandising people. At the time, the one person staffing the information center had built and was managing other information-only databases. These databases were much smaller databases focusing mostly on store operations. The mentality at the time was that this represented an experiment, not a production system. The database space was allocated to the information center to keep the information pests out of the production systems. The database was updated daily and weekly with as much information as could possibly fit into that small space. The database was stuffed full of information from different production systems and connected with a front-end query application. While all of this still ran on the same computer system, this new MIS was the next step toward building a data warehouse. Now that the data was out of the production system, it was easier to allow more people access.

As the company began to use this information, more information was needed. The appetite for information was driven higher as more detailed data became available. As more applications were implemented, such as the automatic replenishment application, the data became more accurate and reliable too. The data volume was increasing with the demand for information. We had the store operations data in one database, the article information in another database, the replenishment information in another database, and so on. We even had heated discussions about which data was correct if some had come from a different system or, even worse, a spreadsheet. The information needs were definitely approaching a critical point.

**The appetite for information was driven higher as more detailed data became available.**

Suddenly, Kmart announced they were building a merchandising database. Sales information would be maintained down to the article and store level for every week. They were using this new database MPP technology from Teradata Corporation. Wal-Mart had a Teradata machine installed for about a year but had not done much with it. It was an experiment. We were learning about the new technology. A competitor had started already, and there was demand from the business side for this information. Wal-Mart's management decided to take some competitive action. Of course, their information technology (IT) department did not have the option of making the required investment in this technology as it was very expensive at the time. They needed a way to satisfy the needs of the other business organizations. IT needed to convince management to make the investment in this technology as opposed to investing the money in other areas of the company such as merchandise. Finally, IT would have to sell this to the Wal-Mart board of directors before the spending would be approved.

The only way to get beyond this lack-of-funding obstacle was to build a business case study and a prototype of the system. The Teradata Corporation was essentially asked to do this for Wal-Mart, and they did. They used a process similar to the one I described in Chapters 3 and 4 to get this business information and document it. Specifically, they built a prototype system. At this time (around 1990), Wal-Mart didn't really have the expertise to build this type of a system. PCs were just becoming a part of the organization along with the PC network systems. We were using one of the first releases of Microsoft Windows. Most people still thought a mouse was a rodent (☺). This was all-new technology. Wal-Mart needed a technology partner badly, so the people from Teradata built a prototype system using a product called ToolBook (from Asymetrix). This was integrated into Microsoft Excel spreadsheets for grids and graphing. After the prototype was completed, a business case study was constructed based on the prototype. This business case study was the selling document that the IT department needed to communicate the information desires of the merchandising organization. This document became the basis for the initial $20 million investment that was needed for the first implementation. It was used as a selling document to convince other Wal-Mart executives to invest in this technology. It worked.

## THE FIRST IMPLEMENTATION

After we received the approval to build this huge database, the team members were identified. This was the first concerted effort to provide information-based analyses on all of the historic merchandising data. It wasn't easy starting this project. We really did not know what we were supposed to be building. We actually wasted a lot of time trying to decide what should be delivered first. We had JAD sessions. We had meetings. We designed a lot of stuff. We got off track. We were not focusing on the business case study. Truly, we were beginning to falter. About a month later, there was a shakedown. The team was narrowed to a much smaller group of people. We had a new and clear focus: deliver the POS data. All of this time was not completely wasted. We were learning a lot, learning the new technology. We spent a great deal of time studying the data, which became valuable later. We now had a clear quest. We were going to deliver what is known today as a data mart. Of course, it was a really big data mart!

With our fresh new focus, we essentially had four teams: a database team, an application team, a GUI team, and the Teradata team. The Teradata team had the most people. I have no idea how many, but Wal-Mart was a very important account for this growing technology company. Each of the other teams only comprised a couple of people. The database team was responsible for designing, building, and maintaining the database. The application team was responsible for loading, maintaining, and extracting the data in the database. The GUI team was responsible for building the front-end application so that the buyers could easily analyze this data. Finally, the Teradata team did everything we did, plus train us. At one time or another, every team created analyses for the user community or extracted data from the database for special projects. Unlike in other companies, being assigned to one team did not mean that we were assigned only one job function. In fact, we each performed one another's job occasionally. This was another point characteristic of our successful implementation: we were a team and we behaved like a team. We worked together to deliver the solution. Each of us had unique strengths, and our collective strengths were enough to cover the team's weaknesses. We worked together well and had fun while we were working. Teamwork is very important for such a massive undertaking. When your company builds your big data warehouse, be sure to select your team members carefully.

## The Database Design

After what appeared to be a loss of time, we were directed to build this thing and make decisions. One vital process that was almost completely eliminated because of this self-inflicted time crunch was data modeling. Data modeling is the process of documenting and understanding the relationships of the data entities and data attributes. If you logically design the database first, the physical implementation will be much easier to maintain in the longer term. The data modeling concept was new for Wal-Mart. A colleague and I were able to convince the manager that he could benefit from our understanding this data better. He would get a better database that would not have to be constantly changed. One serious problem we faced was that the data volume was larger than the computer's capacity, if we implemented exactly what was in the prototype. The database was to be built on a machine that was already purchased. The first database machine was about 600 gigabytes, and we had to fit our data on this machine. Reluctantly, he gave us two weeks to finalize the data model.

> If you logically design the database first, the physical implementation will be much easier to maintain in the longer term.

Our approach to data modeling was a bit different from that of other companies. It was different from Wal-Mart's approach today too. We focused much of our time on the ability to save, maintain, and retrieve this huge amount of data. We did provide value—a lot of value! The user community was asking for weekly sales data. Through our design and technology implementation efforts, we were able to provide daily data. And this was with a database design that was smaller than the original design. We were able to do this because we studied the data. We determined the number of days it would take for the average Wal-Mart product to sell within a week: 2.3. So when an article was sold, it would sell 2.3 times in that week. That meant there were many articles that would sell only one time in a week. Specifically, there were 4.7 days where no articles were sold in a week. Learning that only 5000 unique articles would sell each day, 20,000 in a week, and 40,000 in a month was important information, given that the database was too big to fit in the machine. Using our knowledge of the data and the database, we used the database compression extensions to reduce the volume even more, by compressing on 0. "Compressing on zero" means the database assumes a default value of zero and therefore does not need to store, or allocate physical space, on the disk drive for the value of zero. This is important because it requires as much space to save a large integer value, like 1,233,540, as the value 0—unless you can not save a frequently repeated value, like zero. Zero is assumed to be a default value. We also used a technique that allowed us to store more information than was originally planned, by storing the selling action attributes in a separate smaller table and relating them with a key. Both of these added a tremendous value to the project. These innovations were important enough that Wal-Mart created, and still has, a data administration group.

The main table we focused on was the POS table. Originally, the base POS table had the data elements listed below:

Store number

Item number

Week number

Department number

Activity sequence number

Selling units quantity

Selling amount

Selling cost

Monday unit quantity

Tuesday unit quantity

Wednesday unit quantity

Thursday unit quantity

Friday unit quantity

Saturday unit quantity

Sunday unit quantity

Of course, we had implemented all of the support tables, such as store, article, department, weeks, and selling activity. These support tables are essentially the same for all retail companies I have worked with (see Chapters 10 and 11 for some samples). We basically created a data mart with a so-called *star schema*. Ralph Kimball, in his book *The Data Warehouse Toolkit*, defines the star schema concept in great detail.[2] The concept is so named because there is a central fact table and all the

---

2. Ralph Kimball. *The Data Warehouse Toolkit: Practical Techniques for Building Dimensional Data Warehouses.* John Wiley & Sons, 1996.

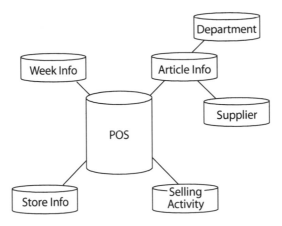

**Figure 8.1** The first Wal-Mart implementation.

support tables surrounding it; when the entities are drawn and connected, they look like a star. We quickly turned the star into a snowflake by adding more reference tables such as supplier information (Figure 8.1). The *snowflake schema*, then, consists of a large fact-based table (POS) surrounded by smaller support tables (store, article, date, etc.), which are also surrounded by yet smaller support tables (region, district, supplier, week, etc.). The entity-relationship diagram, if reduced to a single page, looks very similar to a snowflake under a microscope.

Most of the data elements in the POS table are self-explanatory except for the activity sequence number. The activity sequence number was a unique number that corresponded to another table—the selling activity table. This table had all of the associated selling information. It maintained how an article was sold: Was it was sold with a discount? Was it was sold as a special promotion? Was it sold at a normal price? It also included additional information such as the merchandising department number. We learned there was a finite combination of information because most articles were sold with no special advertisement at a normal price with no discount. The implementation of the selling activity table freed up space that enabled us to add the daily quantities. We were able to compress the daily quantities on zero, because when an article was sold it would sell only 2.3 times in that week, so the value in the daily quantity fields was normally zero.

If you have not fallen asleep yet, you should ask yourself what you can learn from this. A year after I left Wal-Mart, an employee from another retailer told me about my design. He actually thought it was a great design. I was shocked that he already knew of it. I asked him what he did with this design; did he use it? He answered, no, he did not use it. This is the difference between the Wal-Mart culture and other company cultures: the difference between learning and using. The culture of Wal-Mart was to focus on using what they learned. Other companies learn but never ask how they can apply what someone else has created. They don't take action. This is a key success factor in implementing an enterprise data warehouse.

> **This is the difference between the Wal-Mart culture and other company cultures: the difference between learning and using.**

The person at this other retail company never asked me *why* the database was designed like that. Nor was I asked if I thought it was a good idea to implement this design into his company. The truth is, I would never again design a database like this because I doubt I will be in the same situation again. The price of hardware is much less expensive today so I would not want to alter the database design because of a hardware limitation. I can guess that a comparable computer to that same $20 million system would cost less than $1 million today. It would also be more powerful. If cost were not an issue, I would design the POS table with almost no references to other tables. Certainly, there would be no selling activity table, as these attributes would be maintained with the POS table. The selling activity table in Wal-Mart's original design actually caused a performance problem about two years later. It was eliminated and the attributes were added back to the main table. This was the first time that table was changed since the implementation. The next major change was the addition of a selling-time attribute to that table several years later.

The most important issue for your company is to decide what information is needed. You have to perform the analyses and understand your company's data. You have to decide what subject area is important to implement first. You need to design and build the database for your company's data warehouse. If you do not already understand your data, then you should take action to learn it. There is value in understanding your data. It will help you use it.

## The Update Process

So, we had created the "perfect" design (☺), and now the application team had to maintain the data in this database. This was not an easy task because of the high volume and the space-conscious database design. The application team could use the database load utilities for most of the smaller tables. But our first design was more complex, and the volume of data was too large to be loaded with the simple load utilities. The team needed to program in parallel so the volume of data could be processed. They needed to insert records as well as update records. The utilities simply were not designed to do this. Another complexity was the insert and update mix. If you recall, we had determined that when an article sold, it would sell 2.3 times in a week. Therefore, there would be 1 insert record and 1.3 updates to existing records in the database. The next issue to resolve was the article file. Because the merchandising people had reused some of the article numbers over time for different articles, we had to assign a new unique number to each of the articles. I will discuss why we needed a new identifier for articles in the following paragraphs, but this new unique number was the article number that would be in all of the tables in the data warehouse. Finally, because we wanted the selling activity data to fit onto this machine, the team had to create a new process for it. This means they had to create a unique identifier for every selling event combination of an article. Most articles would be sold without any special selling event, but there were millions of combinations for the articles that had some type of selling action. The POS maintenance process (Figure 8.2) was difficult to create.

When you are processing sequentially, one record at a time, as you do in most computer databases, this POS process is still a complex application. We were using MPP technology. To process these POS records daily, the process had to be updated in parallel. This added even more complexity because MPP was new to us. When you update a database in parallel, you essentially want a single process running for each CPU (Figure 8.3). Actually, you want as many of these processes running as the computer can manage—the maximum throughput. This means you must have lots of independent tasks connected to the database at one time. One of the major complexity issues with massively parallel processing is the checkpoint and restart procedure. Checkpoint

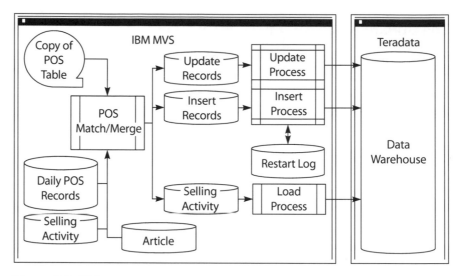

**Figure 8.2** POS maintenance process.

and restart is the process of recovering work that was active when a program failed. For example, if the power fails and the program fails, you need to start processing at the point of failure, not at the beginning, because you have already processed those records. You want to apply the figures only one time to the database. With MPP systems you are processing thousands of transactions at the exact same moment. Therefore, the restart procedures are much more complex than are sequential database checkpoint and restart procedures. A special application interface code had to be developed that enabled this type of processing, with restart capabilities in the event of a failure. The Teradata team developed this new Cobol interface and then taught the Wal-Mart application team how to use it.

This application team was also responsible for maintaining the smaller tables, too, but most of these used standard load utilities. The major exception was the article data, for which special processing was required. We quickly learned that we had a lot of problems with the article data, the biggest being that the unique article numbers were not unique but had been reused for different articles over time. Like every other retailer in the world, Wal-Mart had a "readable" article number. This means that the first two digits signified the department, the next few digits meant something else, and the last two digits meant some-

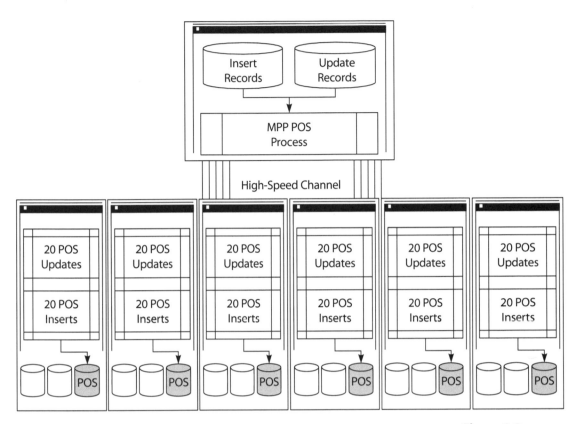

**Figure 8.3**
MPP processing.

thing else again. The problem was not the readable number but that they ran out of those numbers and had to reuse some of them. Every year, there was a mix-up of the article numbers: an article number in the historical sales data might not represent the same product as the identical number in the current article file. This is not a problem until you want to compare the history. If you have different products with the same number, you will be comparing the sales history of two different products. We had to create a new unique article number for every article. This unique number was matched with an expiration date, which had to be created too. The business people did not see this unique article number, but it had to be there to associate the proper sales history to each article.

> We quickly learned that we had a lot of problems with the article data, the biggest being that the unique article numbers were not unique.

There were other issues with the article files, such as substitute articles that were sold as the same product. This added further complexity to maintaining the article file.

## GUI Application

The GUI team was responsible for building the graphical user interface (GUI) that the user community would use. They were responsible for getting the data out of the database and presenting the analysis to the user. This application was called the *buyer decision support system* or BDSS. The team started development of the application shortly after we had completed the physical design. They had to create an application using PCs running on Microsoft Windows. This was a huge challenge because, at the time, only a few people knew how to do this, and they were not working at Wal-Mart. Once again, it was completely new technology. Another big problem the GUI team faced daily was the new network systems. I will discuss more about the network problems later. One of the first major problems they had to address was that they could not retrieve *sets* of records. They had to have all of the primary key values to retrieve a record. They could retrieve one record, or many single records, but not a set of records. For the POS table, the key values needed to access a record were article number, store number, and week number. If you knew the value of the keys (e.g., article number = 10001, store number = 10, and week number = 9301), then the response time to get the record was very fast. If you wanted all records for article 10001 and store 10, then you wanted a set of sales records for all weeks. Initially, if you didn't know this entire key, the database would scan the entire database to find the records that matched. This is okay if you have a small database, but when you have 1 billion records, this is a problem.

For Wal-Mart, this was a big problem. Faced with a similar problem, a team member would take responsibility to solve it. "Taking responsibility" is very different from being assigned the responsibility. This is the way the team worked. We each took responsibility. A person on the Teradata team took responsibility and solved this particular problem, but it did take a couple of weeks. The solution was to make a Cartesian product to create the keys that were needed. Using the example above in which you lack the week key, a Cartesian product is the joining of all of the possible week key values. There are only 52 weeks in a year, so if you join the week table with no constraints, then you have all the needed key values to directly retrieve the records. This is set mathematics, meaning that you UNION the key values for week with the other known key values, thereby creating every possible key combination. Unfortunately, this solution still did not work unless you knew two of the keys. For example, if you wanted to know sales for article 10001, all weeks, for all stores in region 5, the database wanted to scan the very large POS table first, then join it to the smaller tables. Finally, a resolution to this problem was found, but it was not pretty. What was devised was a statement that would be executed with every SQL statement to force the Cartesian product. The silly little statement was something like this:

```
((Article number = Store number or Article number
    NOT = Store number) or
(Store number = Week number or Store number NOT =
    Week number))
```

This strange statement forced the database to join the smaller tables first (to get the key values); then it could directly and easily retrieve the records from the very large database. These lines of code were in nearly every SQL statement that retrieved data from the large tables.

The reason I described this solution here is because it remained in all the application code for years. It might still be in code today. Other companies might have stopped the project at this point and waited for the technical problem to be solved. The culture at Wal-Mart at this time demanded that we take responsibility for the problem, solve the problem, and move on. Getting the information into the hands of the business people, so they could make better decisions, was the focus entirely. Another interesting technical side point is that we learned (because of this problem) that the query response time was directly related to the number of records in the Cartesian product. Now we could predict response times too!

> The culture at Wal-Mart at this time demanded that we take responsibility for the problem, solve the problem, and move on.

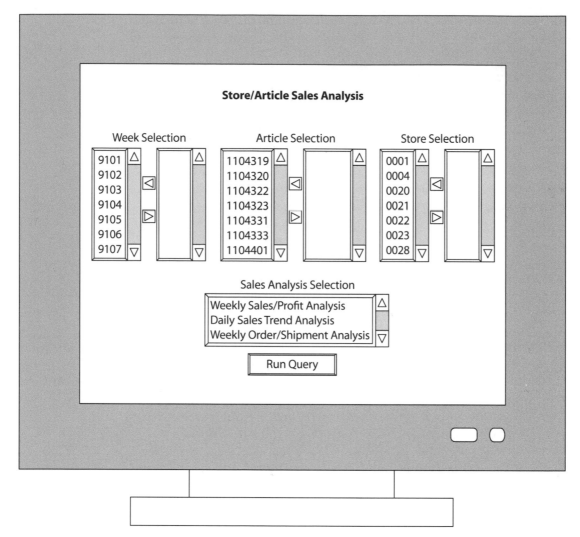

**Figure 8.4**
Recreated sample of the first GUI application.

Even though creating it was not easy, the first BDSS GUI implementation was really a very simple design. Keeping it simple became the theme of development throughout Wal-Mart's information systems division. Of course, the first application has been rewritten and rewritten, but it looked something like what is shown in Figure 8.4. Users would select the analysis they wanted to see. They could select articles, stores, and weeks. When they had provided enough for the query to run, the Run Query button would be highlighted. They would press this button and run their query. When the query completed, the results were placed in a formatted Excel spreadsheet. That was it. Of course, that was not the end of the development. The development has continued endlessly from 1990 until today.

I have mentioned buying an off-the-shelf front-end tool in Chapter 6 and have noted that keeping it simple and flexible is difficult for a multi-industry tool. One of the features we developed later that made the BDSS simple to use was the dynamic use of buttons. You could only press buttons that you were allowed to select. This means you could not press the Run Query button unless all the proper criteria for the analysis were selected. For example, if you were doing a store profitability analysis for an article, then you had to select some articles. If you did not select articles, the application would not allow you to run the query. When enough criteria were there (i.e., you selected some articles), then the Run Query button would be shown, the user could push the button, and the query would execute. If you purchase an off-the-shelf front-end tool, this simplistic approach is difficult to implement and maintain.

The buyers and the buyer analyst were the first to receive this application. The rollout procedure was long because it was done manually, though it was later automated. This simple application was improved upon weekly. It was rewritten and was constantly changing. Wal-Mart did not stop the development after the system was functional. After we got all the pieces of the data warehouse functioning together, we quickly added new subjects to the database. It is not possible to draw a line and say the project ended here, and we started another project. What I can say is the first implementation was POS, and then we added warehouse shipments, store receipts, and purchase orders very quickly afterward. Included in this were all of the reference tables (e.g., store, article, UPC, week) that were needed to support the base fact tables. These same subject areas, plus inventories, are those that other retailers have built in their first data warehouses too. Wal-Mart was a bit slow to add inventory figures because they did not have them until after the replenishment system was fully implemented. It was after this, around 1991, that we upgraded this single

> It is not possible to draw a line and say the project ended here, and we started another project.

system to beyond a terabyte. This is also when this database implementation began to draw attention from the media. It was called the "world's largest commercial database," and it is still called that today. In the next chapter, I am going to discuss the ROI and the construction and integration that followed, which allowed Wal-Mart to move beyond the data mart and into the enterprise data warehouse.

# 9

# Postimplementation of the Wal-Mart Data Warehouse

As I have said before, the Wal-Mart data warehouse project is never finished. It is like the TV commercial selling batteries with the pink bunny: "It keeps going and going and going. . . ." Other companies clearly stop after their first implementation of the data warehouse. Why didn't Wal-Mart stop development? There are some key differentiating points—such as company culture, a desire to improve the business, innovation, and hunger for information—that contribute to the continual development of the data warehouse into an enterprise data warehouse. Culture is a driving factor, but for Wal-Mart, one of the main motivators was their ROI analysis, which quantified the payback. After they understood the payback, it was used as a key part of other newly developed applications.

There are two sections in this chapter. The first, "The ROI Surrounded by Chaos," reveals the events that unfolded after Wal-Mart realized the data warehouse was very successful. I will discuss some of the events leading up to the ROI analyses, the ROI, and how they planned to integrate the data warehouse after the ROI was completed. The second section, "Integrating Operational Applications," describes another differentiation between Wal-Mart and other companies, namely, the way that they have integrated their data warehouse into all the facets of their operation. With the ROI, Wal-Mart understood the value of the information and took further action to exploit this information. I am going to discuss some classical applications that were integrated into the data warehouse. There are many examples of enterprise data warehouse integration, but I will discuss the replenishment process, the traiting system, the perpetual inventory process, and how these applications integrated with the data warehouse. At the end of this chapter, you will be able to understand the synergy created after building an enterprise data warehouse. Along the way, I hope to give you more details on the cultural aspects of Wal-Mart.

## THE ROI SURROUNDED BY CHAOS

After we began to roll out the system, more and more people wanted access to that system. We still had numerous very serious technical problems—of the kind that caused people's PC systems to crash. We had problems in every area of the implementation. There was no single biggest problem. All of them were very big problems. We had occasions when the database would shut down and restart for no apparent reason. The local area network (LAN) we had would suddenly stop functioning, and everybody would be disconnected or they could not connect. On the front-end application, the Windows application would "hang" for no apparent reason. All of these things typically caused the users' PCs to lock up, and they had to reboot. If they were lucky, they could connect after they rebooted.

After many understandable complaints about the errors, something had to be done. In an effort to quantify the problem, we developed an auditing process. We simply wanted to ensure that the query would run properly. If the query did not run, we wanted to know where it was failing. We defined the key points in the query execution process and built a system to track the queries. This application was called *query statistics*. Initially, it performed very simple tracking: the query has been submitted, the query is running, the query has finished. For every query that ran, we tracked it through to completion. As time went on, this became a very elaborate system. We essentially maintained the duration, or run times, of each step in the query execution process, but we also kept the query text, number of stores selected, number of items, number of weeks, application that created, and so on. We had many operational issues to solve before we could clearly understand and resolve the query problem. One problem was that everyone was using the same user-ID and password to log on and run queries. If everyone has the same ID, how do you know who is running which query? We fixed it so that everyone had a different user-ID, but they all still had the same password: "walmart." (This should frighten any security administrator. I know this password by heart because I created hundreds of user-IDs for people, or maybe it was the catchy phrase? ☺) We eventually required people to change their passwords, but that was a much later priority. We could deal with that later, perhaps in the second year.

The reason that I am telling you this is because this was another part of the culture. We were not concerned about people having complete access to all the data. Anyway, the query statistics application was also used as the key success measurement for improvements and upgrades to the system. After it was implemented, the extent of our problem became very, very clear. Approximately 50% of the queries failed! That means that every other time a user tried to execute a query, it failed. In any other company, the development would have been stopped until the problems had been resolved. The Wal-Mart culture was not to stop, but to find a solution that would allow them to continue. The rollout continued. There were early indicators for success happening at the same time. More and more people in the merchandising department were receiving their new PCs

> **The Wal-Mart culture was not to stop, but to find a solution that would allow them to continue.**

with the BDSS installed. People were running queries on every free PC workstation. When someone was out of the office, the PC on her desk was usually running a query because someone else knew she was gone. It was not uncommon to find one individual running long complex queries on four different workstations. People liked it so much that they were asking for the system to be installed in supplier negotiating rooms too. They were using BDSS directly in front of the supplier to leverage the pricing agreements. This was a very powerful negotiating tool, and it was obviously powerful. Finally, they decided to calculate the ROI.

I have dedicated an entire chapter (Chapter 4) to detailing the key elements needed in an ROI study. Creating an ROI is an important part of the data warehouse project. It is important to understand how Wal-Mart did it too. A year after the data warehouse was implemented, company executives began to question the value of the investment they had made. Even though there were problems, the overall support for the system was positive. The only way to quantify results was to do an ROI analysis. There needed to be an assessment of the influence this data warehouse had on Wal-Mart. So, rather simply, some of the users were asked what they had done with the system, how they had used it. All successful users were asked to document their successes. Not everyone's activities were documented, only those of a handful of people. Management knew who was using the system. They knew which people were relying on the analyses because they had contact with them very often. Most of these people were the power users of the BDSS workbench. Some of them were really good at identifying the problems within the system, too. Some took great pride in their ability to find problems. Finally, there were audits of who was doing the most work on the system. Through the query statistics application, it was possible to know how many queries were run and by whom. Building on the initial question, the users were asked: How were you able to improve the business? What analyses did you use? What was the financial benefit? Then they got down to the most important question: Could you have done this without the BDSS workstation? When a financial benefit was found and it could not have been achieved without the BDSS, it was documented. The success stories were consolidated into a single document listing the person, his or her job, the analysis that was performed (charts and graphs), the conclusion that was made, the action that was taken, and the financial benefit. All of these were accumulated into an

ROI document. All told, only a handful of people were involved in the study, yet the total ROI for these people exceeded the cost of the initial implementation, which was about $20 million. To drive home the value of the system, they broke the number down even further, on a per-query basis. The company earned over $12,000 per query. Moreover, they were running over 1000 queries per day! Of course, not all queries were from these experienced power users. Regardless of the percentage of power users, that is a huge ROI. With an ROI of $12,000 per query, you can see why Wal-Mart continued its data warehouse development.

We were still having performance problems after the ROI was completed. We were working to resolve these issues but it simply took time. We had added something we called *deferred queries* to enable a more stable environment for users. Deferred queries meant exactly what the name implied: it allowed the user community to defer the execution of a query until later. That way, they would not have to stay connected to our bouncing network and database. Teradata actually developed the code, and Wal-Mart did the alpha, beta, and production testing on it. We did the alpha, beta, and production testing at the same time because we put the application directly into production when it was functional. Instead of simply allowing the user to press the Run Query button, the BDSS workbench was modified to allow the execution of the query without staying connected, a Defer Query button. The BDSS workbench would simply insert the query into some special tables. The deferred queries application would run the query and save the results in the database. The users were allowed to see the status of the query and could retrieve the results after the query completed. Deferred queries also allowed users to run the queries overnight if they wished, as well as a few other options. The important part of deferring a query was that users did not have to leave it on their PC. They could submit the query and check it later, whenever they wanted. This is important because we had a lot of problems with the network. When users did not have to stay connected to the network for the duration of the query run time, the query didn't fail as often. This increased user

> We did the alpha, beta, and production testing at the same time because we put the application directly into production when it was functional.

confidence, but the performance was still not good. Response time was bad, too. It was not uncommon to have a query run longer than 20 minutes. Many ran for hours. Many never ran!

If you are just now starting to build your data warehouse, there are some benefits to starting now. One of them is that many off-the-shelf DSS applications have much of the functionality that Wal-Mart had to create. The deferred query application, for example, is now a standard part of many off-the-shelf applications. You can buy the product and have this functionality immediately. It is easier now to catch up to the technology advances of companies like Wal-Mart. Companies that adopt technology early will solve many technical problems before other companies will adopt the technology. Almost everything that we built regarding data warehousing over the years is now available in an off-the-shelf product. Enterprise integration of the data warehouse still requires a major investment of time and money. The integrated customized applications are the best and the most powerful in the industry, and they too will get easier to build and maintain.

We had to address the high failure rate, and we did. We did it the Wal-Mart way. I have mentioned that the Wal-Mart culture is such that their people really don't want to stop but prefer to find a solution so they can continue. The way they addressed the problems with BDSS was very different from the way other companies would do it. They brought the buyers into the auditorium, which seats several hundred, to talk about the BDSS workbench problems. They started by talking about the history of the application, then went directly into the benefits of the system. They had the buyers present their successes to the group. They highlighted their success, which was the ROI. They continued showing the different ways they had achieved positive results. They presented the ROI and then talked about the application shortfalls. This was mostly focused around the ability to execute a query. At that time, we had improved substantially. We were up to a 60% success rate! This means that one-third of all the queries failed and did not run to completion! This was made worse because often there was no indication of a failure. It might be hours before someone realized that the workstation was doing nothing. The merchandising people were told clearly that we did not know how to fix the problems. We knew the problems existed, and we were working on them. They were told it would take about a year to bring that 60% success rate into the 90% range. The merchandising organization was directly asked, "Do you want us to stop and fix the problem? Or do you want more PCs on your desks and to continue the rollout process?" They chose the latter. They preferred more failing BDSS applications on their desks up and running to waiting for stable technology. They wanted more BDSS workstations! The data warehouse team was completely comfortable with this result because we were focusing on the business. Today, I clearly understand that this is the profound difference in the culture of Wal-Mart versus other companies. Other companies would have stopped the development to stabilize the application. Wal-Mart, by contrast, began to invest even more heavily in this technology. They wanted more people to have access to this application.

The buyers, with their newfound analyses in the negotiation room, were much stronger during negotiations with suppliers. Some of the suppliers were supposed to be partners and working with the buyers directly. Every time they would travel to visit Wal-Mart, they were sent home without a deal. They did not have the information that the buyers had and were always caught off-guard after they arrived. At this time, it was not uncommon for the big suppliers to be sent away unexpectedly. I encountered an example of this after I left Wal-Mart. I was helping perform a business exploration at a large photo film manufacturer, when an employee who worked with the Wal-Mart account approached me. He told me about the time that Wal-Mart put the BDSS application into the negotiating room. He said that they had always been able to count on Wal-Mart purchasing their overmanufactured, or overstocked, film for the quarter. The only thing they had to do was get the price down low enough. When the price got low enough, Wal-Mart would buy. This happened several times a year—that is, until the BDSS application was installed in the negotiation rooms. When Wal-Mart could plainly see that they had more than enough inventory to last for a very long time, they did not bite at the low price. Wal-Mart would not be able to sell the film, at any price. The salesman was sent back without a deal. He also told me that this was normally a $4 million deal. Now, if you add up the number of suppliers that might have experienced something like this, you will accumulate a nice ROI for a single application.

As you can imagine, the suppliers were not happy with the BDSS workbench. They complained that they could not see what the buyer was seeing. They wanted to do the same analysis as the buyer. In fact, Wal-Mart didn't really want to send salespeople away. They were happy to have a strong information base, but they really did not want to waste time. The suppliers should have come prepared. The information should not have been a surprise, but rather a tool that the suppliers could use to improve sales and profit, too. After all, both the retailer and the manufacturer had the same objective—to sell more merchandise. So Wal-Mart decided to develop the workbench for the suppliers. This was going to be nearly identical to the BDSS workbench, but for the suppliers. Renamed Retail Link, it was essentially the same data warehouse application but without the competitor's product cost information. Of course, there were other limitations but not too many. With Retail Link, suppliers were able to view almost everything that the buyer could see. Most importantly, they could perform the same analyses and exchange ideas for improving the business. They were, and still are, given the Retail Link software for free. Well, it is not exactly free because they must use it. But now the supplier performance expectations are higher. They expect better operating results. When I left Wal-Mart, there were thousands of suppliers that were given access to this application. (We made them change the passwords too. ☺) Of course, this was just the beginning of the data warehouse integration into the business. A new theme was created because of this. The theme was "get the information into the hands of the decision maker."

## INTEGRATING OPERATIONAL APPLICATIONS

Just over a year after the data warehouse implementation was completed, the Information Systems Division decided to deliver the most important new application development, in terms of ROI, to the business. The business had already requested various applications and had developed the priorities of each based on projected ROI to the business. All were to be completed in 18 months. The number one priority on the list was the completion of the replenishment application, with a projected first-year ROI of $178 million.

It is interesting to note that many of the requested applications were to be integrated into the data warehouse. The theme of getting the information into the hands of the decision maker was certainly a high driving factor for further integration. These systems had information that was valuable to people throughout the company. For example, the replenishment system maintained inventory figures that did not exist anywhere else. There were also technical reasons driving integration: it was easy to get data out of the data warehouse database. Because it was easy, the data warehouse was fast becoming a transportation vehicle for data. We had already built the technology that allowed us to pull data from the data warehouse and into all the different types of computers throughout the company. It was becoming clear that there were benefits to using the power of the data warehouse to transport the data. For the replenishment system, each store computer was to receive data from the home office daily. We built a structure that allowed each store to pull this new information from the data warehouse. It was effective because we were designing this to run in parallel, meaning that many hundreds of stores could pull data at the same time. This same technique also applied to other applications.

**The theme of getting the information into the hands of the decision maker was certainly a high driving factor for further integration.**

Another point of value was that different people throughout the company could use the same information for different analyses. Although the traiting application was initially only a replenishment process used to determine distribution, it contained an informational aspect that was valuable too. Traits provided information regarding the active articles in each store. This information is quite helpful when you want to determine a proper allocation of that article. The perpetual inventory system likewise provided more than one benefit. It provided a business operational solution to help manage inventory, and it also delivered extra information that could be used by the entire company. These applications needed to be integrated into the data warehouse so that this new information could be used in analyses. It was this type of integration that created our enterprise data warehouse. So now I will discuss each application specifically, and how each was integrated into the enterprise data warehouse.

## Replenishment

Automatic replenishment delivered the biggest ROI after the implementation of the data warehouse. The expected ROI was $178 million in the first year. The replenishment application was functioning in 500 stores already and had been up and running for several years. When the operational procedures were implemented properly, the store would show an obvious operational improvement. Therefore, the operational aspects of implementing a replenishment system were definitely mature. The problem was that the current technical implementation had essentially reached its technical limits. One of the technology challenges of a rapidly growing company is designing systems that will continue to function when the company doubles in size. In Chapters 6 and 7 I discussed designing systems for linear growth, messaging, and parallel processing. The replenishment application needed to be redesigned for linear growth as well as other enhancements. At this time, the stores of Wal-Mart were mostly in the USA and were just beginning their expansion into Mexico. The main limiting factor of the replenishment system was its ability to process the replenishment records in the nightly window. The constraints had a lot to do with the growth of the company and the different time zones. The replenishment process would begin after the last store would close. The typical store in America closes at 9 P.M. When you consider the time zones, processing could begin only after midnight. There were no stores on the west coast of the USA when the replenishment system was built, so the time crunch was not an issue initially. Additional functionality was being added so each store could be processed independently while enabling the easier-to-use handheld radio frequency (RF) technology. In order to understand the enterprise data warehouse integration of the replenishment application, you need to understand the basic replenishment process. I will explain the basic operational process first so you can better understand the implementation of technology; then I will describe the technical data flow so you can understand how it was integrated.

**The Wal-Mart replenishment system was part of the store department manager's daily job.**

The Wal-Mart replenishment system was part of the store department manager's daily job. Every morning, at 6 A.M., she got a list of suggested orders for articles. (This list was originally on paper. Currently, it appears on a handheld RF terminal directly connected to the backroom computer.) The department manager's job was to review those orders and to accept, reject, or modify them. She had until noon that same day to make these modifications; otherwise the orders would be placed. Of course, this person had other tasks, too, such as counting the merchandise, pricing the merchandise, and stocking the merchandise, and, at times, assisting customers. There were obvious similarities in the tasks of product pricing and counting of merchandise, so tasks such as these were to be integrated. Replenishment was a key focus to integrating these tasks and making them flow more easily with technology. New technology, like the RF handheld devices and the "backroom" merchandising system, were enabling this type of integration. The backroom merchandising system, which Wal-Mart calls the SMART system, was a Unix-based system with a much larger processing and storage capacity than the recently replaced system. The replenishment system was one of the first applications to exploit this new power and much of the new technology. For an article to be on the suggested order list, it had to be represented in the replenishment application, which was run at the home office. When an article was placed into the replenishment process, an order review point was established. An order review point sets the date for the next time that the inventory for a store and article will be reviewed for an order. This was typically based on sales trends and the lead time of that article. A fast-selling article with a short lead time needs to be reviewed more often. Lead time was projected from each individual store's delivery cycle. The lead time for supplier delivery was certainly part of the equation. This process was an obvious effort to maintain a lower inventory. This lead-time process was implemented in the home office on a classical OLTP application. When a store/article reached the order review threshold, the replenishment system determined if an order should be placed. If an order was necessary, a suggested order quantity was calculated and a future order review point was established. No order was placed at this time, just a suggested list of orders. This is the list that the store department manager reviewed every morning.

As I mentioned before, the department manager had other, similar tasks to do at the same time. This time was also used to visually review the shelf quantities. New orders could be placed at any time, by scanning the bar codes on the shelf or product. The department managers could also review the flow of goods. They could inquire about the article sales trends, order trends, article profiles, corporate information, and so on. The RF terminal could do all of these tasks. The majority of the information was available on the in-store processors. These might be considered data marts, but inquiries could travel to the home office computers. (This type of inquiry, regardless of where the information resides, is both OLTP and decision support.) The user was not aware of the complexities of these systems or the location of the data or system that might be doing the processing. The store application was designed for the store's specific needs to help solve problems as quickly as possible, no matter where the data resided. For performance reasons, it is obviously better when the data is closer to the user, so the most vital information is on the local system. This type of processing began the corporatewide integration of the data warehouse—the beginning of the enterprise data warehouse.

For more clarification of this process, we should discuss the data flow through the systems (Figure 9.1). The essential part of the automatic replenishment system ran in the home office. It reviewed articles, based on the order review point, for orders. If the system determined that an order was needed, it would create a suggested order record for this article and store. These suggested order records were loaded into the data warehouse and then transmitted from the home office to the store. The store department manager used the RF device to review the suggested orders, change prices, count inventory, and so on. The manager could make inquiries on articles she was reviewing, or she could scan a shelf label or a product bar code to inquire about other articles to find the flow of goods. The application used the backroom computer to find information, or optionally to retrieve information from the home office computer (the data warehouse), about the flow of goods. Once the orders were finalized, they were returned to the home office computers. The replenishment system placed an order. If the order could be filled via one of the Wal-Mart warehouses, the order would be placed there; otherwise the order was directed to the supplier via electronic data interchange (EDI). The orders were placed in the order systems and into

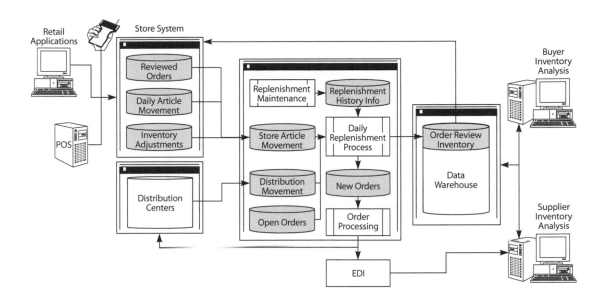

**Figure 9.1**
Replenishment
data flow.

the data warehouse. When a Wal-Mart warehouse received goods from the supplier to fill an open order, the warehouse system would "allocate" the articles to the store. The "allocated" records in the warehouse computer were transmitted to the data warehouse system. The data warehouse system, via the replenishment application, moved that "allocated" record to the in-store system. When the warehouse shipped that order, the article was "in transit" and that record flowed through the systems. When the store received the article, the "received" article record was transmitted back through the system, filling the order.

It is very important to understand that each store manager was responsible for the inventory quantity. No computer system can count the inventory on the shelf, determine shrinkage, mislabeling, misstocking, and so forth—at least not yet. Even though the replenishment system was very effective, there were stores that did not receive an immediate return on investment from the replenishment system. Careful study of each store revealed that the operational procedures for managing inventory were not followed. Once the replenishment procedures were followed, financial benefits followed. Some common problems included manipulation of the on-hand inventory numbers to initiate an order, and inadequate backroom management that resulted in no orders being placed. The system had done exactly what it was designed to do, but store operations had failed to manage the inventory properly. Data integrity became more important as more people began to rely on the data. When the suppliers and the buyers used the financial figures, the data manipulation that I just described had a far-reaching effect beyond the operational systems (such as automatic replenishment). So the business operations (the department manager in this case) must be held accountable for their inventory figures that reside in a computer. This technology is very powerful, but it does not eliminate the need to create and maintain operational procedures. The computer can assist and enable the business operation in many ways, but it can use only what is put into it. When people use and maintain the technology, the technology can enable better decisions. The "enable the business" philosophy was replicated throughout Wal-Mart systems. The replenishment system was no exception.

> **Once the replenishment procedures were followed, financial benefits followed.**

There is one more point to consider in Figure 9.1: the external data. The data flows out of the systems in various places. One place is from the data warehouse to the store system, as the order review and warehouse information moves to the store system. Another place the data flows is from the data warehouse into the buyer and supplier inventory analyses, their decision support systems. Orders can be placed directly via EDI and to a distribution center. Information does flow to other systems that are not illustrated, but the point is that the data warehouse is a key data distribution technology. At any time anyone within the system can easily review quantity on order with lead time, quantity in the warehouse allocated to them, quantity in transit to the store, or quantity on hand, via the data warehouse. Figures can be obtained from each individual system, but the data warehouse has them all. The enterprise data warehouse shields the user from the complexity of the various systems.

**Table 9.1    Store traits.**

| | Pharmacy | Fresh Deli | Bakery | Beach | Retirement | University | <60K Sqft | >120K Sqft | Kmart Comp | Target Comp | Real Comp | etc. |
|---|---|---|---|---|---|---|---|---|---|---|---|---|
| 2105 | N | N | N | N | Y | Y | N | Y | Y | N | N | ... |
| 2106 | Y | N | N | N | N | N | N | Y | Y | Y | N | ... |
| 2107 | Y | Y | N | N | N | N | N | Y | Y | Y | N | ... |
| 2108 | Y | Y | Y | N | Y | Y | N | Y | N | Y | N | ... |
| 2109 | Y | Y | N | N | N | N | N | Y | N | N | N | ... |

## Distribution via Traits

The *traiting* concept was developed as a key part of the replenishment system. It was used to determine the distribution (not allocation) of an article to the stores. However, traits have some very valuable informational aspects that apply directly to data warehousing. I will describe the traiting concept first, then I will show you how it relates to the data warehouse. A trait is simply a characteristic of a store or an article; there are store traits (Table 9.1) and article traits (Table 9.2). For example, if a store is near a university, it has the trait of a "university store." If a store is on the beach, then it has the trait of a "beach" store. These traits are used for classifying stores into manageable units. Traits can be any characteristic at all, as long as it is somewhat permanent. A store can have a fresh deli, it can have a pharmacy, it can be over 120,000 square feet, it can have wide aisles, and so on. A trait can be used to identify the competition in the area. For example, a trait might be having Kmart and Target as neighborhood competitors. Articles can have traits, too. They can be perishable, consumable, hazardous, clothing, furniture, chemical, drug, and so forth. Wal-Mart maintained several thousand traits for stores and articles. An article can have the same trait as a store: for example, a "university article," or a "beach article."

It is important to note that there are only two values to these traits: they either have the trait (TRUE) or they do not have the trait (FALSE). Trait descriptions with more than two values are not allowed. For example, a store with both a meat deli and a salad deli would have

**Table 9.2  Article traits.**

| | Pharmacy | Fresh Produce | Bakery | Beach | Retirement | University | Candy | Electronic Basics | Electronic HiFi | Cosmetic | Replenish | etc. |
|---|---|---|---|---|---|---|---|---|---|---|---|---|
| 40184287 | Y | N | N | Y | N | Y | N | N | Y | N | Y | ... |
| 40184777 | N | Y | N | N | Y | N | N | N | N | Y | Y | ... |
| 40184912 | N | Y | N | Y | N | N | Y | N | N | N | N | ... |
| 40185007 | Y | N | N | N | N | Y | N | N | N | Y | Y | ... |
| 40185412 | N | Y | N | Y | N | N | Y | N | N | N | N | ... |

three distinct traits defined: deli, meat deli, and salad deli. Translated, the store has a deli of some sort, the store specifically has a meat deli, and the store specifically has a salad deli. Another example of this is store size. Store size traits must be defined clearly—for instance, greater than 120,000 square feet or less than 60,000 square feet. Then you use the traits like YES and NO. The trait exists (Y) or it does not exist (N).

Traits are used to match an article to a store in the replenishment system. When you match the article trait to the store trait, the system will create a distribution and a stock keeping unit (SKU). After the distribution is created, inventory for that article can be allocated to that store. Orders can be placed for that article. This process is very dynamic. Basically, a store will get the article if the traits match. This is so dynamic that a human error in maintaining traits can be very costly. Let us assume the "university" trait is removed from the system. Any articles that were being replenished for that trait will be discontinued, and a severe out-of-stock will occur. This same process can be used to positive ends, such as for article closeouts. The flow of goods starts or ceases based on the traits. Changes to the traits could be excellent for seasonal articles and disastrous for "never-out" articles. The traiting concept, therefore, is both powerful and fragile. The traits are maintained centrally with input from store operations and merchandise managers. There is flexibility, meaning you can always choose to override the defaults. For instance, you could choose to stock a specific article that performs well locally but not nationally. However, this is rare. The point is that there is give-and-take in the replenishment from store operations and merchandising; each can set the traits.

> **Traits are used to match an article to a store in the replenishment system.**

There is a more powerful aspect to the traiting concept than simply matching the corresponding traits of the stores and articles. Every article can have a distribution replenishment formula based on many of these traits. This distribution formula is a Boolean formula, meaning that it will have only two values. This is just like the standard light switches in your home: the light can be ON or OFF. The Boolean formulas in traiting are either TRUE (Y) or FALSE (N). If the result of the formula is TRUE, then the store will be allowed to receive that article. If it is TRUE, an SKU record will be created, and the store will be part of the article distribution.

As you can imagine, these distribution formulas can become very complex. Let's look at an example. We have a new product and we want it to be distributed to all stores that have a pharmacy, a fresh deli, and a bakery, but they must be larger than 60,000 square feet. The distribution formula would look something like this:

```
(Pharmacy * Fresh Deli * Bakery * ¬ <60K sqft)
```

In Boolean algebra the * symbol means AND, the + symbol means OR, and the ¬ symbol means NOT. The values that we are hunting for are Pharmacy = Y, Fresh Deli = Y, Bakery = Y, and <60K sqft = N. Using the store chart (Table 9.3), you can see that there is one store that qualifies, store 2108. This store is the only one in the list that would receive this article.

Later you learn that this product also sells well in stores that are in retirement communities. Therefore, you want this article to also go to all of these stores. So you change your formula to distribute to all stores that have a pharmacy, a fresh deli, a bakery, and are smaller than 60,000 square feet, OR they are in a retirement community. The formula would look something like this:

```
((Pharmacy * Fresh Deli * Bakery * ¬ <60K sqft) +
   Retirement)
```

In our example you would now distribute that article to stores 2108 and 2105 (see Table 9.4).

You should be able to understand how powerful this can be, particularly for a large centrally managed retail company like Wal-Mart. There is also another benefit that I have not yet mentioned, but you might have already observed. This process can be used to control the assortment for the various types of stores. You can create a very specific assortment for stores that are in retirement communities versus stores that are in a university community.

The reason for this discussion is to understand how to tie the traiting concept to the enterprise data warehouse. When a distribution formula is created for an article, then an SKU record is created in the database. Therefore, an article will become "active" in a particular store.

**Table 9.3** Store distribution for (pharmacy * fresh deli * bakery * ¬ <60K sqft).

| | Pharmacy | Fresh Deli | Bakery | Beach | Retirement | University | <60K Sqft | >120K Sqft | Kmart Comp | Target Comp | Real Comp | etc. |
|---|---|---|---|---|---|---|---|---|---|---|---|---|
| 2105 | N | N | N | N | Y | Y | N | Y | Y | N | N | ⋯ |
| 2106 | Y | N | N | N | N | N | N | Y | Y | Y | N | ⋯ |
| 2107 | Y | Y | N | N | N | N | N | Y | Y | Y | N | ⋯ |
| 2108 | Y | Y | Y | N | Y | Y | N | Y | N | Y | N | ⋯ |
| 2109 | Y | Y | N | N | N | N | N | Y | N | N | N | ⋯ |

**Table 9.4  Store distribution for ((pharmacy * fresh deli * bakery * ¬ <60K sqft) + retirement)**

|  | Pharmacy | Fresh Deli | Bakery | Beach | Retirement | University | <60K Sqft | >120K Sqft | Kmart Comp | Target Comp | Real Comp | etc. |
|---|---|---|---|---|---|---|---|---|---|---|---|---|
| 2105 | N | N | N | N | Y | Y | N | Y | Y | N | N | ⋯ |
| 2106 | Y | N | N | N | N | N | N | Y | Y | Y | N | ⋯ |
| 2107 | Y | Y | N | N | N | N | N | Y | Y | Y | N | ⋯ |
| 2108 | Y | Y | Y | N | Y | Y | N | Y | N | Y | N | ⋯ |
| 2109 | Y | Y | N | N | N | N | N | Y | N | N | N | ⋯ |

This is valuable information for many reasons, the most obvious of which is allocation. How much merchandise will you need to allocate to the stores? A data warehouse can provide a good estimate based on another, similar product that has the same distribution. The first allocation of a new article can be based on only those stores that will actually receive the goods. This is opposed to a common percentage based on store size, which is used by most retailers. If this is the first time that the product will be in the stores, it can be distributed to a test market using the traiting concept. The entire performance tracking will be done in the data warehouse. A buyer could analyze and adjust the allocation figures on-line and press Create PO when the figures are accurate. The traits could be adjusted, based on the performance tracking in the data warehouse, until the distribution formula is perfected. The category performance can be monitored to ensure that the new article, and perhaps a new distribution, is improving the entire category and not just rearranging the sales figures. The ways to apply these two technologies (OLTP and data warehouse represented here with traiting and allocation) are immeasurable. They go together and they belong together. These applications complement each other. The best solution is to provide a common user interface so that users have no concept of which system they are using. It should be the same system to the user. Total seamless technology integration is the concept of an enterprise data warehouse.

> The best solution is to provide a common user interface so that users have no concept of which system are using.

## Perpetual Inventory

Another application that falls between functionality and information access is the perpetual inventory (PI) system. The PI system is used to maintain the inventory for all articles, not just the articles that participate in automatic replenishment. The perpetual inventory system is designed to see the entire flow of goods for all articles in the company, including replenishment articles. This system was developed to manage flow of goods as well as other elements such as location of inventory. Like the replenishment system, the PI system is both an OLTP and an

OLAP system. The data is available in the store and at the home office. The PI system provides information about the flow of merchandise without the heavy baggage of replenishment, so to speak. So, using both the replenishment and PI systems, the department managers can maintain everything electronically about the inventory in their store.

One of the main benefits of the PI system is that it will track every transaction throughout the system processing. Another benefit is that it can be enabled to show the exact location of the articles in a store. The transaction tracking capability is used to track every action that is placed on an article. Every transaction is assigned a unique identifier for each store/article. This identifier will remain with the transaction throughout the processing. Essentially, the identifier is applied at the source, where the transaction is created, and will be used to verify processing at every critical processing point. Most of these transactions originate from the store, but some do not. When a product is damaged and removed from the inventory, for example, there should be an adjustment reflecting the product removal. Of course, there is a financial impact as well as an impact to the replenishment process that needs to be documented when an item is damaged. Procedurally, the clerk should scan the bar code, using the RF handheld device, and remove the product from inventory. This transaction is assigned a unique identifier and will flow through the system, being tracked and confirmed at every relevant point within each system. When this record leaves the store, it will flow through the systems, triggering various actions based on the record type. When the inventory figures have been returned from the home office to the store, they will be confirmed as processed. Every modifying inventory figure will have an audit trail from the originating source. This is important for several reasons. First, you can determine if transactions were lost. Second, you can see what actions were taken against an article. Finally, you can see the sequence of events that drove an inventory change.

> One of the main benefits of the PI system is that it will track every transaction throughout the system processing. Another benefit is that it can be enabled to show the exact location of the articles in a store.

There are a substantial number of informational analyses that can be created when you have this information in your data warehouse. If you want to analyze the sequence of events for an article, you can do so very easily. The flow of goods can be analyzed for an article and an entire category. The time between each transaction can help you determine the operational cost of changes. If used properly, the PI system can tell you exactly where the product is located within a store. This can help in creating "plan-o-grams" for each store and in making planning more precise. That means that buyers and suppliers can measure the best selling locations without physically going to each store.

There is another benefit of the PI system that applies to the enterprise data warehouse concept. We should use customer service as an example this time. Let's say the department manager is performing daily duties of pricing and counting inventory on the floor. A customer explains that she is looking for a specific article but she wants it in a different color. This is critical because the response that is given will be a purchasing decision for this customer. With the RF handheld PI system, the manager can scan the bar code on the product or shelf and determine if there are more in the back, or in another department. He can determine if there is an open order for that product. He can determine if the product is in transit to the store and when it will arrive. If all of this fails to locate the article for the customer, with an integrated enterprise data warehouse, the manager can still continue to search. He can see if another store nearby has that product. At this point, the local system is bypassed and the search moves through to the home office computers. The system can see if this product is in another city, state, or country. Essentially, it has the capabilities to find that product anywhere in the world. Most importantly, the department manager does not even realize that there are different systems involved. To him, it is one system. This is what I mean by integrating the data warehouse into an enterprise data warehouse.

The Wal-Mart enterprise data warehouse was a complex application designed specifically to enable better decisions. Simplicity and ease of use were the foremost concerns. Advanced technology was applied to enable the decision-making process. They continued to build and improve on their successes. Both OLTP and OLAP were used to assist decision makers in the analysis of their decisions in a timely manner. Finally, technology was applied and designed to enable decision makers to take action immediately after the analysis was complete.

# 10

# Store Operations Sample Analyses

This chapter provides a retailer with the basic analyses that need to be built for the store operations side of the business. Many of the analyses for one group will apply to another group. For example, the basic sales figures used by store operations are important to marketing during a promotion. The basic premise of a data warehouse is that detailed data is available to the entire business. Below I have outlined the basic areas in which store operations could benefit from a data warehouse application. Each application has a small overview, a data element listing, and a sample report.

It is best to use this chapter as a reference for discussion. The sample reports presented here should be used to clarify and to help in the creation of your custom data warehouse. Please take into consideration that some of the analyses build off of one or more similar analyses. An effort has been made to point out these other analyses. As a general rule, the analyses at the beginning of this chapter are simple and get more complex toward the end of the chapter. Instead of repeating data elements for every analysis, they are sometimes referenced to a different section of this chapter. For example, the data elements of a store can be used for almost every type of analysis; these elements are listed once and then referenced thereafter. I have also included a data model skeleton in Appendix B for further data element references.

It is assumed that you will need a calendar or calendar functions. The data structures and functions needed to support the calendar are not included in this chapter. Almost every data element can be presented in a grid or graph. Most retailers will have both. A natural function of a data warehouse is to provide drill-down capabilities. Drill-down capabilities vary depending on the client or presentation tool that is selected. Drilling down is also very difficult to document since there are so many variations, or dimensions, to a single analysis report and, of course, it is difficult to represent more than two dimensions on paper. It is assumed that drill-down through defined hierarchies, such as company, region, and district, will be implemented in a simple, easy-to-use manner.

One more very important point: please do not think these are the only types of analyses available. I have included only the most common types of analyses that retailers around the world are using or want to use. The flexibility to mix and match various parts of the data warehouse is an important function of a data warehouse. I understand that each retailer's business need is different. Additionally, once that need is resolved, there will be many other issues that tend to be very specific to each retailer. Your decision support system (DSS) must be flexible enough to resolve that next business issue in a timely manner.

## BASIC STORE OPERATIONS INFORMATION NEEDS

The store operations management is concerned with the day-to-day business operation of the retail chain. Most of their time is spent reviewing the financial status of stores for the current week. In an ideal situation, they want the same store (comparable store or comp-store) sales to increase this year compared to last year at the same time. Comp-store sales increases are a good indicator of a healthy, growing retailer. They will want to be able to measure these results monthly, weekly, and daily. Along with these comparisons, they will want to review the planned sales versus the actual sales. Some of the following analyses are important to the store operations group:

◆ store sales by day, week (fiscal), and month
◆ comparable (comp-) store sales using this year–this week (TY-TW) versus last year–this week (LY-TW) figures as well as monthly comparisons (TM-TY vs. LM-TY) and year-to-date comparisons (TY-YTD vs. LY-YTD)
◆ flash store sales using hourly sales figures for current day, integrated with store sales above
◆ departmental store sales using a combination of store sales and comp-store sales
◆ current sales as compared with planned sales
◆ competitive comparable store performance

## STORE SALES

Store operations may have the capability to review the sales of every store by day, week, and month. Some retailers still do not retain any daily information about their stores. Some retailers will not have the drill-down capabilities—that is, company sales to regional sales to district sales to store sales—that are almost standard these days when building a data warehouse. In either case, a store sales analysis is a necessary first step in implementing a decision support system for store operations. Store sales analysis is essentially the ranking and grouping of stores into a usable form (Table 10.1).

**A store sales analysis is a necessary first step in implementing a decision support system for store operations.**

The sales can be graphed but will be normally viewed in a tabular fashion. The user will be able to sort and group stores by any number of data elements. Most analyses will be a drill-down from company, through region, to district, then area, and into store for the current week or month. Daily information should be maintained for week-to-date (WTD) and month-to-date (MTD) analyses, and for future functionality.

## Store Sales Data Elements

The data elements listed below are grouped together in terms of data similarity. Data elements shown in italics are optional but could be helpful in the development of other future analyses. The data elements should be used as a basis for a customized data model. The data elements listed under daily store sales are basis for analyzing store sales. For performance reasons, it may be necessary to create a weekly and/or monthly entity. Of course, each retailer will have data elements and terms that are very company specific. In this chapter, the entire definition of every retail operational hierarchy (store, area, region, company, and corporate) has been omitted for simplicity. It is assumed that the operational hierarchy is a clearly defined hierarchy:

- **Store Information**

  Store identifier, store name/address, store state code, store zip code, store manager name, region identifier, region name, district identifier, area identifier, store square foot (Sqft) selling area, *open date, remodel date, pre-remodel Sqft, number of fuel pumps, hours of operation, car-wash code, store size code, other customer store-level data elements*

- **Daily Store Sales**

  Store identifier, fiscal year, fiscal week, date, retail sales, customer count, retail sales per Sqft, fuel sales, labor costs

- **Region Information**

  Region identifier, region name, region manager identifier, *other customer region-level data elements*

- **District Information**

  District identifier, district name, district manager identifier, *other customer district-level data elements*

- **Monthly Store Sales**

  Store identifier, month, fiscal year, retail sales, customer count, fuel sales, labor cost

- **Weekly Store Sales**

  Store identifier, fiscal week, retail sales, customer count, fuel sales, labor cost

**Table 10.1  Store sales sample report.**

| Regn | Distr | Area | Store | Name | Manager | 1000 Sqft | Retail Sales | Rtl Sales $/Sqft | Cust Count | Avg Cust Tran | Rtl Sales % Petro | Fuel Sales | Fuel 92 Sales | Fuel 89 Sales | Fuel 87 Sales |
|------|-------|------|-------|------|---------|-----------|--------------|------------------|------------|---------------|-------------------|------------|---------------|---------------|---------------|
| 2 | 10 | 1 | 2178 | Cupertino | Tim | 10 | 12,765 | $1.28 | 4,401 | $2.90 | 60% | $7,659 | · | · | · |
| | | | 2209 | San Jose North | Kelly | 12 | 18,965 | $1.58 | 3,281 | $5.78 | 42% | $7,965 | · | · | · |
| | | | 2210 | San Jose South | Sally | 18 | 15,998 | $0.89 | 5,007 | $3.20 | 75% | $11,999 | | | |
| | | | 2212 | San Jose East | Terry | 13 | 17,544 | $1.35 | 4,975 | $3.53 | 22% | $3,860 | | | |
| | | | 2234 | Santa Clara | Tommy | 12 | 10,021 | $0.84 | 3,958 | $2.53 | 34% | $3,407 | | | |
| | | | 2239 | Sunnyvale | Lisa | 17 | 20,004 | $1.18 | 2,941 | $6.80 | 78% | $15,603 | | | |
| | | 2 | 2240 | Monterey Bay 1 | Barry | 22 | 17,992 | $0.82 | 1,924 | $9.35 | 62% | $11,155 | · | · | · |
| | | | 2245 | Monterey Bay 2 | Dewane | 8 | 5,482 | $0.69 | 907 | $6.04 | 78% | $4,276 | | | |
| | | | | Totals | | 112 | 118,771 | $1.06 | 27,394 | $4.34 | 56% | $65,924 | · | · | · |

**Table 10.2    Comparable store sample report.**

Generic Retail Store Corp.
Comp-Store Sales Report for Region 2 District 10 Week 9634
District Manager: Larry Hirt

| Region | Distr | Area | Store | Name | Manager | 1000 Sqft | TY Retail Sales | LY Retail Sales |
|--------|-------|------|-------|------|---------|-----------|----------|----------|
| 2 | 10 | 1 | 2178 | Cupertino | Tim | 8 | $12,765 | $13,211 |
| | | | 2209 | San Jose North | Kelly | 12 | $18,965 | $17,666 |
| | | | 2210 | San Jose South | Sally | 9 | $15,998 | $14,893 |
| | | | 2212 | San Jose East | Terry | 13 | $17,544 | $12,332 |
| | | | 2234 | Santa Clara | Tommy | 12 | $10,021 | $6,922 |
| | | | 2239 | Sunnyvale | Lisa | 14 | $20,004 | $17,030 |
| | | 2 | 2240 | Monterey Bay 1 | Barry | 22 | $17,992 | $16,289 |
| | | | 2245 | Monterey Bay 2 | Dewane | 7 | $5,482 | $12,803 |
| | | | | Totals | | 97 | $118,771 | $111,146 |

## COMPARABLE STORE SALES

A comparable store sales analysis builds off the store sales analysis. It uses all the data elements in the store sales analysis, plus comparable figures. There is no need to modify the existing data structures to implement the comparable store sales application. The client application can be created using the existing structures. The front-end implementation is the major difference between these two applications. The only requirement is that the data be maintained for the comparable period. For example, for a weekly comparison, there must be at least 53 full weeks of data, while for quarterly comparisons you must have five full quarters, or 65 weeks, of sales data. Determining the amount of data to be maintained on-line will be the major consideration in designing the flexibility of this data warehouse. For the most flexible and simple implementation, I suggest 65 weeks of daily data and two years of weekly/monthly data. This will provide your company with the most flexible options for the front-end analysis.

> I suggest 65 weeks of daily data and two years of weekly/monthly data.

| Retail % Increase | RTL Sales $\Sqft | LY Cust Count | TY Cust Count | Cust % Incr | TY Fuel Sales | LY Fuel Sales | Fuel % Increase | Rtl Sales % Fuel |
|---|---|---|---|---|---|---|---|---|
| −3.4% | $1.60 | 4,401 | 4331 | −1.6% | $7,659 | $6,799 | 12.6% | 60% |
| 7.4% | $1.58 | 3,281 | 3347 | 2.0% | $7,965 | $8,361 | −4.7% | 42% |
| 7.4% | $1.78 | 5,007 | 5117 | 2.2% | $11,999 | $12,009 | −0.1% | 75% |
| 42.3% | $1.35 | 4,975 | 5413 | 8.8% | $3,861 | $4,500 | −14.2% | 22% |
| 44.8% | $0.84 | 3,958 | 4271 | 7.9% | $3,407 | $5,676 | −40.0% | 34% |
| 17.5% | $1.43 | 2,941 | 3100 | 5.4% | $15,603 | $14,345 | 8.8% | 78% |
| 10.5% | $0.82 | 1,924 | 1987 | 3.3% | $11,155 | $10,921 | 2.1% | 62% |
| −57.2% | $0.78 | 907 | 835 | −7.9% | $4,276 | $4,112 | 4.0% | 78% |
| 6.9% | $1.22 | 27,394 | 28,400 | 3.7% | $65,924 | $66,724 | −1.2% | 56% |

## Comparable Store Sales Data Elements

The comparable store data elements are identical to the aforementioned store sales data elements. No change in the data structure is necessary to deliver the comparable store analyses (Table 10.2). The only difference is in the client application, which will utilize comparable historic data. There may need to be an additional data structure that will identify the comparable dates, weeks, and months. For example, some retailers have a 53rd week every fourth year. Thanksgiving is on a Thursday but could be in a different fiscal week than last year. There are many examples in the calendar of events that will change from year to year. Therefore, a data structure like the following may be necessary:

- **Comparable Weeks**
  TY fiscal week, LY fiscal week

- **Comparable Months**
  Fiscal month, TY fiscal month

- **Comparable Seasons**
  Season, TY fiscal week, LY fiscal week

## FLASH STORE SALES

Store operations must review the sales of stores all during the day. The flash store sales application is an hourly transaction processing application designed to give executives the most up-to-date information regarding sales at each store location. The key word *flash* is used to indicate a quick view of today's business operation. Specifically, this application is the store sales application, but to the user it appears to be maintained in real time. During the day, as sales are occurring in the store, transactions are being accumulated and posted to a central warehouse. These figures are made available to executives immediately. The executives can press the Enter key over and over while watching the sales occur worldwide. They have the option to drill down from the company through and into the store sales. This information is particularly helpful just prior to a store visit.

Each implementation can build upon the previous implementation. I will identify a few types of flash sales: hourly flash sales, departmental hourly flash sales, and real-time transaction flash sales. The hourly flash sales implementation is the most common and the least complex, whereas the real-time transaction flash sales implementation provides the most up-to-the-minute and accurate financial figures possible—and, of course, is also the most complex. With the addition of comparable figures, this analysis is complete. The comparable hourly flash sales implementation is a further extension of this analysis.

The hourly flash sales application provides the executive with sales figures hourly. In essence, the in-store processor initiates a transmission to the central computer hourly. In this brief connection, the cumulative sales figures for the day can be posted to the data warehouse. A final, end-of-day transaction will be sent to the data warehouse that will match the financial end-of-day sales provided at the closing of the POS terminal. This data will be available immediately to the executives as it arrives in the data warehouse. Hourly transmissions are a cost-effective way to provide executives with hourly sales figures. When each store, operating independently, sends transactions by the hour, there is an appearance of real-time sales analysis.

The departmental hourly flash sales application is implemented in a similar manner as hourly flash sales. The difference is that more information is transmitted in the hourly connection. Departmental cumulative sales figures will be transmitted with the total sales figures hourly. This means that the in-store computer will accumulate sales for each department every hour and will transmit those figures to the data warehouse hourly. Those figures will be available immediately for executives. Departmental hourly flash sales can also be used to analyze traffic patterns for the different hours of sales. For example, let's say that beer and wine departmental sales usually increase substantially after 5 P.M. for the entire company. Are there any stores in which beer and wine sales consistently declined after 5 P.M.? If so, it could be an indication of an operational problem where the store clerk is not stocking the beer and wine merchandise properly. This may identify the need for more part-time help in the store for those busy periods.

> **Hourly transmissions are a cost-effective way to provide executives with hourly sales figures.**

The real-time transaction flash sales implementation is true transaction processing. After the sale in a store is finalized with a customer, the transaction is processed in the store system, then processed at the central computer. Unlike the previous flash sales implementations, this system has all the information that is available at the POS. Of course, the processing volume increases substantially as each item the customer purchased is tracked and made available for users to query. As you can imagine, this implementation is good for store operations as well as for merchandising and marketing. Operationally, this POS implementation is the most advanced implementation any retailer can undertake when building a data warehouse. This implementation allows the retailer to focus on using the data, by putting it in a data warehouse, instead of waiting and gathering the data at the end of the day. Interestingly, this can cause a problem with management because the figures change too rapidly for comparisons! If you want to compare a store with the region, the data will change between each analysis. This is a very good position to be in, having too

> **The solution is not to slow down the updating process but to slow down the presentation of the information.**

much information available too fast. The solution is not to slow down the updating process but to slow down the presentation of the information. Display only the figures for intervals of 15, 30, or 60 minutes and allow the managers to do a static comparison.

Here is an example of what might happen. Consider a requirement that the sales figures match exactly when changing between levels in the operational hierarchy. I am not referring to data integrity but timing. For example, if stores 10 and 20 report sales of $200 and $400, respectively, and they belong to area 2, then area 2 should have sales of $600. While the user is reviewing the store sales of stores 10 and 20, store 10 could post a new sales figure of $300, an increase of $100. Therefore, if the user reviews both an area analysis and a store analysis, the first would indicate a total of $600 while the next would indicate the more accurate figure of $700. The executive may get the idea that the figures are misstated. In other words, constantly changing figures may not be conducive to effective decision making. It may be necessary to take a "snapshot" of the sales figures at the top of the hour and maintain a static copy of those figures for the executives. The solution is simple: a duplicate copy. One copy is static for the hour, while the other is active. There may be another reason for a duplicate copy. If the database on which this is implemented does provide simultaneous updates and inquiries, two sets of these tables may be necessary. Some databases do not allow what is known as a *dirty read*. This allows the user to read the data records in the database while updates are taking place at the same time. If data contention could be an issue, there should be duplicate copies.

## Flash Store Sales Data Elements

Flash store sales data elements will be used in conjunction with their supporting reference entities, such as store information. The analysis will also need the operations hierarchy data elements: region information, district information, area information. For performance reasons, summaries may also be called for when accumulating the sales for a district, region, or company. Basically, there will be two sets of entities. One, flash store sales, will maintain all the transmitted records historically. The other, current flash store sales, will maintain only the most up-to-date or *current* records. The historical entities will be used for more comparative and decision support purposes, whereas the current entities will be used to show the most current sales figures. If you recall, the records will be cumulative throughout the day so there will be only one record per store per day, the most recent, in the current entity. The current entities will be smaller and provide a much faster response time for the executives:

- **Flash Store Sales**

  Store identifier, date of sale, transmission timestamp, cumulative retail sales dollars, cumulative customer count, cumulative fuel sales dollars, post timestamp

- **Current Flash Store Sales**

  Store identifier, current date of sale, last reported hour, cumulative retail sales dollars, cumulative customer count, cumulative fuel sales dollars, post timestamp

To implement a departmental flash store sales analysis, you will need the following data elements in addition to the entities outlined above:

- **Current Departmental Flash Store Sales**

  Store identifier, date of sale, last hour reported, department, cumulative retail sales dollars, cumulative customer count, cumulative fuel sales dollars, post timestamp

- **Departmental Flash Store Sales**

  Store identifier, date of sale, transmission timestamp, department, cumulative retail sales dollars, cumulative customer count, cumulative fuel sales dollars, post timestamp

For real-time transaction flash sales analyses, all of the aforementioned entities will be needed for summary tables. In addition, you will need store transaction, store transaction merchandise, and store transaction tender data elements:

- **Store Transaction**

  Store identifier, transaction sequence number, register number, transaction timestamps (tender or stop timestamp), operator identifier, scan time (start and stop transaction timestamp), number of items in transaction, total dollar sale, fuel sales, discount amount, customer type, customer identifier, customer zip code, total tax paid amount, post timestamp

- **Store Transaction Merchandise**

  Store identifier, transaction timestamps (tender or stop timestamp), transaction sequence number, register number, transaction type (sale, return, coupon, etc.), item identifier, quantity, unit retail sell price, unit cost, discount amount

- **Store Transaction Tender**

  Store identifier, transaction timestamps (tender or stop timestamp), transaction sequence number, register number, tender type, tender account, approval code, tender amount

Finally, there may be more data elements that will need to be retained. These data elements will follow closely with the register transaction log (TLOG). Not all TLOG information will be retained (e.g., different country, state, city, or local tax information), but only the most critical data elements. If more data elements are required, they can be added at a later time.

## Flash Store Sales Sample Report

The flash store sales report (see Table 10.3) will be very similar to the store sales report in Table 10.1. However, it will be confined to the information available, which is dependent on the chosen implementation. Included in these samples are a regional flash sales report and a departmental flash sales report. Although there is no comparable flash store sales analysis defined in this chapter, the natural evolution of this analysis is to add comparable figures for the same time period. This evolution is the same as including the store sales analysis in the comparable store sales analysis (see Tables 10.1 and 10.2). Unlike the comparable store sales analysis, the comparable flash store sales figures will

**Table 10.3    Flash store sales sample report.**

Generic Retail Store Corp.
Flash Store Sales Report for Region 2 District 10
District Manager: Larry Hirt

| Regn | Distr | Area | Store | Name | Manager | Retail Sales | Cust Count | Avg Cust Trans | Fuel Sales | Hour |
|------|-------|------|-------|------|---------|-------------|-----------|---------------|-----------|------|
| 2 | 10 | 1 | 2178 | Cupertino | Tim | $765 | 89 | $8.60 | $359 | 9 |
| | | | 2209 | San Jose North | Kelly | $966 | 164 | $5.89 | $465 | 9 |
| | | | 2210 | San Jose South | Sally | $998 | 100 | $9.98 | $898 | 10 |
| | | | 2212 | San Jose East | Terry | $1,544 | 198 | $7.80 | $596 | 10 |
| | | | 2234 | Santa Clara | Tommy | $821 | 78 | $10.53 | $407 | 9 |
| | | | 2239 | Sunnyvale | Lisa | $704 | 61 | $11.54 | $603 | 10 |
| | | 2 | 2240 | Monterey Bay 1 | Barry | $992 | 81 | $12.25 | $855 | 10 |
| | | | 2245 | Monterey Bay 2 | Dewane | $482 | 43 | $11.21 | $474 | 10 |
| | | | | Totals | | $7,272 | 814 | $8.93 | $4,657 | |

be time-of-day comparisons. This will allow the store operations executives to see sales and customer counts in the first hour of operation. They will find that the first couple of hours the store is open represent a very good gauge of the performance of the entire day. As in the comparable store sales analysis, I suggest 65 weeks of daily data and two years of weekly/monthly data. This will provide the retailer with the most flexible options for the front-end (client) development.

As you can see from these sample reports (Tables 10.3, 10.4) the totals are for the current day. The Hour column indicates the last time the data was updated. The Percent Stores Reporting line indicates that all but 3% of stores have reported hourly departmental sales figures.

## DEPARTMENTAL STORE SALES

A departmental store sales analysis will be used by store operations executives to further analyze the performance of an individual store. Typically, after a store is identified as a poor performer, the next step is to determine whether the whole store is performing badly or just specific departments. If a specific department is performing badly, the

**Table 10.4    Departmental flash sales report for a specific region.**

Generic Retail Store Corp.
Departmental Flash Sales Report for Region 2 District 10
District Manager: Larry Hirt

| Regn | Distr | Dept | Dept Name | Retail Sales |
|------|-------|------|-----------|--------------|
| 2 | 10 | 1 | Beer | $1,599 |
|  |  | 2 | Cigarettes | $1,101 |
|  |  | 3 | Petro | $823 |
|  |  | 4 | Candy | $859 |
|  |  | 6 | Drinks | $922 |
|  |  | 7 | Auto Accessories | $319 |
|  |  | 8 | Food | $1,136 |
|  |  | 10 | Misc | $513 |
|  |  |  | Totals | $7,272 |
|  |  |  | Percent Stores Reporting | 97% |

corrective solution may be as simple as moving certain merchandise into a display case. Once again, comparable sales are very important. Information about last year's departmental performance will be a very good gauge to measure against this year's poor performance. If the sales figures have decreased equally this year (TY) versus last year (LY), then there may be a problem with the store's appearance or with staffing. Often the problem can be a single department. This is what the operations executives want to determine.

This information is also valuable to the merchants. The merchants may want to drill further into a store's sales to review the performance of specific categories in a store or group of stores. It may be that store operations has identified a potential selling trend based on geography, such as magazines in a rural area that do not sell as well as in an urban area. Store operations and merchandising would work together to resolve this issue, starting at the departmental level. In saying this, the operational decision support system should be linked directly into the merchandising decision support system. Combined use of this information illustrates the need, once again, for a single enterprisewide data warehouse. Otherwise, you will spend a great deal of time and effort trying to combine data from two different data marts—a store operations data mart and a merchandising data mart.

Of course, there are many ways to make a departmental comparison.

Every level of the store operational hierarchy should be able to compare (TY-LY) departmental figures at a minimum for each fiscal week and month. Daily detail is very important because it gives you the flexibility to compare specific date ranges like holidays and events. Daily detail is also very important for excluding specific events. Daily information is good for asking very pointed questions such as, "What would the sales be if sales around the Halloween event are excluded?"

## Departmental Store Sales Data Elements

In addition to the following data elements, you will also need the store sales data elements listed earlier to do a departmental store sales analysis. For performance reasons, you may need to summarize these data elements. Specifically, store-level data may be summarized into district- or region-level data. The monthly departmental sales entity may not be needed; it will depend on the retail accounting method used. If fiscal weeks fall directly into a fiscal month, then you should simply add a month code to the weekly departmental sales entity and do not use the monthly entity. For a sample report, see Table 10.5.

- **Daily Departmental Sales**

  Store identifier, department, date, TY sales, LY sales, TY gross margin, LY gross margin

- **Monthly Departmental Sales**

  Store identifier, department, fiscal month, TY sales, LY sales, TY-YTD sales, LY-YTD sales, TY gross margin, LY gross margin, TY-YTD gross margin, LY-YTD gross margin

- **Weekly Departmental Sales**

  Store identifier, department, fiscal week, TY sales, LY sales, TY-MTD sales, LY-MTD sales, TY-YTD sales, LY-YTD sales, TY gross margin, LY gross margin, TY-MTD gross margin, LY-MTD gross margin, TY-YTD gross margin, LY-YTD gross margin

## PLANNED SALES

Retailers annually plan the sales performances for the next year. These figures typically are calculated for the entire company and then are

**Table 10.5** Departmental store sales sample report.

Generic Retail Store Corp.
Departmental Store Sales Report for Region 2 District 10 Week 9644
District Manager: Larry Hirt

| Regn | Distr | Dept | Dept Name | LY-TW Sales | TY-TW Sales | Pct Incr | LYTM-MTD Sales | TYTM-MTD Sales | Pct Incr | LY-YTD Sales | TY-YTD Sales | Pct Incr |
|---|---|---|---|---|---|---|---|---|---|---|---|---|
| 2 | 10 | 1 | Beer | $85,977 | $90,276 | 5% | $83,054 | $92,984 | 12% | $280,367 | $305,600 | 9% |
| | | 2 | Cigarettes | $12,012 | $12,132 | 1% | $11,162 | $13,298 | 19% | $230,087 | $253,096 | 10% |
| | | 3 | Petro | $36,008 | $33,848 | −6% | $37,110 | $34,863 | −6% | $377,781 | $336,225 | −11% |
| | | 4 | Candy | $14,220 | $34,839 | 145% | $17,762 | $35,884 | 102% | $234,571 | $340,128 | 45% |
| | | 6 | Drinks | $27,710 | $24,385 | −12% | $32,921 | $25,116 | −24% | $271,121 | $233,164 | −14% |
| | | 7 | Auto Accessories | $11,888 | $13,790 | 16% | $14,490 | $14,204 | −2% | $181,157 | $190,215 | 5% |
| | | 8 | Food | $22,224 | $27,558 | 24% | $25,353 | $28,384 | 12% | $232,211 | $283,297 | 22% |
| | | 10 | Misc | $10,365 | $12,645 | 22% | $10,700 | $13,025 | 22% | $106,234 | $127,481 | 20% |
| | | | Totals | $220,404 | $249,472 | 13% | $232,551 | $257,759 | 11% | $1,913,529 | $2,069,206 | 8% |

driven down to the store level. Therefore, every store has a performance objective. These performance objectives are usually defined in terms of sales and profit for a store, area, district, region, and so on. People from store operations and store planning may adjust these figures monthly. This planning analysis will only use the most current planning figures. While some executives may want to analyze the past plans to improve the new plans, most are only interested in the current finalized plan. Using the current store sales information, many retailers plan for the month; some will have a plan for every week. Weekly and monthly planning analysis data structures and analyses are very similar. Similar data structures and processes can be implemented for both. Operations executives will want to analyze the stores, areas, districts, and so on that are far below planned sales or extremely above planned sales. Therefore, these exceptions may need to be highlighted or broken into a separate analysis.

## Planned Sales Data Elements

Planning data is typically maintained in the home office computer. Adding planning data (listed below) to store sales data elements (described previously) will provide enough information to deliver an analysis of planned versus actual sales. Once again, all of the store sales data elements will be needed for this analysis. For a sample planned sales report, see Table 10.6.

- **Monthly Planned Sales and Profit**

  Store identifier, department, fiscal month, planned retail sales, planned retail gross margin, planned fuel sales, planned fuel gross margin

- **Weekly Planned Sales and Profit**

  Store identifier, department, fiscal week, planned retail sales, planned retail gross margin, planned fuel sales, planned fuel gross margin

## COMPETITIVE STORE SALES

A competitive store sales analysis is identical to a comparable store sales analysis, but with a focus on competition in the area. Executives

**Table 10.6  Planned sales sample report.**

Generic Retail Store Corp.
Planned Store Sales Report for Region 2 District 10 Week 9634
District Manager: Larry Hirt

| Distr | Area | Store | Name | Manager | TY Retail Sales | Planned Sales | Sales % to Planned | TY Fuel Sales | Planned Sales | Sales % to Planned | Rtl Sales % Fuel |
|-------|------|-------|------|---------|-----------------|---------------|--------------------|---------------|---------------|--------------------|------------------|
| 10 | 1 | 2178 | Cupertino | Tim | $11,392 | $13,211 | −13.8% | $6,835 | $6,799 | 0.5% | 60% |
| | | 2209 | San Jose North | Kelly | $17,592 | $17,666 | −0.4% | $7,389 | $8,361 | −11.6% | 42% |
| | | 2210 | San Jose South | Sally | $14,625 | $14,893 | −1.8% | $10,969 | $12,009 | −8.7% | 75% |
| | | 2212 | San Jose East | Terry | $16,171 | $12,332 | 31.1% | $3,558 | $4,500 | −20.9% | 22% |
| | | 2234 | Santa Clara | Tommy | $8,648 | $6,922 | 24.9% | $2,940 | $5,677 | −48.2% | 34% |
| | | 2239 | Sunnyvale | Lisa | $18,631 | $17,030 | 9.4% | $14,532 | $14,345 | 1.3% | 78% |
| | 2 | 2240 | Monterey Bay 1 | Barry | $16,619 | $16,289 | 2.0% | $10,304 | $10,921 | −5.7% | 62% |
| | | 2245 | Monterey Bay 2 | Dewane | $4,109 | $12,803 | −67.9% | $3,205 | $4,112 | −22.1% | 78% |
| | | | Totals | | $107,787 | $111,146 | −3.0% | $59,732 | $66,724 | −10.5% | 55% |

may want to draw a correlation between competition and sales performance. Let's say a competitor is rapidly expanding its fresh foods department. When this competitor opens a larger fresh foods department, shops that compete with this retailer might show a sales drop of more than 20%. Store operation executives would like to know these patterns and develop a strategy to recoup sales or minimize the impact. Therefore, if an expansion pattern exists for a specific competitor, executives want to immediately know the impact on the operation.

## Competitive Store Sales Data Elements

All of the store sales data elements and comparable store sales data elements outlined previously, as well as the following data elements, will be needed for a competitive store sales analysis. For performance reasons and ease of use, another entity has been defined: store competition codes. This entity is more difficult to maintain, but provides serious performance and flexibility in reporting and queries. It will allow store operations to include or exclude any combination of competition using a standard relational database. For a sample competitive store sales report, see Table 10.7.

- **Store Competition Codes**

  Store identifier, P66, 7-11, BP, Texaco, Amoco, Gulf, Exxon, fuel, Chevron, Wal-Mart, Metro, local other

- **Competition**

  Competition identifier, competition name, competition abbreviation

- **Store Competition**

  Store identifier, competition identifier

**Table 10.7  Competitive store sales sample report.**

Generic Retail Store Corp.
Competitive Store Sales Report for Region 2 District 10 Week 9634
With Phillips 66 as a Competitor
District Manager: Larry Hirt

| Area | Store | Name | Manager | 1000 Sqft | TY Retail Sales | LY Retail Sales | Retail % Increase | Rtl Sales $/SQFT | TY Fuel Sales | LY Fuel Sales | Fuel % Increase | Rtl Sales % Fuel |
|---|---|---|---|---|---|---|---|---|---|---|---|---|
| 1 | 2178 | Cupertino | Tim | 8 | $12,765 | $13,211 | −3.4% | $1.60 | $7,659 | $6,799 | 12.6% | 60% |
| | 2209 | San Jose North | Kelly | 12 | $18,965 | $17,666 | 7.4% | $1.58 | $7,965 | $8,361 | −4.7% | 42% |
| | 2210 | San Jose South | Sally | 9 | $15,998 | $14,893 | 7.4% | $1.78 | $11,999 | $12,009 | −0.1% | 75% |
| 2 | 2240 | Monterey Bay 1 | Barry | 22 | $17,992 | $16,289 | 10.5% | $0.82 | $11,155 | $10,921 | 2.1% | 62% |
| | 2245 | Monterey Bay 2 | Dewane | 7 | $5,482 | $12,803 | −57.2% | $0.78 | $4,276 | $4,112 | 4.0% | 78% |
| | | Totals | | 58 | $71,202 | $74,862 | −4.9% | $1.23 | $43,054 | $42,202 | 2.0% | 60% |

Competition

| Store | 66 | BP | TX | AM | GF | XX | PT | CV | OC |
|---|---|---|---|---|---|---|---|---|---|
| 2178 | X | | | | | X | | X | |
| 2209 | X | | X | X | | | | | |
| 2210 | X | X | X | X | | | | | |
| 2240 | X | | | X | X | | | | X |
| 2245 | X | | | X | X | | X | | |

LEGEND: 66=Phillips 66 BP=British Petroleum TX=Texaco AM=Amoco GF=Gulf XX=Exxon PT=Petro CV=Chevron OC=Other Competitor

# 11

# Merchandising Sample Analyses

This chapter continues the theme of the previous chapter but for a different subject area, merchandising. In this chapter you will find the basic analyses that most retailers will be building for the merchandising department. As mentioned before, many of these analyses build on what has already been defined in other areas, such as store operations analyses. The basic premise of a data warehouse is that detailed data is available to the entire business. As in the previous chapter, each application is given a small overview, a list of data elements, and a sample report. These analyses build upon themselves and get more complex toward the end of the chapter.

## BASIC MERCHANDISING INFORMATION NEEDS

From a retail perspective, merchandising is very broad. A data warehouse can quickly provide a retailer with several key analyses to improve the business. I have identified many common areas for retailers to focus in order to improve their merchandising position. Of course, each retailer has a unique set of merchandising challenges. Below is a list of analyses that many merchants perform or want to be able to perform:

- basic article POS analysis
- article selling versus planned selling analysis
- fast-selling article analysis
- slow-selling article analysis
- vendor performance analysis
- category performance analysis
- article selling by geographic locations
- comparative article sales (article vs. article)
- store and article grouping
- basic affinity selling
- out-of-stock analysis

After mastering some of these analyses in a data warehouse, the merchants can provide better in-stock, faster turns, a better merchandise mix, and more accurate inventory allocation for the entire chain. Additionally, the research time needed for merchants to perform these types of analyses should decrease substantially. Some retailers spend 80% of their time researching to perform these analyses. That time can be reduced to 20% or less for retailers that do not already have a data warehouse.

> Some retailers spend 80% of their time researching to perform these analyses. That time can be reduced to 20% or less for retailers that do not already have a data warehouse.

## BASIC ARTICLE POS ANALYSIS

This analysis will provide the merchant with the basics to better understand article movement. This analysis is limited to a single article. The selling performance of that article is studied via the standard organizational hierarchy (company, region, district, etc.) within the company. This is the building block for other, more complex analyses. This fundamental analysis requires the use of point-of-sale (POS) data. Other data, such as receipts and inventory, is valuable but not required for the first implementation of a data warehouse. The idea is to get a snapshot of the article performance over time in terms of units sold, dollars sold, gross margin, sell-through, and the like. The analysis can be output as both a tabular report and in graphical form. The tabular report will show some of the basic retail measurements, whereas the graph will show the trends. Used together, they become a very powerful management tool for inventory.

## Basic Article POS Data Elements

Along with the following data elements, the store hierarchies (as defined in "Store Sales" in the previous chapter) will be used for this analysis. There are several sales tables defined here. Not all need to be defined and created. The data usually exists in some form within every retail operation. However, some retailers will not have some of this data. Store transaction, store transaction merchandise, and store transaction tender data elements were defined in Chapter 10 and are not repeated here, but are the basis for these sales summaries. For performance reasons, other summary tables may be necessary. I believe you will need to maintain 65 week of daily and weekly data. If implemented, monthly data should be maintained for two full years. A basic article sample report and accompanying bar graph are shown in Table 11.1.

- **Article Information**

  Article identifier, article description, article cost, suggested retail price, article retail price, department identifier, supplier identifier, supplier pack quantity, supplier pack cost,

  color identifier, size identifier

- **Article UPC Cross-Reference**

  Article identifier, UPC, activity code

- **Weekly Company Sales Summary**

  Article identifier, fiscal week, selling code, selling event, units sold, retail dollars, unit retail price, unit cost

*(continued on page 222)*

**Table 11.1   Basic article sample report and bar graph (on facing page).**

Generic Retail Store Corp.
Christmas Truck—Item #533434
Department 4 Class 55

| Week | Selling Price | Unit Cost | Units Sold | Cum Units Sold | Sales | Margin | Sell Thru |
|------|---------------|-----------|------------|----------------|-------|--------|-----------|
| 35 | $13.97 | $6.51 | 0 | 0 | $0 | $0 | 0% |
| 36 | $13.97 | $6.51 | 1,751 | 1,751 | $24,461 | $13,062 | 1% |
| 37 | $13.97 | $6.51 | 18,123 | 19,874 | $253,178 | $135,198 | 6% |
| 38 | $13.97 | $6.51 | 25,667 | 45,541 | $358,568 | $191,476 | 14% |
| 39 | $13.97 | $6.51 | 30,199 | 75,740 | $421,880 | $225,285 | 23% |
| 40 | $13.97 | $6.51 | 40,598 | 116,338 | $567,154 | $302,861 | 35% |
| 41 | $13.97 | $6.51 | 38,333 | 154,671 | $535,512 | $285,964 | 46% |
| 42 | $13.97 | $6.51 | 42,708 | 197,379 | $596,631 | $318,602 | 59% |
| 43 | $9.97 | $6.51 | 35,812 | 233,191 | $357,046 | $123,910 | 70% |
| 44 | $9.97 | $6.51 | 36,120 | 269,311 | $360,116 | $124,975 | 80% |
| 45 | $9.97 | $6.51 | 33,771 | 303,082 | $336,697 | $116,848 | 90% |
| 46 | $9.97 | $6.51 | 16,499 | 319,581 | $164,495 | $57,087 | 95% |
| 47 | $9.97 | $6.51 | 9,241 | 328,822 | $92,133 | $31,974 | 98% |
| 48 | $9.97 | $6.51 | 5,294 | 334,116 | $52,781 | $18,317 | 100% |
| 49 | $9.97 | $6.51 | 695 | 334,811 | $6,929 | $2,405 | 100% |
| 50 | $9.97 | $6.51 | 0 | 334,811 | $0 | $0 | 100% |
| 51 | $9.97 | $6.51 | 0 | 334,811 | $0 | $0 | 100% |
| 52 | $9.97 | $6.51 | 0 | 334,811 | $0 | $0 | 100% |
| | | | $334,811 | | $4,127,582 | $1,947,962 | |

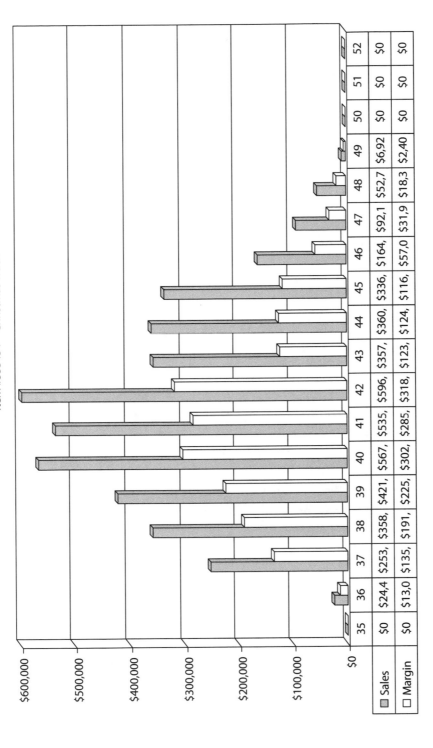

Item #533434—Christmas Truck

| | 35 | 36 | 37 | 38 | 39 | 40 | 41 | 42 | 43 | 44 | 45 | 46 | 47 | 48 | 49 | 50 | 51 | 52 |
|---|---|---|---|---|---|---|---|---|---|---|---|---|---|---|---|---|---|---|
| ■ Sales | $0 | $24,4 | $253, | $358, | $421, | $567, | $535, | $596, | $357, | $360, | $336, | $164, | $92,1 | $52,7 | $6,92 | $0 | $0 | $0 |
| □ Margin | $0 | $13,0 | $135, | $191, | $225, | $302, | $285, | $318, | $123, | $124, | $116, | $57,0 | $31,9 | $18,3 | $2,40 | $0 | $0 | $0 |

- **Daily Store Sales Summary**

  Store identifier, article identifier, date of sale, selling code, selling event, units sold, retail dollars, unit retail price, unit cost

- **Daily Company Sales Summary**

  Article identifier, date of sale, selling code, selling event, units sold, retail dollars, unit retail price, unit cost

- **Weekly Store Sales Summary**

  Store identifier, article identifier, fiscal week, selling code, selling event, units sold, retail dollars, unit retail price, unit cost

## TOP 25, BOTTOM 25 ANALYSIS

This analysis, another basic but very important reporting feature, will rank the top 25 and bottom 25 articles in terms of units sold, retail dollars, and gross profit for the company and the higher levels in the organizational hierarchy (e.g., region and district). The analysis can be created dynamically, for example, on demand for a specific week, if the product of stores and articles (the number of stores times the number of articles) is relatively small. The other organizational levels (such as the region) will need to be produced weekly. Of course, another way to look at the top 25 articles is via the merchandising hierarchy. This means the 25 top-selling articles for each department in terms of units sold, retail dollars, and gross profit for the company and the next organizational level (e.g., region). This data should be produced weekly.

Certainly, there are many different ways to rank the top and bottom 25. Many retailers will want more restrictions on this analysis, such as ranking the articles that have a profit margin of more than 40%. This is an important part of the flexibility of the data warehouse. Care should be taken in the design to ensure that there is sufficient flexibility to create many top and bottom 25 analyses.

### Top 25, Bottom 25 Data Elements

In addition to the following data elements, the data elements defined previously for the basic article POS data analysis will be used. A sample top 25, bottom 25 report is shown in Table 11.2 on page 224.

- **Company Top/Bottom 25 Articles**

  Arthcle identifier, fiscal week, ranking type, ranking sequence code, units sold, retail dollars, gross margin

- **Company Department Top/Bottom 25 Articles**

  Article identifier, department identifier, fiscal week, ranking type, ranking sequence code, units sold, retail dollars, gross margin

- **Region Top/Bottom 25 Articles**

  Article identifier, region identifier, fiscal week, ranking type, ranking sequence code, units sold, retail dollars, gross margin

## ARTICLE INVENTORY ANALYSIS

Article inventory is the study of current and historic inventory levels. There are many different types of analyses for inventory, including some that are very sophisticated. For decision support, inventory analysis is typically used in conjunction with other analyses, such as the basic article POS analysis. In the sample report (Table 11.3, pages 226–227), I show both sales and receipts with inventory figures (which in this case reveals a habitual inventory flow problem; see discussion later in this chapter). Inventory is not flowing properly—it is not being maintained to match demand. Some inventory figures (including purchase orders) used by retailers are maintained or created through an automated replenishment process for basic inventory (retailers often call that process *BARS* for basic automated replenishment System, or *CARS* for computer automated replenishment system). For this analysis, there will be no attempt to replace or even simulate this calculation. The data warehouse should utilize the inventory figures already available. Although it appears deceptively easy, calculating the accurate inventory figures requires constant attention from the store employees. Operationally, it may take several years to implement an

**Table 11.2   Top 25, bottom 25 sample report.**

Generic Retail Store Corp.
Top 25 Items Sold Total Company by Gross Margin
Week 42 Department 1—Pack Liquor

| Rank | Item ID | Description | Dept | Class | Unit Retail | Unit Cost | Mkup Pct | Units Sold | Retail Sales | Gross Margin | Dept Contr Rtl Sls | Dept Contr Grs Mrgn |
|---|---|---|---|---|---|---|---|---|---|---|---|---|
| 1 | 19927 | Miller Lite 12 PK 12oz Cans | 1 | 2 | $13.99 | $6.51 | 115% | 16,072 | $224,847 | $120,219 | 15% | 20% |
| 2 | 19819 | Bud 12 PK 12oz Cans | 1 | 2 | $13.99 | $6.51 | 115% | 15,971 | $223,434 | $119,463 | 15% | 20% |
| 3 | 19821 | Bud 12 PK 12oz Bottles | 1 | 2 | $12.99 | $6.30 | 106% | 17,509 | $227,442 | $117,135 | 15% | 20% |
| . . . | . . . | . | . . . | . . . | . . . | . . . | . . . | . . . | . . . | . . . | . . . | . . . |
| 23 | 20188 | Fruit Coolers 6 PK 12oz Foil | 1 | 7 | $5.99 | $2.75 | 118% | 11,566 | $69,280 | $37,474 | 5% | 6% |
| 24 | 17442 | Fruit Coolers 6 PK 12oz Bottles | 1 | 7 | $6.99 | $3.50 | 100% | 9,845 | $68,817 | $34,359 | 5% | 6% |
| 25 | 19820 | Bud Lite 6 PK 12oz Bottles | 1 | 2 | $5.25 | $3.60 | 46% | 18,277 | $95,954 | $30,157 | 6% | 5% |

Top 25 Totals     $909,775    $458,807
Department 1 Totals  $1,499,872  $598,881
Top 25% Department       61%      77%

automated replenishment system with accurate inventory. The discipline necessary to maintain accurate inventory figures is ultimately the responsibility of the people in each store and not of a computer. For instance, one of the most obvious reasons for an inventory figure to become inaccurate is shoplifting. (Most thieves are not kind enough to scan the inventory they have stolen. If they did this before they left the store, the computer could determine the correct inventory as well as record the necessary markdowns. ☺) The point is, maintaining the accurate inventory is a difficult process. Fortunately, the computer is a tool that can enable and assist this inventory management process. That said, I recommend that the data warehouse implementation not be related to the creation of inventory figures, as this will dramatically impact the time it will take to construct the system. For the first implementation, especially, I suggest you focus on using those inventory figures that already exist to understand and better manage the inventory.

> **Although it appears deceptively easy, calculating the accurate inventory figures requires constant attention from the store employees.**

There are two basic areas of data for inventory analysis, current and historic. Current inventory data refers to the inventory in the store today. Many retailers maintain data, in one form or another, on current inventory. Historic inventory data is more costly to maintain; it may not be available, or it may be maintained only for a few weeks. Many retailers maintain the historic inventory data with the POS data. This might be a good way to maintain the inventory figures depending on the type of stores and the frequency of articles selling. For example, if a retail company has only a few thousand articles and sells each article every day, the sales and inventory data might need to be together in the same data structure. On the other hand, if a retailer sells only a few of the thousands of articles, it might not be a good idea to maintain the inventory figures with the sales figures. The reason is simple. The analyses on inventory usually require the existence of an inventory record regardless of whether an article sold or not. For these retailers, the inventory record will be created weekly, which is based on time passing and not on the action of selling an article. The result can be a very different data structure. Each retailer will have to determine how to maintain the inventory figures as well as how long they will retain that information.

**Table 11.3   Article inventory sample report and graph (on facing page).**

Generic Retail Store Corp.
Inventory Analysis for Item #22378—Fancy Ice Scraper
Store 1811 North Maine

| Week | Retail Price | Unit Cost | Sold Units | Receipt Units | Ending On-Hand Units | Sales | Gross Margin | Planned Units Sold | Planned Sales |
|------|------|------|------|------|------|------|------|------|------|
| 01-Sep-96 | $8.99 | $2.53 | 2 | 24 | 22 | $17.98 | $12.92 | 8 | $71.92 |
| 02-Sep-96 | $8.99 | $2.53 | 18 | 0 | 4 | $161.82 | $116.28 | 8 | $71.92 |
| 03-Sep-96 | $8.99 | $2.53 | 4 | 0 | 0 | $35.96 | $25.84 | 8 | $71.92 |
| 04-Sep-96 | $8.99 | $2.53 | 0 | 0 | 0 | $0.00 | $0.00 | 8 | $71.92 |
| 05-Sep-96 | $8.99 | $2.53 | 10 | 24 | 14 | $89.90 | $64.60 | 8 | $71.92 |
| 06-Sep-96 | $8.99 | $2.53 | 14 | 0 | 0 | $125.86 | $90.44 | 8 | $71.92 |
| 07-Sep-96 | $8.99 | $2.53 | 0 | 0 | 0 | $0.00 | $0.00 | 8 | $71.92 |
| 08-Sep-96 | $8.99 | $2.53 | 0 | 0 | 0 | $0.00 | $0.00 | 8 | $71.92 |
| 09-Sep-96 | $8.99 | $2.53 | 5 | 24 | 19 | $44.95 | $32.30 | 8 | $71.92 |
| 10-Sep-96 | $8.99 | $2.53 | 10 | 0 | 9 | $89.90 | $64.60 | 8 | $71.92 |
| 11-Sep-96 | $8.99 | $2.53 | 9 | 0 | 0 | $80.91 | $58.14 | 8 | $71.92 |
| 12-Sep-96 | $8.99 | $2.53 | 0 | 0 | 0 | $0.00 | $0.00 | 8 | $71.92 |
| 13-Sep-96 | $8.99 | $2.53 | 8 | 24 | 16 | $71.92 | $51.68 | 8 | $71.92 |
| 14-Sep-96 | $8.99 | $2.53 | 13 | 0 | 3 | $116.87 | $83.98 | 8 | $71.92 |
| 15-Sep-96 | $8.99 | $2.53 | 3 | 0 | 0 | $26.97 | $19.38 | 8 | $71.92 |
| 16-Sep-96 | $8.99 | $2.53 | 0 | 0 | 0 | $0.00 | $0.00 | 8 | $71.92 |
| 17-Sep-96 | $8.99 | $2.53 | 5 | 24 | 19 | $44.95 | $32.30 | 8 | $71.92 |
| 18-Sep-96 | $8.99 | $2.53 | 8 | 0 | 11 | $71.92 | $51.68 | 8 | $71.92 |
| | Totals | | 109 | 120 | 7 | $979.91 | $704.14 | 144 | $1,294.56 |

Item #22378—Fancy Ice Scraper

| | 01-Sep-96 | 02-Sep-96 | 03-Sep-96 | 04-Sep-96 | 05-Sep-96 | 06-Sep-96 | 07-Sep-96 | 08-Sep-96 | 09-Sep-96 | 10-Sep-96 | 11-Sep-96 | 12-Sep-96 | 13-Sep-96 | 14-Sep-96 | 15-Sep-96 | 16-Sep-96 | 17-Sep-96 | 18-Sep-96 |
|---|---|---|---|---|---|---|---|---|---|---|---|---|---|---|---|---|---|---|
| Sold units | 2 | 18 | 4 | 0 | 10 | 14 | 0 | 0 | 5 | 10 | 9 | 0 | 8 | 13 | 3 | 0 | 5 | 8 |
| Receipt units | 24 | 0 | 0 | 0 | 24 | 0 | 0 | 0 | 24 | 0 | 0 | 0 | 24 | 0 | 0 | 0 | 24 | 0 |
| Ending on-hand units | 22 | 4 | 0 | 0 | 14 | 0 | 0 | 0 | 19 | 9 | 0 | 0 | 16 | 3 | 0 | 0 | 19 | 11 |

## Article Inventory Data Elements

Even though many retailers will maintain the inventory data elements with the POS data elements, I show the inventory data elements as a separate entity from POS. Retailers often combine the two because the majority of the inventory adjustments are POS transactions (sales and returns). This is almost common sense when every article in a store sells every day. However, since this scenario does not apply for every retailer, I will discuss it separately. The stock keeping unit (SKU) entity is used to maintain the current inventory data as well as other attributes related specifically to that store and article. Inventory history can be a very complex data entity. However, I have greatly simplified this to maintain only the key elements needed for inventory analysis. You may have noticed the elements for beginning, ending, and next inventory dates. These time periods may differ among various retailers and even within a retail organization. If all inventory is always calculated every day or week, only the ending inventory date may be necessary. In either case, the retailer must decide the time element that is best to use.

- **Stock Keeping Unit (Current Inventory)**

  Store identifier, article identifier, current inventory quantity, retail price, cost, life-to-date retail sales, life-to-date units sold, location identifier, minimum presentation quantity, maximum shelf quantity, maximum facing quantity, perishable code, replenishment code

- **Inventory History**

  Store identifier, article identifier, inventory type, beginning inventory date, ending inventory date, next inventory date, inventory qty, retail price, cost

## Article Inventory Sample Report

As you can see from the sample report (Table 11.3), this retailer most definitely has a flow-of-goods problem. Store 1811 is habitually selling out of the fancy ice scraper. This article could achieve the planned sales, perhaps even sell more, if the product were consistently stocked. The chart clearly shows that there is a problem maintaining sufficient inventory.

## ARTICLE SELLING VERSUS PLANNED SELLING

One way to detect an over- or underperforming article is by comparing the actual sales to the planned sales. If actual sales are exceeding planned sales, the article is selling faster than expected and inventory may be depleted. This could be a very big problem if there is a promotion on that article. Conversely, if the article is selling below the plan, then the retailer may have to deal with larger than expected markdowns. Even worse, shipments of the slow-selling article may continue! This analysis compares actual sales to planned sales in a graphical presentation that will allow the merchandiser to quickly identify deviations from the plan.

### Article Selling versus Planned Data Elements

This analysis will use all the data elements in the basic article POS analysis. Included as well, usually from the home office computers, will be the planning information by article, given below. Weekly information is more than adequate to get a good analysis. Unfortunately, many retailers do not create merchandising plans down to the article level. It may be possible to extrapolate the planning figures down to the article level, with substantial guidance from the retailer's merchandise planning group. For starters, this information at the company level will be more than adequate. Article planning at the store level is a future enhancement for many retailers.

- **Weekly Article Planned Sales**
  Article identifier, fiscal week,
  planned units, planned selling
  price, planned cost

Let's take a look at a sample report (Table 11.4) and accompanying charts (Figures 11.1 and 11.2). Judging from the sell-through

**Table 11.4  Article selling versus planned sample report.**

Generic Retail Store Corp.
Planned vs. Actual Analysis for Christmas Truck—Item #533434
Department 4 Class 55

| Week | Unit Retail | Planned Retail | Unit Cost | Units Sold | Cum Units Sold | Retail Sales | Gross Margin | Actual Sell-Thru | Planned Sell-Thru | Cumm Planned Unit Sell-Thru | Planned Units Sold | Planned Sales |
|---|---|---|---|---|---|---|---|---|---|---|---|---|
| 35 | $13.97 | $13.97 | $6.51 | 0 | 0 | $0 | $0 | 0% | 0% | 0 | 0 | $0 |
| 36 | $13.97 | $13.97 | $6.51 | 1,751 | 1,751 | $24,461 | $13,062 | 1% | 1% | 3,350 | 3350 | $46,800 |
| 37 | $13.97 | $13.97 | $6.51 | 18,123 | 19,874 | $253,178 | $135,198 | 6% | 2% | 6,700 | 3350 | $46,800 |
| 38 | $13.97 | $13.97 | $6.51 | 25,667 | 45,541 | $358,568 | $191,476 | 14% | 5% | 16,750 | 10050 | $140,399 |
| 39 | $13.97 | $13.97 | $6.51 | 30,199 | 75,740 | $421,880 | $225,285 | 23% | 10% | 33,500 | 16750 | $233,998 |
| 40 | $13.97 | $13.97 | $6.51 | 40,598 | 116,338 | $567,154 | $302,861 | 35% | 20% | 67,000 | 33500 | $467,995 |
| 41 | $13.97 | $13.97 | $6.51 | 38,333 | 154,671 | $535,512 | $285,964 | 46% | 30% | 100,500 | 33500 | $467,995 |
| 42 | $13.97 | $13.97 | $6.51 | 42,708 | 197,379 | $596,631 | $318,602 | 59% | 40% | 134,000 | 33500 | $467,995 |
| 43 | $9.97 | $13.97 | $6.51 | 35,812 | 233,191 | $357,046 | $123,910 | 70% | 50% | 167,500 | 33500 | $333,995 |
| 44 | $9.97 | $13.97 | $6.51 | 36,120 | 269,311 | $360,116 | $124,975 | 80% | 60% | 201,000 | 33500 | $333,995 |
| 45 | $9.97 | $13.97 | $6.51 | 33,771 | 303,082 | $336,697 | $116,848 | 90% | 70% | 234,500 | 33500 | $333,995 |
| 46 | $9.97 | $13.97 | $6.51 | 16,499 | 319,581 | $164,495 | $57,087 | 95% | 80% | 268,000 | 33500 | $333,995 |
| 47 | $9.97 | $13.97 | $6.51 | 9,241 | 328,822 | $92,133 | $31,974 | 98% | 85% | 284,750 | 16750 | $166,998 |
| 48 | $9.97 | $13.97 | $6.51 | 5,294 | 334,116 | $52,781 | $18,317 | 100% | 90% | 301,500 | 16750 | $166,998 |
| 49 | $9.97 | $13.97 | $6.51 | 695 | 334,811 | $6,929 | $2,405 | 100% | 95% | 318,250 | 16750 | $166,998 |
| 50 | $9.97 | $13.97 | $6.51 | 0 | 334,811 | $0 | $0 | 100% | 100% | 335,000 | 16750 | $166,998 |
| 51 | $9.97 | $13.97 | $6.51 | 0 | 334,811 | $0 | $0 | 100% | 100% | 335,000 | 0 | $0 |
| 52 | $9.97 | $13.97 | $6.51 | 0 | 334,811 | $0 | $0 | 100% | 100% | 335,000 | 0 | $0 |
| | | | | $334,811 | | $4,127,582 | $1,947,962 | | | | 335000 | $3,875,950 |

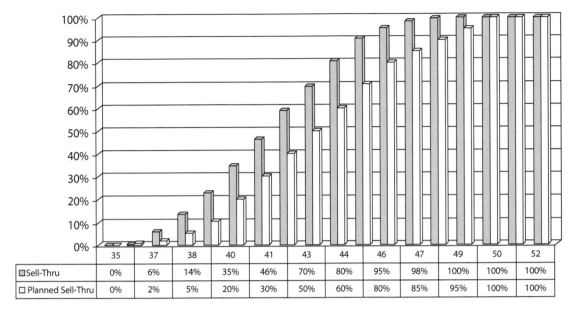

| | 35 | 37 | 38 | 40 | 41 | 43 | 44 | 46 | 47 | 49 | 50 | 52 |
|---|---|---|---|---|---|---|---|---|---|---|---|---|
| ▨ Sell-Thru | 0% | 6% | 14% | 35% | 46% | 70% | 80% | 95% | 98% | 100% | 100% | 100% |
| ☐ Planned Sell-Thru | 0% | 2% | 5% | 20% | 30% | 50% | 60% | 80% | 85% | 95% | 100% | 100% |

**Figure 11.1**
Sell-through
percentage chart.

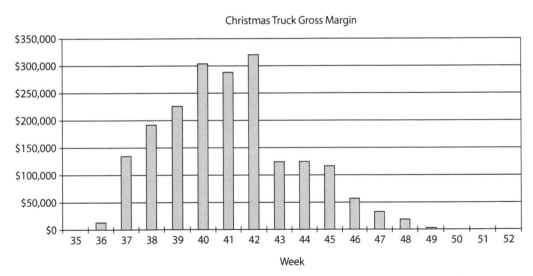

**Figure 11.2**
Gross margin
analysis

percentage chart (Figure 11.1), this article was clearly out of stock in many stores by week 43, with a 70% sell-through. The gross margin, shown in Figure 11.2, reflects a price change that was made. Perhaps this price change should not have happened. The article was selling nicely, and there was no need for the price change. Clearly, it would have sold out without any pricing actions.

## FAST-SELLING ARTICLE ANALYSIS

The basic idea behind the analysis of fast selling is to maintain that fast-selling pace without running out of merchandise in the store. This analysis is most often used during the introduction of new articles, seasonal articles, or article exception analysis. If fast-selling articles are not monitored closely, they can quickly become a marginal or slow-selling article because of out-of-stock conditions. Actions to take for fast-selling articles include purchasing more inventory, canceling promotional price changes, or increasing the price of the product. Therefore, if you are building an enterprise data warehouse, the ability to provide these functions may need to be integrated from the beginning.

It is important to differentiate this analysis from the top 25 analysis. Fast-selling articles may not be the most frequently sold article in the company, nor the most profitable, nor the one with the largest gross sales. The fast-selling article is an article that has unexpectedly sold more than planned. In a typical retail operation, these fast-selling articles may never make the top 25 because of out-of-stock conditions. If the retailer is using only averages and monthly or weekly information, it could falsely appear to the merchant that the article has an average selling pattern. For example, if the article was received in a store on Monday and sold out by Thursday, then the weekly selling average would appear about 50% lower than what could actually be achieved.

There are several variables that will determine if an article is moving fast. For seasonal articles, the measure could be sell-through greater than 20% in

**If the retailer is using only averages and monthly or weekly information, it could falsely appear to the merchant that the article has an average selling pattern.**

the first week of selling. For other articles, the measure could be a stock-to-sales ratio of less than two weeks. Maybe the turns are up to 15 a month. The point here is that every retailer will have a definition of a fast-selling article, and this definition is the one that should be used for this implementation.

## Fast-Selling Data Elements

This analysis will use the data elements from the previously discussed basic article POS data analysis and the article inventory analysis. Most likely, each retailer will have specific metrics (formulas for calculating) that will be used to define a fast-moving article. No additional data entities will be needed. However, some data elements may need to be added to the existing entities. A sample report on fast-selling articles is shown in Table 11.5.

## SLOW-SELLING ARTICLES

The analysis for slow-selling articles is the exact opposite of the fast-selling analysis. What a retailer will do with a slow-selling analysis is to determine the poorly performing articles. After it is determined that an article is a slow mover, the merchant has several opportunities for action to improve the business. If there are any outstanding purchase orders, they should be canceled or pushed back to a later date. It may be necessary to work with marketing to create a promotion to help stimulate sales. The merchant could also make a price change to move the merchandise faster. If the information is available, the merchant may work with store operations to find a new location for the article in the stores.

As with the fast-selling analysis, each retailer will have its own measurements to determine which articles are slow moving. It may be that each merchandising department will have a different standard for defining what is a slow-selling article. For example, beer will generally sell faster than novelty merchandise, so a stock-to-sales ratio of 4 would be unacceptable for beer, whereas that same ratio would indicate a fast mover for novelty merchandise. The point is that manage-

**Table 11.5   Fast-selling sample report.**

Generic Retail Store Corp.
Fast-Selling Items Total Company by Turns
Week 42

| Description | Dept | Class | Unit Retail | Unit Cost | Mkup Pct |
|---|---|---|---|---|---|
| Beefy Cigars 2 PK | 2 | 8 | $4.99 | $1.12 | 346% |
| Big Stick Candy | 1 | 2 | $2.99 | $0.63 | 375% |
| Christmas Model Truck w/Trailer | 5 | 4 | $29.99 | $9.50 | 216% |
| Christmas Pickup Truck | 5 | 4 | $8.99 | $2.75 | 227% |
| Novelty Coffee Cup | 6 | 2 | $3.99 | $0.35 | 1040% |
| Braves Baseball Cap | 6 | 1 | $6.99 | $3.50 | 100% |

ment may need to establish different performance objectives for each department.

## Slow-Selling Data Elements

This analysis uses the data elements from the basic article POS data analysis and from the article inventory data analysis. Again, it is likely that each retailer will have specific metrics or formulas to define a slow-moving article. No additional data entities are needed. However, some data elements may need to be added to an existing entity. A sample report of slow-selling articles is shown in Table 11.6.

## VENDOR PERFORMANCE ANALYSIS

Vendor (or supplier) performance analysis is very important to a retailer. Many retailers have no idea how well a vendor is supplying their stores. They may have the perception that the vendor knows more about their merchandise than they do. Perhaps the vendor does know more about their products, but the retailer knows more about the customers and what they buy. A supplier will measure its own performance based on how much merchandise is moved from the supplier's

| Units Sold | Retail Sales | Gross Margin | Beginning Inv Units | Beginning Inv Dollars | Weekly Turn | Stock to Sales |
|---|---|---|---|---|---|---|
| 15,971 | $79,695 | $61,808 | 16,000 | $79,840 | 100% | 1.0 |
| 16,072 | $48,055 | $37,930 | 17,266 | $51,625 | 93% | 1.1 |
| 8,909 | $267,181 | $182,545 | 12,500 | $374,875 | 71% | 1.4 |
| 11,566 | $103,978 | $72,172 | 16,447 | $147,859 | 70% | 1.4 |
| 18,277 | $72,925 | $66,528 | 28,802 | $114,920 | 63% | 1.6 |
| 9,845 | $68,817 | $34,359 | 20,000 | $139,800 | 49% | 2.0 |

warehouse to the retailer. The retailer measures its sales based on customer purchases. Obviously, there is a small conflict of interest when the vendor is allowed to manage the merchandise. This is the retailer's challenge.

This conflict of interest is exactly why I recommend that each retailer establish performance standards for each supplier or group of suppliers. Standard performance levels need to be defined for each variable so that the retailer can highlight the exceptions. For example, returns greater than 10% are not acceptable for any supplier. These standards need to be established and communicated clearly to the vendors. Effective communication is very important, as many suppliers may not even be aware that there is a performance problem. Other performance standards need to be placed on a supplier individually or on a class of suppliers. The suppliers need to know that the retailer wants them to constantly improve. Retailers need to push lead times down for all vendors based on individual vendor performance. This means that vendors with a 20-day lead time should be pushed to 10 days, and vendors with a 30-day lead time should be pushed to 15 days. Of course, suggesting improvements will do nothing. There must be measurements in place,

> **Obviously, there is a small conflict of interest when the vendor is allowed to manage the merchandise. This is the retailer's challenge.**

**Table 11.6  Slow-selling sample report.**

Generic Retail Store Corp.
Slow-Selling Items Total Company by Stock to Sales
Week 42 Stock to Sales >35

| Item ID | Description | Dept | Class | Unit Retail | Unit Cost | Mkup Pct | Units Sold | Retail Sales | Gross Margin | Beginning Inv Units | Beginning Inv Dollar | Weekly Turn | Stock to Sales |
|---|---|---|---|---|---|---|---|---|---|---|---|---|---|
| 19927 | Extra Length Marlboro Cig | 2 | 8 | $2.99 | $1.76 | 70% | 19 | $57 | $23 | 29,881 | $89,344 | 0% | 1573 |
| 19819 | Coconut Chocolate Bars | 3 | 1 | $0.99 | $0.40 | 148% | 29 | $29 | $17 | 13,098 | $12,967 | 0% | 452 |
| 19820 | Ultra Thin 50 Count Wipes | 4 | 1 | $0.99 | $0.35 | 183% | 55 | $54 | $35 | 22,844 | $22,616 | 0% | 415 |
| 19821 | Thanksgiving Model Truck | 5 | 1 | $12.99 | $9.00 | 44% | 13 | $169 | $52 | 698 | $9,067 | 2% | 54 |
| 20188 | ½ Pint 10W50 Motor Oil | 5 | 2 | $1.99 | $0.78 | 155% | 187 | $372 | $226 | 9,112 | $18,133 | 2% | 49 |
| 17442 | Braves Baseball T-shirt | 6 | 12 | $13.99 | $6.50 | 115% | 20 | $280 | $150 | 700 | $9,793 | 3% | 35 |

with supporting information to substantiate your position with the vendor, so the vendor can be compensated (or penalized) accordingly. But, this is up to each retailer. The data warehouse is certainly a good place to maintain the measurements.

I recommend that vendor data be updated at least weekly, and daily for exception reporting and notification. Without weekly figures, the human response time to resolve a supply problem might be impossible. The exception analysis should monitor supplier variables, such as accurate fills and lead times, and notify the responsible buyer when an exception occurs. This will allow the buyer to take immediate action with the supplier. It is also strongly recommended that some of these figures be calculated down to the store/product level. This way, a simple problem with a product, like a quality issue, can be identified, perhaps contained, and quickly resolved with the supplier's help. Reallocation of existing data is another benefit, but I will not discuss much about this. The point is that data must exist at the store level to make the best decisions.

The retailer will be able to query the vendor information, using the predefined limits for a department, and a list of vendors that qualify will be displayed. The user will have the option to further restrict the list and continue this process, driving down to a manageable number of poorly performing vendors. The analysis can continue by drilling down to the store/vendor level or vendor/PO level. The PO tracking entity details the current status of each PO for decision support, mostly to calculate number of days for each step in the PO fulfillment process.

## Vendor Performance Data Elements

This analysis uses the data elements from the basic article POS data analysis and perhaps the inventory information listed previously in the article inventory data elements. PO tracking, supplier information, and supplier performance data elements (listed below) are also needed. Weekly data, when including current week-to-date (WTD) data, is sufficient for the analysis. The monthly data entity is nearly identical to the weekly entity and will be used to enhance query performance. The exact data element will vary depending on the needs of each retailer, but these elements will provide a very good starting point. A sample vendor performance report is shown in Table 11.7.

**Table 11.7  Vendor performance sample report.**

Generic Retail Store Corp.
Vendor Performance Analysis—Lead Times
Weeks 42, 43

| Vendor | Vendor Name | Dept | Avg Days Lead | EDI | Current On-Order | Retail Period Receipts | Retail Period Sales | Period Grs Sls Margin | Period Gross Mkup | Period Sales % to Dept | Period Sales % to Corp | Period Total Dept Sales |
|---|---|---|---|---|---|---|---|---|---|---|---|---|
| 59983 | Anheuser-Busch | 1 | 1 | Y | $62,000 | $285,503 | $283,981 | $171,120 | 60% | 6% | 1% | $4,733,017 |
| 20024 | Coca-Cola | 2 | 1 | Y | $126,870 | $305,877 | $312,772 | $162,223 | 52% | 8% | 1% | $4,025,672 |
| 20026 | Pepsi Cola | 2 | 1 | Y | $98,667 | $279,993 | $298,009 | $158,201 | 53% | 7% | 1% | $4,025,672 |
| 39611 | RJR | 5 | 3 | Y | $12,887 | $200,988 | $178,221 | $79,662 | 45% | 5% | 0% | $3,877,721 |
| 82813 | Hershey Chocolate | 3 | 7 | N | $3,200 | $172,249 | $128,776 | $68,689 | 53% | 11% | 0% | $1,204,540 |

Generic Retail Store Corp.
Vendor Performance Analysis—PO Tracking
Hershey Chocolate, Weeks 42, 43

| PO # | Entry Date | Cancel Date | Approve Date | Ship Date | Receipt Date | Ordered Units | Retail Total | Cost Total | # Days Approve | # Days Ship | # Days in Trans | # Days Receipt (Lead) | Total Days |
|---|---|---|---|---|---|---|---|---|---|---|---|---|---|
| 8923498 | 11/5/96 | 12/5/96 | 11/11/96 | 11/12/96 | 11/15/96 | 36,144 | $38,665 | $20,492 | 6 | 1 | 3 | 4 | 10 |
| 8923515 | 11/5/96 | 12/5/96 | 11/11/96 | 11/12/96 | 11/15/96 | 24,288 | $29,229 | $15,491 | 6 | 1 | 3 | 4 | 10 |
| 8923532 | 11/5/96 | 12/5/96 | 11/11/96 | 11/12/96 | 11/15/96 | 48,048 | $47,718 | $25,291 | 6 | 1 | 3 | 4 | 10 |
| 9000275 | 11/12/96 | 12/12/96 | 11/16/96 | 11/17/96 | 11/19/96 | 24,576 | $30,465 | $16,146 | 4 | 1 | 2 | 3 | 7 |
| 9000292 | 11/12/96 | 12/12/96 | 11/16/96 | 12/2/96 | 12/4/96 | 13,152 | $26,172 | $13,871 | 4 | 16 | 2 | 18 | 22 |
| Totals & Averages | | | | | | | $172,249 | $91,292 | 5.2 | 4 | 2.6 | 6.6 | 11.8 |

- **PO Tracking**

  Supplier identifier, PO number, PO tracking number, PO entry date, PO approval date, PO issue date, EDI code, PO first receiving date, PO last receiving date, PO cancel date, unit retail price, unit retail cost, quantity received

- **Supplier Information**

  Supplier identifier, supplier name, supplier address, supplier contact person, supplier phone

- **Monthly Supplier Performance**

  Fiscal month, outstanding on-order dollars, total

sales dollars, total cost dollars, gross margin, total units sold, total customer returns, total returns to vendor, average unit retail, average unit cost, unique number of products shipped, number of accurately filled POs, average lead time, total number of purchase orders issued, total freight costs, purchase discounts, cancellation dollars, markdown dollars, beginning inventory, ending inventory

- **Weekly Supplier Performance**

  Fiscal week, outstanding on-order dollars, total

sales dollars, total cost dollars, gross margin, total units sold, total customer returns, total returns to vendor, average unit retail, average unit cost, unique number of products shipped, number of accurately filled POs, average lead time, total number of purchase orders issued, total freight costs, purchase discounts, cancellation dollars, markdown dollars, beginning inventory, ending inventory

## CATEGORY PERFORMANCE ANALYSIS

Until recently, the main focus for many retailers was the performance of a single article and/or department. This type of analysis is needed and still remains the fundamental essence of retail merchandising. With new technology capable of managing large amounts of data, however, category performance has attracted the attention of many retailers. Category management entails grouping articles together based on similar traits and tracking the sale and margin of the entire category. The big challenge facing the category manager is finding the proper mix of merchandise needed to sustain or grow an entire category. When a new article is introduced to a category, although it may be a stellar-selling product, the question should be, did the sales for the whole category increase? Perhaps the sales simply moved around within the category, increasing sales for the single article while reducing sales for similar articles. Did the profit for the entire category increase or decrease with the introduction of this fast-selling new article?

The essence of category management is grouping articles together and tracking the group performance. Retailers may have a different objective when implementing a category management system. Category management could even entail developing an understanding of how location of the category within a store influences sales. This analysis will focus on the basic performance of the category of merchandise. It is very similar to the basic inventory analysis mentioned earlier. Most retailers already have some type of category management reporting. If you do, you should tailor your analysis to your existing category management. The next step beyond category management is store and article grouping analysis. This will be defined later in this chapter.

> **The essence of category management is grouping articles together and tracking the group performance.**

## Category Performance Data Elements

The data elements needed to track category performance are the same as those for the basic article POS data analysis, but with the addition of a few fields (listed below). There is typically a category code or identifier added as an attribute to the article information entity. Category may already be defined in the merchandising hierarchy as a category, class, or subclass. For a first implementation, summary information may be sufficient to enable category management tools to function properly. An enterprise view of category management will reveal the necessity for the supportive detailed data. For a more dynamic implementation, see the section entitled "Store and Article Grouping" later in his chapter. For a sample analysis of category performance, see Table 11.8.

- **Category Information**

  Category identifier, category description, category manager

- **Article Category Cross Reference**

  Article identifier, category identifier, date added, date removed

## ARTICLE SELLING BY GEOGRAPHIC LOCATIONS

After determining the performance of an article for the entire company, it may be necessary to determine how the article is selling in different areas within the company. The article may be selling very well in the Northeast, while in the Southeast you may not be able to give the merchandise away. This type of analysis breaks down the sales of a particular article into the operational hierarchy. The operational hierarchy is typically divided into such groupings as company, region, district, area, and store. When data is maintained down to the store level, another hierarchy could be used just as easily. This analysis allows the retailer to compare the sales of an article for each region, district, area, and store, thereby helping the merchant to better understand the demographic selling patterns of the article. From this information a merchant can better allocate the initial shipment, better allocate new merchandise, remove or add goods to different areas, better determine if there is an operational difference in the selling, better determine the season of an article by geography, and so on. For a more dynamic approach to geographic analysis, see the section entitled "Store and Article Grouping" later in this chapter.

### Article Selling by Geographic Locations Data Elements

This analysis will use the data elements from the basic article POS data analysis as well as the data elements defined in the operational analyses in Chapter 10. Retailers may have specific geographic areas that are important to them. These areas are in one way or another tied to a store, perhaps by something as simple as a zip code. If a retailer already has

**Table 11.8  Category performance sample report and graph (on facing page).**

Generic Retail Stores
Category Sales Performance Analysis
Category 1427—Holiday Accessories

| Week | Avg Unit Rtl Price | Avg Unit Cost | Total Sold | Cumm Units Sold | Total Sales | Gross Cost | Gross Margin | Maint Markup | Planned Sales | Planned vs Actual | Act Pct to Planned |
|------|-----|-----|-----|-----|-----|-----|-----|-----|-----|-----|-----|
| 35 | $11.27 | $6.54 | 923 | 923 | $10,402 | $6,033 | $4,369 | 58% | $12,894 | ($2,492) | 81% |
| 36 | $13.42 | $7.78 | 1,751 | 2,674 | $23,498 | $13,629 | $9,869 | 58% | $13,677 | $9,821 | 172% |
| 37 | $12.35 | $7.16 | 1,132 | 3,806 | $13,975 | $8,105 | $5,869 | 58% | $15,814 | ($1,840) | 88% |
| 38 | $12.88 | $7.22 | 1,002 | 4,808 | $12,908 | $7,234 | $5,674 | 56% | $13,998 | ($1,090) | 92% |
| 39 | $12.61 | $7.12 | 1,477 | 6,285 | $18,631 | $10,516 | $8,114 | 56% | $15,330 | $3,301 | 122% |
| 40 | $12.75 | $7.02 | 1,501 | 7,786 | $19,135 | $10,537 | $8,598 | 55% | $16,885 | $2,250 | 113% |
| 41 | $12.68 | $6.98 | 1,222 | 9,008 | $15,496 | $8,530 | $6,967 | 55% | $17,071 | ($1,575) | 91% |
| 42 | $12.71 | $7.37 | 1,101 | 10,109 | $13,999 | $8,119 | $5,879 | 58% | $15,381 | ($1,382) | 91% |
| 43 | $12.70 | $7.36 | 1,071 | 11,180 | $13,599 | $7,888 | $5,712 | 58% | $14,962 | ($1,363) | 91% |
| 44 | $12.71 | $7.50 | 1,556 | 12,736 | $19,771 | $11,665 | $8,106 | 59% | $19,700 | $71 | 100% |
| 45 | $12.70 | $7.49 | 1,223 | 13,959 | $15,534 | $9,165 | $6,369 | 59% | $15,822 | ($288) | 98% |
| 46 | $13.87 | $8.99 | 1,787 | 15,746 | $24,786 | $16,065 | $8,721 | 65% | $24,964 | ($179) | 99% |
| 47 | $13.29 | $8.76 | 1,666 | 17,412 | $22,134 | $14,594 | $7,540 | 66% | $16,700 | $5,434 | 133% |
| 48 | $13.58 | $8.01 | 1,287 | 18,699 | $17,475 | $10,310 | $7,165 | 59% | $17,979 | ($505) | 97% |
| 49 | $13.43 | $7.92 | 1,221 | 19,920 | $16,400 | $9,676 | $6,724 | 59% | $17,057 | ($657) | 96% |
| 50 | $13.50 | $7.97 | 1,029 | 20,949 | $13,897 | $8,199 | $5,698 | 59% | $14,375 | ($479) | 97% |
| 51 | $13.47 | $7.95 | 1,446 | 22,395 | $19,475 | $11,490 | $7,985 | 59% | $20,201 | ($725) | 96% |
| 52 | $13.49 | $7.96 | 1,413 | 23,808 | $19,057 | $11,243 | $7,813 | 59% | $19,740 | ($683) | 97% |
|  | $13.03 | $7.69 | 23,808 | 23,808 | $310,172 | $183,000 | $127,172 | 59% | $302,551 | $7,621 | 103% |

Category 1427—Holiday Accessories

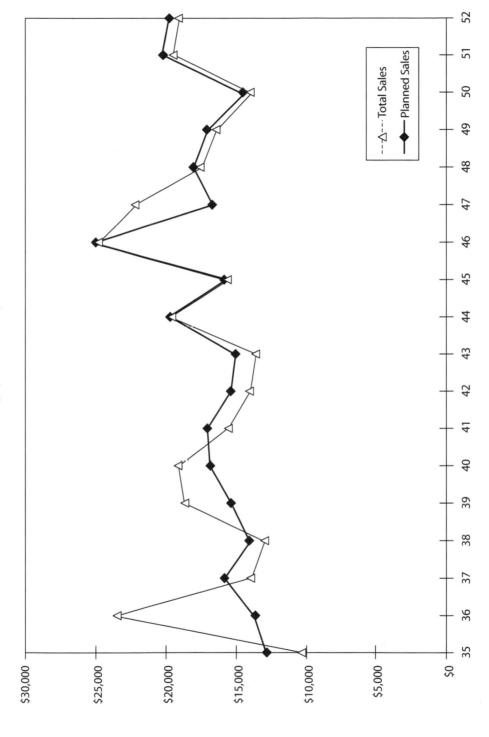

defined these areas, it is a simple task to integrate them into this geographic analysis.

## Article Selling by Geographic Locations Sample Report

The report shown in Table 11.9 enumerates the sales of a specific article across different areas. As you can see, a couple of areas have lowered the retail price by a dollar and were able to improve their stock-to-sales position beyond the other areas. Might a permanent price change be in order? Normally, this information can easily be displayed graphically on a map.

## COMPARATIVE ARTICLE SALES

A comparative article sales analysis is the comparison of two different articles. It is nearly identical to the basic article POS analysis except for the addition of a second, comparative article. It is also important that this analysis compare the performance of one article against the merchandise hierarchy (department, class, subclass) of that article. The greatest value from this analysis can generally be gained from a visual, or graphic, presentation because similar patterns between the comparative articles can most readily be identified in this way. This analysis is important to the merchant when determining which articles complement each other and which articles conflict with each other. It is also good for determining the "fit" of an article into a category of merchandise. Sometimes the sales patterns are very different for different operational areas of the company. So this comparative analysis can also compare two different operational areas for the same article.

## Comparative Article Sales Data Elements

The data elements are the same as those for the basic article POS data analysis and the category performance analysis defined earlier in this chapter. When comparing geographical areas or an operational

**Table 11.9  Sample report of article selling by geographic locations.**

Generic Retail Store Corp.
Item Area Analysis for Item #22378—Fancy Ice Scraper
Area Analysis Region 5 District 2 for Weeks 13 through 26

| Regn | Distr | Area | Area Name | Manager | Sold Units | Receipt Units | Ending On-Hand Units | Retail Price | On-Order Packs | On-Order Units | Total Sales | Stock to Sales for Period |
|------|-------|------|-----------|---------|------------|---------------|----------------------|--------------|----------------|----------------|-------------|---------------------------|
| 5 | 2 | 8 | West Virginia | Billy Ray | 126 | 192 | 66 | $7.99 | 1 | 12 | $1,006.74 | 1.5 |
| | | 2 | Georgia & N. Florida | Dewane | 188 | 288 | 100 | $7.99 | 7 | 84 | $1,502.12 | 1.5 |
| | | 3 | Carolinas | Kelly | 59 | 96 | 37 | $8.99 | 1 | 12 | $530.41 | 1.6 |
| | | 4 | Alabama & Mississippi | Tim | 45 | 96 | 51 | $8.99 | 1 | 12 | $404.55 | 2.1 |
| | | 6 | Tennesse | Terry | 39 | 96 | 57 | $8.99 | 0 | 0 | $350.61 | 2.5 |
| | | 7 | Kentucky | Lisa | 57 | 192 | 135 | $8.99 | 6 | 72 | $512.43 | 3.4 |
| | | 1 | South Florida | Stefan | 25 | 108 | 83 | $8.99 | 5 | 60 | $224.75 | 4.3 |
| | | 5 | Virginia | Sally | 22 | 96 | 74 | $8.99 | 0 | 0 | $197.78 | 4.4 |
| | | | | | 561 | 1,164 | 603 | | 21 | 252 | $4,729.39 | 2.1 |

hierarchy for an article, data elements defined in the previous chapter will be needed.

### Comparative Article Sales Sample Report

As you can see from Table 11.10 (pages 248–249), Miller Lite follows the category sales and gross margin very closely. Any change to the article will most likely affect the entire category.

## STORE AND ARTICLE GROUPING

Store and article grouping is a very dynamic and flexible implementation of article selling by geographic locations and category performance analysis. Fundamentally, the user can establish any relationship with an article or a store. This analysis will allow a user to dynamically

1. create a group of articles and name that group,
2. create a group of stores and name that group, and
3. create a group of articles and stores and name that group.

Once these groups are defined, they can be used to measure the performance of the entire group. Each group can be compared with other groups or individual articles. The attributes of articles and stores are very important for defining these groups. To define a group of articles or stores, the user can construct a query using constraints on the attributes of a store and/or article. In fact, any type of constraint is acceptable that will produce a result set of store, article, or some combination.

There are two types of groups, dynamic and static. A static grouping is exactly that, static, and will not change over time. Once the group is created, it will not change without some human intervention (e.g., deleting the group or changing the grouping query). Dynamic grouping is re-created as the business changes. Groups can change from day to day. To clarify the difference between static and dynamic grouping, let's create an example. First, let's create several groups of stores based on retail square feet. The large store group is greater than 40,000 square feet, the medium store group is 10,000 to 39,000 square feet, and the smallest stores are less than 10,000 square feet. Once these groups are created, I can measure and compare the performance of the store groups using the comparable store sales analysis metrics (defined in Chapter 10). When the analysis is complete, I can save it and rerun it weekly. The big question now is whether or not to include the new stores that are added as the company expands (dynamic) or to just use these exact stores for comparison (static).

I hope this example clarifies the power of store and article groups. Of course, they can become very complex, too. As the user community learns more and more about their companies through their data, this will become a very powerful tool to measure and diagnose store and article performance. You can also take this analysis beyond stores and articles. You could use groupings for the SKU (both stores and articles), departments, regions, districts, geographic boundaries, competitive comparison, sale ratings, promotional advertising, and so on. You could even extend this concept to customers. A retailer may have a specific issue that can be resolved by implementing this grouping strategy. It may be necessary to implement a custom grouping application to resolve a specific retail business problem.

> As the user community learns more and more about their companies through their data, this will become a very powerful tool to measure and diagnose store and article performance.

Groups generally remain private to an individual user or owner. The owner can modify or delete that group at any time. The owner can also promote the group to other users. Therefore, it may be helpful to create a process to elevate some groups into production processes so other users can analyze mutually common groups. Once an owner relinquishes ownership, he or she can no longer delete or modify the group.

## Store and Article Grouping Data Elements

This analysis requires all of the store sales data elements discussed in Chapter 10 and the basic article POS data elements defined in this chpater, in addition to the new data elements listed below. A few of the attributes within the retail grouping entity and the retail grouping creation method need to be explained. The group type, in the retail grouping entity, is a code to identify if this group is a store group, an article

**Table 11.10  Comparative article sales sample report and graph (on facing page).**

Generic Retail Store Corp.
Category 1427—Beer vs. Item 22765—Miller Lite 6 PK Cans
Company Level Weeks 35 through 52

| Week | Catg Avg Unit Rtl Price | Catg Avg Unit Cost | Item Unit Retail | Item Unit Cost | Catg Units Sold | Item Units Sold | Item % Catg Units Sold | Catg Total Sales | Item Total Sales | Item % Catg Total Sales | Catg Gross Margin | Item Gross Margin | Item % Catg Gross Margin |
|---|---|---|---|---|---|---|---|---|---|---|---|---|---|
| 35 | $11.27 | $6.54 | $3.99 | $2.22 | 14,768 | 4,330 | 29% | $166,435 | $17,277 | 10% | $69,903 | $7,664 | 11% |
| 36 | $13.42 | $7.78 | $3.99 | $2.22 | 28,016 | 8,685 | 31% | $375,975 | $34,653 | 9% | $157,909 | $15,372 | 10% |
| 37 | $12.35 | $7.16 | $3.99 | $2.22 | 18,112 | 5,977 | 33% | $223,593 | $23,848 | 11% | $93,909 | $10,579 | 11% |
| 38 | $12.88 | $7.22 | $3.99 | $2.22 | 16,032 | 4,649 | 29% | $206,532 | $18,551 | 9% | $90,781 | $8,229 | 9% |
| 39 | $12.61 | $7.12 | $3.99 | $2.22 | 23,632 | 6,381 | 27% | $298,088 | $25,459 | 9% | $129,828 | $11,294 | 9% |
| 40 | $12.75 | $7.02 | $3.99 | $2.22 | 24,016 | 6,244 | 26% | $306,159 | $24,914 | 8% | $137,567 | $11,052 | 8% |
| 41 | $12.68 | $6.98 | $3.99 | $2.22 | 19,552 | 4,692 | 24% | $247,938 | $18,723 | 8% | $111,465 | $8,306 | 7% |
| 42 | $12.71 | $7.37 | $3.99 | $2.22 | 17,616 | 3,876 | 22% | $223,979 | $15,463 | 7% | $94,071 | $6,860 | 7% |
| 43 | $12.70 | $7.36 | $3.99 | $2.22 | 17,136 | 3,770 | 22% | $217,588 | $15,042 | 7% | $91,387 | $6,673 | 7% |
| 44 | $12.71 | $7.50 | $3.99 | $2.22 | 24,896 | 5,477 | 22% | $316,332 | $21,854 | 7% | $129,696 | $9,695 | 7% |
| 45 | $12.70 | $7.49 | $3.99 | $2.22 | 19,568 | 5,088 | 26% | $248,551 | $20,300 | 8% | $101,906 | $9,005 | 9% |
| 46 | $13.87 | $8.99 | $3.99 | $2.22 | 28,592 | 7,720 | 27% | $396,571 | $30,802 | 8% | $139,529 | $13,664 | 10% |
| 47 | $13.29 | $8.76 | $3.99 | $2.22 | 26,656 | 7,464 | 28% | $354,151 | $29,780 | 8% | $120,644 | $13,211 | 11% |
| 48 | $13.58 | $8.01 | $3.99 | $2.22 | 20,592 | 5,972 | 29% | $279,598 | $23,827 | 9% | $114,635 | $10,570 | 9% |
| 49 | $13.43 | $7.92 | $3.99 | $2.22 | 19,536 | 5,275 | 27% | $262,407 | $21,046 | 8% | $107,587 | $9,336 | 9% |
| 50 | $13.50 | $7.97 | $3.99 | $2.22 | 16,464 | 3,622 | 22% | $222,346 | $14,452 | 6% | $91,162 | $6,411 | 7% |
| 51 | $13.47 | $7.95 | $3.99 | $2.22 | 23,136 | 4,627 | 20% | $311,607 | $18,463 | 6% | $127,759 | $8,190 | 6% |
| 52 | $13.49 | $7.96 | $3.99 | $2.22 | 22,608 | 4,296 | 19% | $304,908 | $17,139 | 6% | $125,012 | $7,603 | 6% |
|  | $13.03 |  | $3.99 |  | 380,928 | 98,143 | 26% | $4,962,758 | $391,592 | 8% | $4,571,166 | $173,714 | 4% |

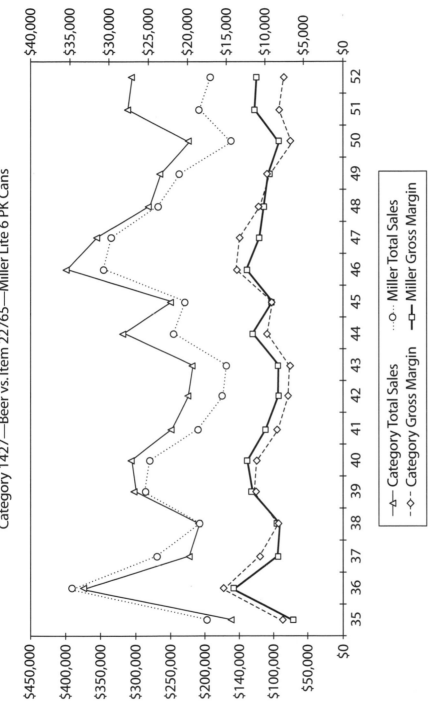

Category 1427—Beer vs. Item 22765—Miller Lite 6 PK Cans

—△— Category Total Sales    ···o··· Miller Total Sales
—◇— Category Gross Margin    —□— Miller Gross Margin

group, both (SKU group), or something else (e.g., department, region). The group update frequency is used to define a static or dynamic group. If it is a dynamic group, then this is used to define the frequency with which this grouping must be updated. The retail grouping creation method entity is used to maintain the SQL that was used to create the grouping. It defines how the group is to be created. The group process procedure name is used in lieu of SQL for complex group processing and for retailers who already have sophisticated stored procedures functioning to produce groupings.

- **Retail Grouping Creation Method**

  Group identifier, group processing type, group process procedure name, group SQL

- **Retail Grouping**

  Group identifier, group name, group type, group update frequency, group creation date, group creator, group public access code

- **SKU Grouping**

  Group identifier, store identifier, article identifier

- **Article Grouping**

  Group identifier, article identifier

- **Store Grouping**

  Group identifier, store identifier

## Store and Article Grouping Sample Report

There is no specific report for store and article groupings. The reports for the groups are typically the same reports as defined previously for store operations (Chapter 10) or merchandising (this chapter), only for the articles or stores defined in the group. In other words, the group is another article or store constraint in each analysis.

## BASIC AFFINITY SELLING

Affinity analysis can be very complex. Data mining tools can help determine the natural affinity among articles and can draw associations with merchandise that are not intuitively obvious. However, a complex analysis is not necessary if you only want to know which articles sold with another specific article. So if one article is already known, this simpler analysis is for you. You will need to input an article identifier, a date range, and optionally a store constraint. All POS transactions will be scanned for that article, date range, and store list to return a list of articles sold with that specific article, ranked by the number of times that each article was sold with the specified article. Because of the complexity of this analysis, response time may be an issue. However, if date and store have been constrained properly, performance should not be an issue. If a query requests all dates in this century and all stores, then (depending on the database) performance may be an issue. It may be necessary to defer these requests for nightly processing.

## Basic Affinity Selling Data Elements

The data elements used in this analysis will primarily be from the store transaction merchandise entity, part of the cash register TLOG, defined in Chapter 10. It may also use entities defined in the store sales analysis and in the basic article POS analysis. No other data elements are necessary. A basic affinity selling analysis is shown in Table 11.11.

## OUT-OF-STOCK ANALYSIS

This analysis is specifically designed to study out-of-stock conditions. While this can be a very complex analysis, I believe I have greatly simplified it. Current inventory data for every store is necessary for the computer to determine the out-of-stock situation. If inventory figures are not available, it still may be possible to calculate current inventory based on receipts and sales of seasonal articles. If the inventory figures are perceived as inaccurate, then this out-of-stock analysis will likewise be perceived as inaccurate. The reason I mention this is because store operations *must* have the discipline to perform inventory counts and adjustments weekly (if not daily). Monthly, quarterly, and annual inventory figures are good for financial figures but not for article performance.

There are several different views on how to calculate out-of-stock,

**Table 11.11    Basic affinity selling sample report.**

Generic Retail Store Corp.
Top Affinity Item for Item 22765—Miller Lite 6 PK Cans
Weeks 22, 23, 24 Entire Company

| Item ID | Item Description | # Total Trans | Affinity Item ID | Affinity Description | Dept | # Trans Affinity | Relation Percent |
|---------|-----------------|---------------|------------------|---------------------|------|------------------|------------------|
| 22765 | Miller Lite 6 PK Cans | 200,107 | 19819 | Mar's M&Ms Peanuts | 2 | 11,291 | 5.642% |
| | | | 19927 | Mar's M&Ms Plain | 2 | 11,198 | 5.596% |
| | | | 19821 | Luv's 12 PK Diapers | 5 | 10,822 | 5.408% |
| | | | 20188 | Beefy Cigars 2 PK | 1 | 1,899 | 0.949% |
| | | | 19820 | Marlboro Regular PK | 3 | 1,872 | 0.935% |
| | | | 17442 | Certs Wintergreen Roll Candy | 2 | 1,690 | 0.845% |

but I calculate it as follows. If a store has no inventory at any time in a time period (let's use a week for this example), it was out-of-stock for that week. An out-of-stock is zero or negative inventory. Of course, negative inventory indicates an operational issue, but I will count it as out-of-stock. I then calculate a percentage of the number of stores in-stock to the number of stores out-of-stock. This figure is the in-stock and/or out-of-stock percentage. With this percentage you should be able to determine the earning potential if inventory levels had been maintained.

> Store operations must have the discipline to perform inventory counts and adjustments weekly (if not daily).

### Out-of-Stock Data Elements

The data elements for this analysis really belong in the company inventory entity by adding the out-of-stock store count and the in-stock store count. You may ask why you need the store count as opposed to one figure or the percentage. The reason is that the number of stores changes over time for almost every retailer. If you maintain a percentage and use it as the basis for calculating the lost revenue potential, it will be wrong next month if a new store opens. The same can be applied to the store counts: you need to know both for historical measurements. I suggest a 65-week retention period for this data to enable a quarter-to-quarter comparison. You could maintain an out-of-stock flag on an entity called weekly store inventory. If inventory figures for the stores are maintained historically, this should be implemented. However, I do believe that the percentage of out-of-stock, as mentioned above, will be more useful.

- **Weekly Company Inventory**

  Article identifier, fiscal week, out-of-stock store count, in-stock store count

## Out-of-Stock Sample Report

The out-of-stock percentage will typically be used in conjunction with the basic inventory analysis data. Table 11.12 shows an out-of-stock condition was starting at least in week 40, much too early in the Christmas season. There is a good opportunity for improvement in sales, and the price change in week 43 was probably not necessary, as the article would have sold out at the regular price.

**Table 11.12    Out-of-stock analysis sample report.**

Generic Retail Store Corp.
Out-of-Stock Analysis for Christmas Truck Item #533434
Department 4 Class 55

| Week | Selling Price | Unit Cost | Units Sold | Cum Units Sold | Sales | Margin | Sell-Thru | Percent In-Stock |
|---|---|---|---|---|---|---|---|---|
| 35 | $13.97 | $6.51 | 0 | 0 | $0 | $0 | 0% | 6% |
| 36 | $13.97 | $6.51 | 1,751 | 1,751 | $24,461 | $13,062 | 1% | 45% |
| 37 | $13.97 | $6.51 | 18,123 | 19,874 | $253,178 | $135,198 | 6% | 98% |
| 38 | $13.97 | $6.51 | 25,667 | 45,541 | $358,568 | $191,476 | 14% | 99% |
| 39 | $13.97 | $6.51 | 30,199 | 75,740 | $421,880 | $225,285 | 23% | 84% |
| 40 | $13.97 | $6.51 | 40,598 | 116,338 | $567,154 | $302,861 | 35% | 71% |
| 41 | $13.97 | $6.51 | 38,333 | 154,671 | $535,512 | $285,964 | 46% | 64% |
| 42 | $13.97 | $6.51 | 42,708 | 197,379 | $596,631 | $318,602 | 59% | 60% |
| 43 | $9.97 | $6.51 | 35,812 | 233,191 | $357,046 | $123,910 | 70% | 55% |
| 44 | $9.97 | $6.51 | 36,120 | 269,311 | $360,116 | $124,975 | 80% | 52% |
| 45 | $9.97 | $6.51 | 33,771 | 303,082 | $336,697 | $116,848 | 90% | 47% |
| 46 | $9.97 | $6.51 | 16,499 | 319,581 | $164,495 | $57,087 | 95% | 38% |
| 47 | $9.97 | $6.51 | 9,241 | 328,822 | $92,133 | $31,974 | 98% | 21% |
| 48 | $9.97 | $6.51 | 5,294 | 334,116 | $52,781 | $18,317 | 100% | 6% |
| 49 | $9.97 | $6.51 | 695 | 334,811 | $6,929 | $2,405 | 100% | 1% |
| 50 | $9.97 | $6.51 | 0 | 334,811 | $0 | $0 | 100% | 0% |
| 51 | $9.97 | $6.51 | 0 | 334,811 | $0 | $0 | 100% | 0% |
| 52 | $9.97 | $6.51 | 0 | 334,811 | $0 | $0 | 100% | 0% |
| | | | $334,811 | | $4,127,582 | $1,947,962 | | |

# 12

# Conclusion

t is always valuable to learn from the success of others. Wal-Mart's data warehouse is certainly a highly visible successful implementation. Sam Walton's remark, "Most everything I've done I've copied from someone else," is a good philosophy that obviously worked well. Although you cannot expect to duplicate Wal-Mart's system, you can certainly learn from and improve upon their successes. There are many things we can learn from Wal-Mart's approach, and these can be placed in four broad categories: focusing on the business, building a team, communicating openly and effectively, and applying technology.

## FOCUS ON THE BUSINESS

Focusing on the business is paramount. Solving a business problem by enabling better decisions is the key to a successful data warehouse implementation. The obsession to solve business problems, the flexibility to change, and a measured return on investment are elements needed for the long-term growth of the data warehouse. Continuously providing your company with new information and merging the data from disparate systems is essential to maximizing the value of an enterprise data warehouse. Remember to build your data warehouse in complete alignment with your company's objectives. Technical obstacles, such as extremely large data and processing volumes, can be managed but are a moot issue if there is no business sponsorship.

## BUILD A TEAM

Building a team is an essential part of the construction process. Pick your team wisely, particularly the project leader. If your company needs help building its data warehouse, then pick your partners carefully and define very clear milestones. You will need to work closely with the people that will use this new system, so they are an essential part of the team.

## COMMUNICATE OPENLY AND EFFECTIVELY

Communicating openly and effectively will help these very different groups of people work together to apply technology that will solve a business problem. It will also help prioritize, maintain focus, and provide a clear direction during the construction of the data warehouse. The business community needs to clearly understand the value of the technology. You may need to build a business case and/or a prototype system for them to clearly understand the value. Twelve months after implementation, measuring the return on investment is paramount for the long-term success of the data warehouse. Gather the ROI conservatively and communicate your success within your company. Give information freely, as this allows more people the chance to profit from the data warehouse investment.

## APPLY TECHNOLOGY

Applying technology to solving a business problem should be the key strength of every technology department. Business people do not want "open" or "standard" systems, they want a technical solution to their business problems. For high-growth companies, designing systems for exponential growth is a learning process and, consequently, has little to do with cost. Do not create self-imposed limitations on accessing your data. When you learn to build linear systems, update in near real time, and run continuously, you will have additional time to focus on solving the business problems.

I wish you and your company the best of luck in building your data warehouse. Finally, when you are building your company's enterprise data warehouse, I hope you can become as obsessed with providing business value to your company as Wal-Mart was.

# A

# Retail Formulas

Here are some commonly used formulas that can be used during the business exploration. I obtained these formulas from various people in the retail industry. Every retailer will use formulas similar to these. Sometimes a retail company will use the same name for a different formula. It is for this reason that these formulas should be documented and distributed so that everyone in the business can use a "common language" when referring to a calculated value.

## INVENTORY FORMULAS

### Net Receipts

(Purchases + Transfers in + Returns from customers + Overages)

− (Transfers out + Returns to vendors)

= Net receipts

## Ending Inventory at Retail

Beginning inventory
- − Sales
- − Transfers out
- − Returns to vendor
- − Markdowns
- − Employee discounts
- − Shrinkage
- + Purchases
- + Returns from customers
- + Transfers in
- + Markups
- = Ending inventory

## Average Inventory

For six months:     BOM inventory added for past 7 months / 7

For a year:         BOM inventory added for past 13 months / 13

Note: BOM = Beginning of month

## Turnover

Season =    $ Total sales for season/$ Average inventory for season

Year =      $ Total sales for year/$ Average inventory for year

## Stock-to-Sales Ratio

$ Retail beginning inventory / $ Sales

## Fresh Goods Factor

$ Receipts of the past two months / $ BOM inventory for current month

## Open to Buy

For current month:    Planned BOM inventory for next month

      + Planned sales for current month

      + Planned markdowns for current month

      + Planned shrinkage for current month

      − Open orders for current month

      − Actual BOM inventory for current month

      = Open to buy for current month

For future months:    Planned purchase for the month

      − Open orders for the month

      = Open to buy for the months

## Purchases Needed for a Season

If season has not begun:    Planned end-of-season inventory

      + Planned sales for season

      + Planned markdowns for season

      + Planned shrinkage for season

      − Planned beginning-of-season inventory

      = Purchase required for season

If season is in progress:    Planned end-of-season inventory

      + Actual sales for season

      + Actual markdowns for season

      + Actual shrinkage for season

      − Actual beginning-of-season inventory

      = Purchases required for season

## KEY PERCENTAGE RELATIONSHIPS

### Percentage change this year (TY) from last year (LY)

(TY − LY) / LY

### Percentage change this year from plan (PL)

(TY − PL) / PL

### Shrinkage as a percentage of sales

$ Shrinkage / $ Sales

### Markdowns as a percentage of sales

$ Markdowns / $ Sales

### Employee discounts as a percentage of sales

$ Employee discounts / $ Sales

### Monthly percentage distributions

Sales:   $ Sales for the month / $ Sales for the season = Monthly %

$ Sales for the Season * Monthly % = $ Sales for the month

Markdowns:   $ Markdowns for the month / $ Markdowns for the season = Monthly %

$ Markdowns for the season * Monthly % = $ Markdowns for the month

## MARGIN AND PROFIT FORMULAS

### Gross Margin

Sales − Cost of goods sold (COGS) = Gross margin

or

Sales − Cost complement = Initial markup − Reduction at cost

= Gross margin

Reductions at cost = (Markdown $ + Employee discount $ + Shrink $)

* Cost complement

### Merchandise Margin

Gross margin + Vendor discounts

### Merchandise Margin as a Percentage of Sales

$ Merchandise margin / $ Sales

### Vendor Discounts

Invoice amount of goods * Shipping term % = Vendor discount $

### Return on Inventory Investment at Cost (ROII)

(Merchandise margin % * Turnover) / Cost complement = ROII

or

(Merchandise margin $ / Average inventory) / Cost complement %

# B

# Retail Data Model

When your company is creating a data warehouse, it is important to create a logical design for your database. This is important for several reasons. First, you want to be able to communicate openly about what will be in the data warehouse. The user community will want to know which elements are going to be included. If there are multiple implementations, they will want to know which elements will be available for each implementation. Next, a logical data model facilitates the creation of a low maintenance physical database design that will require only minor modifications after implementation. Assuming your business does not change dramatically, the physical implementation based on the logical model should last for many years without modification. Finally, the data model is an excellent way to contain the scope of a data warehouse project. To contain the scope of the data warehouse using the logical data model, you would select subject areas that are included in the first and later implementations. Then you would build a timeline based on the creation of those subject areas.

The following data model has very clear subject areas: time hierarchy, operational hierarchy, merchandise hierarchy, point-of-sale (POS), inventory, planned inventory, markdown markup, merchandise summaries, operational summaries, and orders. To prioritize the implementation, the first implementation could be the POS subject area plus the supporting time hierarchy, operational hierarchy, and merchandise hierarchy. The second data warehouse implementation could be another subject area, like inventory. Of course, you will want to implement each subject area according to the needs and priorities of your company.

Most retailers will have three basic hierarchies that they use most often: time hierarchy, operational hierarchy, and merchandise hierarchy. They will want to drill up, down, and across with almost every combination of these to better understand the events happening in their business. The operational hierarchy normally defines the operational management hierarchy starting with a department manager and going up to the corporate level. It identifies the operationally responsible areas of the company. As you can see in the operational hierarchy diagram, the hierarchy clearly includes managers at the division, region, district, store, and department level. I have also included a STORE_FLOOR_LOCATION entity because some retailers are working towards physically managing the location of the inventory within a store. In order to manage inventory at this level, the department within each store must be further divided into specific locations where an article can be placed.

The merchandising hierarchy, like the operational hierarchy, is associated with an individual having specific merchandising responsibilities. This includes some aspects of article pricing, but the analysis of pricing is so large it should be in a completely different subject area.

The time hierarchy should be simple to understand, but unfortunately it is not. Within a retailer, there can easily be four different time scales (operational, financial, marketing, and merchandising), plus the normal calendar events, like Christmas and Easter. Every retailer will have some deviation of these. For example, store operations may begin their week on Sunday, merchandising may begin their week on Monday, finance may begin their weeks based on January 1, and marketing may begin their week on Wednesday. They all want to analyze sales and most, at one time or another, want to see the sales (or returns) of an individual article. Moving holidays (like Easter) further complicates the time hierarchy.

There are five merchandising subject areas that I have included in the following data model: point-of-sale (POS), inventory, planned inventory, markdown markup, and orders. The POS and the inventory are the most complex. I have chosen to separate them because they can be substantially different to maintain.

The POS primarily consists of historical facts while the inventory numbers are up-to-the-minute figures. The POS essentially tracks the customer actions. For example, a transaction (POS_TRANSACTION) is initiated when a customer (CUSTOMER) requests to purchase one or more articles (POS_MERCHANDISE) and wishes to pay (TENDER) for it in one or more ways. POS comprises all of the key elements needed for an article to sell. Inventory management, on the other hand, can be based on the selling transaction as well as on other transactions not relating to customers, and has both current and historical value. The CURRENT_INVENTORY entity maintains the most up-to-date information on inventory. These entities essentially focus on the entire flow of goods, both currently and historically. Article sales via POS is the single largest transaction volume in the flow-of-goods and this will adjust inventory, but inventories can be adjusted without selling. Articles move from the manufacturer (on a truck) to a distribution center, to the stores (on a truck), then into the back room, and finally to the sales floor. During this time inventory adjustments can occur, like when articles are damaged or returned. Finally, a department store manager can manually adjust the inventory for a myriad of reasons. For many analyses, like price management, only the current inventory is needed while other forecasting applications, such as automatic replenishment, require the use of historical inventory data. Analyses using the data elements in the inventory planning subject area will use historical inventory while analyses for price changes will use current inventory and may result in a markdown or markup (markdown markup subject area). The orders subject area is oversimplified here but is an important aspect of inventory management. Articles must be ordered, received from the supplier, distributed to the stores, and eventually paid for. This in turn adjusts open-to-buy figures.

Finally, a data warehouse would not be complete without summary tables. This is more of a physical aspect of the design than a logical design. Logically, summary tables should not exist if you have the detailed source data. Unfortunately, the technology to instantaneously summarize millions (and for some systems billions) of records has not arrived yet. I would look for this technology after computer systems move away from mechanically operated disk drives. Until this new technology arrives, we will need summary tables to provide the user community with a reasonable response time to their queries. The merchandise summaries subject area and the operational summaries subject area are summary tables that might be used by a typical retailer.

# OPERATIONAL HIERARCHY

**DIVISION**

| DIVISION_ID | INTEGER |
|---|---|
| DIVISION_NAME | CHAR(35) |
| DIVISION_MGR | CHAR(35) |

**REGION**

| REGION_ID | INTEGER |
|---|---|
| DIVISION_ID | INTEGER |
| REGION_NAME | CHAR(35) |
| REGION_MGR | CHAR(35) |

**DISTRICT**

| DISTRICT_ID | INTEGER |
|---|---|
| REGION_ID | INTEGER |
| DIVISION_ID | INTEGER |
| DISTRICT_NAME | CHAR(35) |
| DISTRICT_MGR | CHAR(35) |

**STORE**

| STORE_ID | SMALLINT |
|---|---|
| DISTRICT_ID | INTEGER |
| REGION_ID | INTEGER |
| DIVISION_ID | INTEGER |
| STORE_NAME | CHAR(20) |
| STORE_MGR | CHAR(35) |
| ADDRESS_1 | VARCHAR(50) |
| ADDRESS_2 | VARCHAR(50) |
| CITY_NAME | CHAR(40) |
| STATE_CODE | CHAR(2) |
| COUNTRY_CODE | CHAR(2) |
| ZIP_CODE | CHAR(7) |
| QUIET_OPEN_DATE | DATE |
| GRAND_OPEN_DATE | DATE |
| CLOSE_DATE | DATE |
| FINAL_CLOSE_DATE | DATE |
| REMODEL_DATE | DATE |
| REMODEL_REVIEW_DATE | DATE |
| SIZE_CLASS_CODE | SMALLINT |
| SALES_CLASS_CODE | SMALLINT |
| TOTAL_SQFT | INTEGER |
| SELLING_SQFT | INTEGER |
| BACKROOM_SQFT | INTEGER |
| LEASE_SQFT | INTEGER |
| OWN_SQFT | INTEGER |
| PRIMARY_WHS_ID | INTEGER |
| HARDLINE_WHS_ID | INTEGER |
| SOFTLINE_WHS_ID | INTEGER |
| FRESH_WHS_ID | INTEGER |
| 24FILM_FLAG | CHAR(1) |
| VIDEO_RENTAL_FLAG | CHAR(1) |
| CAMERA_SALES_FLAG | CHAR(1) |
| APOTHEKE_FLAG | CHAR(1) |
| VISION_FLAG | CHAR(1) |
| GROCERY_FLAG | CHAR(1) |
| DELI_FLAG | CHAR(1) |
| FABRICS_FLAG | CHAR(1) |
| AUTOMOTIVE_FLAG | CHAR(1) |
| PASTRY_FLAG | CHAR(1) |
| BUTCHER_FLAG | CHAR(1) |
| WINE_FLAG | CHAR(1) |
| BAKERY_FLAG | CHAR(1) |
| OPERATION_HOURS | SMALLINT |
| CAR_WASH_FLAG | CHAR(1) |
| FUEL_FLAG | CHAR(1) |

**STORE_DEPT**

| STORE_ID | SMALLINT |
|---|---|
| OPER_DEPT_NBR | INTEGER |
| STORE_DEPT_MGR_NAME | CHAR(35) |
| STORE_DEPT_SQFT | SMALLINT |

**STORE_FLOOR_LOCATION**

| FLOOR_LOCATION_ID | INTEGER |
|---|---|
| STORE_ID | SMALLINT |
| OPER_DEPT_NBR | INTEGER |
| FLOOR_LOCATION_DESC | CHAR(25) |
| FLOOR_LOCATION_AISLE | SMALLINT |
| FLOOR_LOCATION_TAG | DECIMAL(16) |
| FLOOR_LOCATION_SQFT | INTEGER |

**OPERATIONAL_DEPT**

| OPER_DEPT_NBR | INTEGER |
|---|---|
| OPER_DEPT_NAME | CHAR(35) |

# MERCHANDISE HIERARCHY

**MERCHANT GROUP**

| MDS_GRP_ID | SMALLINT |
|---|---|
| MDS_GRP_NAME | CHAR(35) |
| MDS_GRP_MGR_NAME | CHAR(35) |

**MERCHANT SUBGROUP**

| MDS_SGRP_ID | INTEGER |
|---|---|
| MDS_GRP_ID | SMALLINT |
| MDS_SGRP_NAME | CHAR(35) |
| MDS_SGRP_MGR_NAME | CHAR(35) |

**DEPARTMENT**

| DEPT_ID | SMALLINT |
|---|---|
| MDS_SGRP_ID | INTEGER |
| MDS_GRP_ID | SMALLINT |
| DEPT_NAME | CHAR(35) |
| ABBR_NAME | CHAR(12) |
| DEPT_TYPE | CHAR(2) |
| MULT_BUYER_FLAG | CHAR(1) |
| SR_BUYER_ID | CHAR(32) |

**CLASS**

| CLASS_ID | SMALLINT |
|---|---|
| DEPT_ID | SMALLINT |
| CLASS_CODE | CHAR(4) |
| CLASS_NAME | CHAR(35) |
| BUYER_ID | CHAR(32) |

**VENDOR**

| VNDR_ID | INTEGER |
|---|---|
| VNDR_NAME | CHAR(30) |
| VNDR_ADDR_1 | CHAR(45) |
| VNDR_ADDR_2 | CHAR(45) |
| VNDR_CITY | CHAR(35) |
| VNDR_COUNTRY | CHAR(3) |
| VNDR_ZIP | CHAR(12) |
| VNDR_CONTACT_NAME | CHAR(35) |
| VNDR_CONTACT_PHONE | DECIMAL(15) |
| VNDR_CONTACT_FAX | DECIMAL(15) |
| VNDR_CONTACT_EMAIL | CHAR(80) |
| VNDR_2nd_PHONE | DECIMAL(15) |
| EDI_FLAG | CHAR(1) |
| EDI_ROUTING_CODE | CHAR(30) |
| EDI_VENDOR_ID | CHAR(12) |

**PRODUCT**

| ITEM_ID | INTEGER |
|---|---|
| VNDR_ID | INTEGER |
| CLASS_ID | SMALLINT |
| DEPT_ID | SMALLINT |
| ITEM_STATUS | CHAR(1) |
| ITEM_DESC | CHAR(50) |
| PRIMARY_ITEM_FLAG | CHAR(1) |
| PRIMARY_ITEM_ID | INTEGER |
| POS_DESC | CHAR(12) |
| CREATE_DATE | TIMESTAMP |
| ORDERABLE_FLAG | CHAR(1) |
| PRIVATE_LABEL_FLAG | CHAR(1) |
| ITEM_STYLE_CODE | INTEGER |
| ITEM_COLOR_CODE | CHAR(3) |
| ITEM_SIZE_CODE | CHAR(5) |
| PRICE_STRAT_CODE | CHAR(1) |
| PRE_PRICED_AMT | DECIMAL(9,2) |
| MIN_RETL_AMT | DECIMAL(9,2) |
| MAX_RETL_AMT | DECIMAL(9,2) |
| STORE_ORD_FLAG | CHAR(1) |
| DEFECT_CODE | CHAR(1) |
| PRIM_DISTB_MODE_CODE | SMALLINT |
| PRICE_REMARK_FLAG | CHAR(1) |
| TKT_TYPE_CODE | CHAR(1) |
| UPC_ON_TKT_CODE | CHAR(1) |
| RETAIL_ON_TKT_FLAG | CHAR(1) |
| HANG_RACK_CODE | CHAR(1) |
| PEG_HOOK_CODE | CHAR(1) |
| DSPL_TRAY_FLAG | CHAR(1) |
| DSPL_CASE_FLAG | CHAR(1) |
| EMP_DISC_FLAG | CHAR(1) |
| QA_TEST_REQD_FLAG | CHAR(1) |
| HAZARD_ITEM_FLAG | CHAR(1) |
| FLAMABLE_CODE | CHAR(1) |
| HAZARD_CODE | CHAR(1) |
| HAZARD_CLASS_CODE | SMALLINT |
| LIQUID_CAPACITY_QTY | INTEGER |
| ACTIVITY_DATE | DATE |
| UPDATE_DATE | DATE |
| CONTROLLED_ITEM_FLAG | CHAR(1) |
| ENVIRONMENT_SENSITIVE_CODE | CHAR(1) |
| RETAIL_TKT_FLAG | CHAR(1) |
| ROYALTY_PERCENT | DECIMAL(5,5) |
| WEIGH_FLAG | CHAR(1) |
| UOM | CHAR(2) |
| SIZE_PER_UNIT_QTY | INTEGER |
| BRAND_NAME | CHAR(35) |
| SELLABLE_FLAG | CHAR(1) |
| X_AXIS_MEASURE | INTEGER |
| Y_AXIS_MEASURE | INTEGER |
| Z_AXIS_MEASURE | INTEGER |

**UPC XREF**

| UPC | DECIMAL(13,0) |
|---|---|
| ITEM_ID | INTEGER |
| UPC_STATUS_FLAG | CHAR(1) |
| UPC_ACTIVITY_DATE | DATE |

**PRICING REMARKS**

| REMARK_ID | INTEGER |
|---|---|
| ITEM_ID | INTEGER |
| REMARK_1 | CHAR(80) |
| REMARK_2 | VARCHAR(80) |
| REMARK_3 | VARCHAR(80) |

**RETAIL PRICE**

| ITEM_ID | INTEGER |
|---|---|
| STORE_ID | SMALLINT |
| EVENT_ID | INTEGER |
| PRICE_AMT | NUMERIC(9,2) |

**EVENT**

| EVENT_ID | INTEGER |
|---|---|
| EVENT_DESC | CHAR(35) |
| EVENT_TYPE | CHAR(1) |
| EVENT_START_DATE | DATE |
| EVENT_END_DATE | DATE |

# TIME HIERARCHY

**YR_DT**

| YR_ID | SMALLINT |
|---|---|
| YR_END-DESCR | CHAR(21) |
| YR_BEG_DT | DATE |
| YR_BEG_JUL_DT | INTEGER |
| YR_END_DT | DATE |
| YR_END_JUL_DT | INTEGER |

**QTR_DT**

| QTR_ID | SMALLINT |
|---|---|
| YR_ID | SMALLINT |
| QTR_END_DESCR | CHAR(21) |
| QTR_BEG_DT | DATE |
| QTR_BEG_JUL_DT | INTEGER |
| QTR_END_DT | DATE |
| QTR_END_JUL_DT | INTEGER |
| YR_QTR_NBR | SMALLINT |
| YR_END_DT | DATE |

**MO_DT**

| MO_ID | SMALLINT |
|---|---|
| QTR_ID | SMALLINT |
| YR_ID | SMALLINT |
| MO_END_DESCR | CHAR(21) |
| MO_BEG_DT | DATE |
| MO_BEG_JUL_DT | INTEGER |
| MO_END_DT | DATE |
| MO_END_JUL_DT | INTEGER |
| QTR_MO_NBR | SMALLINT |
| YR_MO_NBR | SMALLINT |
| QTR_END_DT | DATE |
| YR_END_DT | DATE |
| MO_NAME | CHAR(9) |

**WK_DT**

| WK_END_DT | DATE |
|---|---|
| WK_END_DESC | CHAR(21) |
| WK_END_JUL_DT | INTEGER |
| WK_BEG_DT | DATE |
| WK_BEG_JUL_DT | INTEGER |
| MO_WK_NO | SMALLINT |
| QTR_WK_NO | SMALLINT |
| YR_WK_NO | SMALLINT |
| MO_ID | SMALLINT |
| MO_END_DT | DATE |
| QTR_ID | SMALLINT |
| QTR_END_DT | DATE |
| YR_ID | SMALLINT |
| YR_END_DT | DATE |

**DAY_DT**

| ACCT_DT | TIMESTAMP |
|---|---|
| WK_END_DT | DATE |
| HOLIDAY_ID | INTEGER |
| ACCT_JUL_DT | INTEGER |
| WK_DAY_NBR | SMALLINT |
| MO_DAY_NBR | SMALLINT |
| QTR_DAY_NBR | SMALLINT |
| YR_DAY_NBR | SMALLINT |
| DAY_DESC | CHAR(9) |
| STORE_CLOSED | SMALLINT |

**HOLIDAY**

| HOLIDAY_ID | INTEGER |
|---|---|
| HOLIDAY_DESC | INTEGER |

**HOUR_TIME**

| ACCT_DT | TIMESTAMP |
|---|---|
| HOUR_CODE | INTEGER |
| HOUR_NAME | INTEGER |

# POINT-OF-SALE

## POS_TRANSACTION

| | |
|---|---|
| TRAN_SEQ_NBR | INTEGER |
| REGISTER_NBR | INTEGER |
| TRAN_TIMESTAMP | TIMESTAMP |
| TRAN_TYPE | INTEGER |
| ACCT_DT | TIMESTAMP |
| STORE_ID | SMALLINT |
| OPERATOR_ID | SMALLINT |
| START_TRAN_TIMESTAMP | TIMESTAMP |
| END_TRAN_TIMESTAMP | TIMESTAMP |
| TTL_ITEM_CNT | INTEGER |
| TTL_SALES_AMT | DECIMAL(9,2) |
| TTL_UNITS_QTY | INTEGER |
| TTL_TAX_AMT | DECIMAL(9,2) |
| DISCOUNT_AMT | DECIMAL(9,2) |
| ASSOC_DISCOUNT_AMT | DECIMAL(9,2) |
| TTL_COUPON_AMT | DECIMAL(9,2) |
| TTL_CASH_AMT | DECIMAL(9,2) |
| TTL_CHECK_AMT | DECIMAL(9,2) |
| TTL_CC_AMT | DECIMAL(9,2) |
| TTL_DEBIT_AMT | DECIMAL(9,2) |
| TTL_OTHER_AMT | DECIMAL(9,2) |
| CARD_TYPE | CHAR(2) |
| AUTH_CODE | CHAR(12) |

## DISCOUNT

| | |
|---|---|
| DISCOUNT_TYPE | INTEGER |
| DISCOUNT_DESC | CHAR(25) |
| DISCOUNT_OFF_AMT | DECIMAL(9,2) |
| DISCOUNT_PCT | DECIMAL(5,5) |

## PCS_MERCHANDISE

| | |
|---|---|
| TRAN_SEQ_NBR | INTEGER |
| REGISTER_NBR | INTEGER |
| TRAN_TIMESTAMP | TIMESTAMP |
| TRAN_TYPE | INTEGER |
| ACCT_DT | TIMESTAMP |
| STORE_ID | SMALLINT |
| UPC | DECIMAL(13,0) |
| DISCOUNT_TYPE | DECIMAL(13,0) |
| MDS_TRAN_TYPE | SMALLINT |
| SELL_QTY | INTEGER |
| SELL_RETAIL | DECIMAL(9,2) |
| SELL_COST_AMT | DECIMAL(9,2) |
| DISC_AMT | DECIMAL(9,2) |

## UPC_XREF

| | |
|---|---|
| UPC | DECIMAL(13,0) |
| ITEM_ID | INTEGER |
| UPC_STATUS_FLAG | CHAR(1) |
| UPC_ACTIVITY_DATE | DATE |

## CUSTOMER

| | |
|---|---|
| CUSTOMER_ID | INTEGER |
| CUST_NAME | CHAR(35) |
| CUST_TYPE | SMALLINT |
| CUST_ADDR_1 | CHAR(45) |
| CUST_ADDR_2 | CHAR(45) |
| CUST_CITY | CHAR(32) |
| CUST_COUNTRY | CHAR(3) |
| CUST_ZIPCODE | CHAR(7) |

## FREQ_SHOPPER

| | |
|---|---|
| TRAN_SEQ_NBR | INTEGER |
| REGISTER_NBR | INTEGER |
| TRAN_TIMESTAMP | TIMESTAMP |
| TRAN_TYPE | INTEGER |
| ACCT_DT | TIMESTAMP |
| STORE_ID | SMALLINT |
| CUSTOMER_ID | INTEGER |
| FS_REBATE_AMT | DECIMAL(9,2) |
| FS_AUTH_CODE | CHAR(12) |
| FS_DISC_PCT | DECIMAL(5,5) |

## CUSTOMER_TENDER_XREF

| | |
|---|---|
| CUST_CARD_NBR | INTEGER |
| CUST_CARD_EXP_DATE | DATE |
| CUSTOMER_ID | INTEGER |
| CUST_CARD_TYPE | CHAR(1) |
| SHOPPING_VELOCITY | INTEGER |
| FIRST_SHOP_TIMESTAMP | TIMESTAMP |
| LAST_SHOP_TIMESTAMP | TIMESTAMP |
| CUST_CARD_NAME | CHAR(35) |
| TTL_PURCH_AMT | DECIMAL(9,5) |
| TTL_DAILY_AMT | DECIMAL(9,2) |
| SECURITY_CODE | CHAR(12) |

## TENDER

| | |
|---|---|
| TRAN_SEQ_NBR | INTEGER |
| REGISTER_NBR | INTEGER |
| TRAN_TIMESTAMP | TIMESTAMP |
| TRAN_TYPE | INTEGER |
| ACCT_DT | TIMESTAMP |
| STORE_ID | SMALLINT |
| TENDER_TYPE | SMALLINT |
| TENDER_AUTH_CODE | CHAR(12) |

## COUPON

| | |
|---|---|
| TRAN_SEQ_NBR | INTEGER |
| REGISTER_NBR | INTEGER |
| TRAN_TIMESTAMP | TIMESTAMP |
| TRAN_TYPE | INTEGER |
| ACCT_DT | TIMESTAMP |
| STORE_ID | SMALLINT |
| COUPON_BARCODE | DECIMAL(16) |
| FACE_VALUE_AMT | DECIMAL(9,2) |
| REDEMPTION_CODE | INTEGER |
| REDEMPTION_VALUE_AMT | DECIMAL(9,2) |

## CASH

| | |
|---|---|
| TRAN_SEQ_NBR | INTEGER |
| REGISTER_NBR | INTEGER |
| TRAN_TIMESTAMP | TIMESTAMP |
| TRAN_TYPE | INTEGER |
| ACCT_DT | TIMESTAMP |
| STORE_ID | SMALLINT |
| CURRENCY_TYPE | SMALLINT |
| CURRENCY_AMT | DECIMAL(12,2) |
| CURRENCY_EXCH_RATE | DECIMAL(9,5) |

## OTHER_TENDER

| | |
|---|---|
| TRAN_SEQ_NBR | INTEGER |
| REGISTER_NBR | INTEGER |
| TRAN_TIMESTAMP | TIMESTAMP |
| TRAN_TYPE | INTEGER |
| ACCT_DT | TIMESTAMP |
| STORE_ID | SMALLINT |
| TENDER_AMT | DECIMAL(9,2) |
| TENDER_KEY | CHAR(40) |
| TENDER_OTHER | VARCHAR(200) |

## CREDIT_CARD

| | |
|---|---|
| TRAN_SEQ_NBR | INTEGER |
| REGISTER_NBR | INTEGER |
| TRAN_TIMESTAMP | TIMESTAMP |
| TRAN_TYPE | INTEGER |
| ACCT_DT | TIMESTAMP |
| STORE_ID | SMALLINT |
| CUST_CARD_NBR | INTEGER |
| CUST_CARD_EXP_DATE | DATE |
| CC_AMT | DECIMAL(9,2) |
| CC_AUTH_CODE | CHAR(12) |

# INVENTORY

### STORE_FLOOR_LOCATION

| | |
|---|---|
| FLOOR_LOCATION_ID | INTEGER |
| STORE_ID | SMALLINT |
| OPER_DEPT_NBR | INTEGER |
| FLOOR_LOCATION_DESC | CHAR(25) |
| FLOOR_LOCATION_AISLE | SMALLINT |
| FLOOR_LOCATION_TAG | DECIMAL(16) |
| FLOOR_LOCATION_SQFT | INTEGER |

### INVENTORY_ADJUSTMENT_TYPE

| | |
|---|---|
| ADJUSTMENT_CODE | INTEGER |
| ADJUSTMENT_DESC | CHAR(18) |

### CURRENT_INVENTORY

| | |
|---|---|
| ITEM_ID | INTEGER |
| FLOOR_LOCATION_ID | INTEGER |
| STORE_ID | SMALLINT |
| OPER_DEPT_NBR | INTEGER |
| ON_ORDER | INTEGER |
| IN_WHS_QTY | INTEGER |
| IN_TRANSIT_QTY | INTEGER |
| ON_HAND | INTEGER |
| EST_DELIVERY_DATE | DATE |
| LAST_POS_DATE | DATETIME |
| LAST_RECEIPT_DATE | DATETIME |
| CURRENT_ACTIVITY_SEQ_NBR | INTEGER |
| MAX_SHELF_QTY | INTEGER |
| MIN_PRESENTATION_QTY | INTEGER |
| SAFETY_SHOCK_QTY | INTEGER |
| MULTI_LOCATION_FLAG | CHAR(1) |
| MIN_ORDER_QTY | INTEGER |
| MAX_ORDER_QTY | INTEGER |
| SELLING_VELOCITY_CODE | SMALLINT |
| REPLENISHMENT_PROFILE_CODE | INTEGER |

### INVENTORY_ADJ_TRANS

| | |
|---|---|
| ACTIVITY_SEQUENCE_NBR | INTEGER |
| ADJUSTMENT_CODE | INTEGER |
| ITEM_ID | INTEGER |
| FLOOR_LOCATION_ID | INTEGER |
| ACCT_DT | TIMESTAMP |
| STORE_ID | SMALLINT |
| OPER_DEPT_NBR | INTEGER |
| ADJUSTMENT_QTY | INTEGER |
| ON_HAND_QTY | INTEGER |
| OLD_RETAIL_AMT | DECIMAL(9,2) |
| NEW_RETAIL_AMT | DECIMAL(9,2) |
| OLD_COST_AMT | DECIMAL(9,4) |
| NEW_COST_AMT | DECIMAL(9,4) |
| ADJUSTMENT_SOURCE | CHAR(12) |
| ADJUSTMENT_USER_ID | CHAR(30) |

### INVENTORY_HISTORY

| | |
|---|---|
| ITEM_ID | INTEGER |
| FLOOR_LOCATION_ID | INTEGER |
| STORE_ID | SMALLINT |
| ACCT_DT | TIMESTAMP |
| OPER_DEPT_NBR | INTEGER |
| INVENTORY_TYPE | SMALLINT |
| EOP_ON_ORDER_QTY | INTEGER |
| EOP_IN_WHS_QTY | INTEGER |
| EOP_IN_TRANSIT_QTY | INTEGER |
| EOP_ON_HAND_QTY | INTEGER |
| EOP_DATE | DATE |
| NEXT_ACTIVITY_SEQ_NBR | INTEGER |
| NEXT_ACTIVITY_DATE | DATE |

Note:
EOP=End of Period

# PLANNED INVENTORY

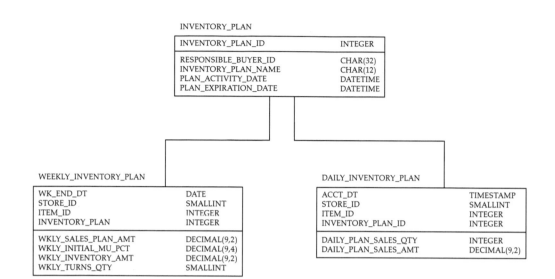

INVENTORY_PLAN

| INVENTORY_PLAN_ID | INTEGER |
|---|---|
| RESPONSIBLE_BUYER_ID | CHAR(32) |
| INVENTORY_PLAN_NAME | CHAR(12) |
| PLAN_ACTIVITY_DATE | DATETIME |
| PLAN_EXPIRATION_DATE | DATETIME |

WEEKLY_INVENTORY_PLAN

| WK_END_DT | DATE |
|---|---|
| STORE_ID | SMALLINT |
| ITEM_ID | INTEGER |
| INVENTORY_PLAN | INTEGER |
| WKLY_SALES_PLAN_AMT | DECIMAL(9,2) |
| WKLY_INITIAL_MU_PCT | DECIMAL(9,4) |
| WKLY_INVENTORY_AMT | DECIMAL(9,2) |
| WKLY_TURNS_QTY | SMALLINT |

DAILY_INVENTORY_PLAN

| ACCT_DT | TIMESTAMP |
|---|---|
| STORE_ID | SMALLINT |
| ITEM_ID | INTEGER |
| INVENTORY_PLAN_ID | INTEGER |
| DAILY_PLAN_SALES_QTY | INTEGER |
| DAILY_PLAN_SALES_AMT | DECIMAL(9,2) |

# MARKDOWN MARKUP

MARKDOWN_TYPE_DESC

| MD_TYPE | INTEGER |
|---|---|
| MD_DESC | CHAR(30) |
| MD_MU_FLAG | CHAR(1) |

MARKDOWNS

| STORE_ID | SMALLINT |
|---|---|
| ACCT_DT | TIMESTAMP |
| ITEM_ID | INTEGER |
| MD_TYPE | CHAR(1) |
| MARKDOWN_UNIT_QTY | INTEGER |
| MARKDOWN_AMT | DECIMAL(9,2) |

# ORDERS

**VENDOR**

| VNDR_ID | INTEGER |
|---|---|
| VNDR_NAME | CHAR(30) |
| VNDR_ADDR_1 | CHAR(45) |
| VNDR_ADDR_2 | CHAR(45) |
| VNDR_CITY | CHAR(35) |
| VNDR_COUNTRY | CHAR(3) |
| VNDR_ZIP | CHAR(12) |
| VNDR_CONTACT_NAME | CHAR(35) |
| VNDR_CONTACT_PHONE | DECIMAL(15) |
| VNDR_CONTACT_FAX | DECIMAL(15) |
| VNDR_CONTACT_EMAIL | CHAR(80) |
| VNDR_CONTACT_2nd_PHONE | DECIMAL(15) |
| EDI_FLAG | CHAR(1) |
| EDI_ROUTING_CODE | CHAR(30) |

**PURCHASE ORDER**

| PO_NBR | INTEGER |
|---|---|
| VNDR_ID | INTEGER |
| ACCT_DT | TIMESTAMP |
| PO_STATUS | CHAR(1) |
| SHIP_DATE | DATE |
| CANCEL_DATE | DATE |
| ENTRY_DATE | DATE |
| APPROVAL_DATE | DATE |
| APPROVER_NAME | CHAR(35) |
| TERMS_CODE | CHAR(15) |
| SHIPPING_CODE | INTEGER |
| ISSUE_DATE | DATE |
| FIRST_FILL_DATE | DATE |
| LAST_FILL_DATE | DATE |
| SUBTOTAL_AMT | DECIMAL(9,2) |
| TOTAL_DISC_AMT | DECIMAL(9,2) |
| TOTAL_AMT | DECIMAL(9,2) |
| TOTAL_UNITS | INTEGER |
| TOTAL_UNITS_RECEIVED | INTEGER |
| EDI_XFER_FLAG | CHAR(1) |

**PURCHASE_ORDER_LINE**

| PO_LINE_NBR | INTEGER |
|---|---|
| ITEM_ID | INTEGER |
| PO_NBR | INTEGER |
| VNDR_ID | INTEGER |
| ACCT_DT | TIMESTAMP |
| PO_LINE_STATUS | CHAR(1) |
| VENDOR_REF_NBR | CHAR(20) |
| ORDER_QTY | INTEGER |
| UNIT_COST_AMT | DECIMAL(9,5) |
| SUBTOTAL_COST_AMT | DECIMAL(9,2) |
| DISC_PCT | DECIMAL(5,5) |
| TOTAL_COST_AMT | DECIMAL(9,2) |
| UNITS_RECEIVED | INTEGER |

**STORE_PO_DISTRIBUTION**

| STORE_ID | SMALLINT |
|---|---|
| PO_LINE_NBR | INTEGER |
| ITEM_ID | INTEGER |
| PO_NBR | INTEGER |
| VNDR_ID | INTEGER |
| ACCT_DT | TIMESTAMP |
| ALLOCATED_UNITS | INTEGER |
| STORE_RECEIVED_UNITS | INTEGER |
| 1st_STORE_RECEIPT_DATE | DATE |
| LAST_STORE_RECEIPT_DATE | DATE |

# MERCHANDISE SUMMARIES

### DAILY_STORE_ITEM_SALES

| | |
|---|---|
| STORE_ID | SMALLINT |
| ITEM_ID | INTEGER |
| ACCT_DT | TIMESTAMP |
| EVENT_ID | INTEGER |
| DAILY_SALES_UNIT_QTY | INTEGER |
| DAILY_SALES_AMT | DECIMAL(9,4) |
| SELL_RETAIL_AMT | DECIMAL(9,2) |
| DAILY_COST_AMT | DECIMAL(9,4) |

### WEEKLY_REGION_ITEM_SALES

| | |
|---|---|
| EVENT_ID | INTEGER |
| ITEM_ID | INTEGER |
| WK_END_DT | DATE |
| REGION_ID | INTEGER |
| DIVISION_ID | INTEGER |
| WEEKLY_SALES_UNIT_QTY | INTEGER |
| WEEKLY_SALES_AMT | DECIMAL(9,2) |
| WEEKLY_AVG_RETAIL_AMT | DECIMAL(7,2) |
| WEEKLY_COST_AMT | DECIMAL(7,4) |
| EOW_OH_QTY | INTEGER |
| EOW_OO_QTY | INTEGER |
| REGION_IN_STOCK_PCT | DECIMAL(5,4) |

### DAILY_STORE_ITEM_RECEIPTS

| | |
|---|---|
| STORE_ID | SMALLINT |
| ITEM_ID | INTEGER |
| ACCT_DT | TIMESTAMP |
| DAILY_RECEIPT_QTY | INTEGER |
| DAILY_RECEIPT_RETAIL_AMT | DECIMAL(9,2) |
| DAILY_RECEIPT_COST_AMT | DECIMAL(9,4) |

### WEEKLY_STORE_ITEM_SALES

| | |
|---|---|
| EVENT_ID | INTEGER |
| STORE_ID | SMALLINT |
| ITEM_ID | INTEGER |
| WK_END_DT | DATE |
| WEEKLY_SALES_UNIT_QTY | INTEGER |
| WEEKLY_SALES_AMT | DECIMAL(9,2) |
| EOW_RETAIL_AMT | DECIMAL(9,2) |
| WEEKLY_COST_AMT | DECIMAL(9,4) |
| EOW_OH_QTY | INTEGER |
| EOW_OO_QTY | INTEGER |
| OUT_OF_STOCK_FLAG | CHAR(1) |

### WEEKLY_ITEM_SALES

| | |
|---|---|
| ITEM_ID | INTEGER |
| WK_END_DT | DATE |
| DIVISION_ID | INTEGER |
| EVENT_ID | INTEGER |
| WEEKLY_SALES_UNIT_QTY | INTEGER |
| WEEKLY_SALES_AMT | DECIMAL(9,2) |
| WEEKLY_COST_AMT | DECIMAL(9,4) |
| EOW_OH_QTY | INTEGER |
| EOW_OO_QTY | INTEGER |
| DIV_IN_STOCK_PCT | DECIMAL(5,4) |

### DAILY_STORE_ITEM_ORDERS

| | |
|---|---|
| ITEM_ID | INTEGER |
| STORE_ID | SMALLINT |
| ACCT_DT | TIMESTAMP |
| OO_STATUS_CODE | INTEGER |
| DAILY_OO_QTY | INTEGER |
| DAILY_OO_AMT | INTEGER |
| PLAN_RECEIPT_DATE | DATE |

### MONTHLY_STORE_ITEM_SALES

| | |
|---|---|
| STORE_ID | SMALLINT |
| ITEM_ID | INTEGER |
| EVENT_ID | INTEGER |
| MO_ID | SMALLINT |
| MONTHLY_SALES_UNIT_QTY | INTEGER |
| MONTHLY_SALES_AMT | INTEGER |
| MONTLY_AVG_RETAIL_AMT | DECIMAL(9,2) |
| MONTHLY_COST_AMT | DECIMAL(9,4) |
| EOM_OH_QTY | INTEGER |

Note:
EOW=End of Week
OO=On Order
OH=On Hand

HOURLY_STORE_SALES

| | |
|---|---|
| STORE_ID | SMALLINT |
| ACCT_DT | TIMESTAMP |
| HOUR_CODE | INTEGER |
| THTY_GROSS_SALES_AMT | DECIMAL(9,2) |
| THTY_CUMULATIVE_DAILY_SALES_AMT | DECIMAL(9,2) |
| THLY_GROSS_SALES_AMT | DECIMAL(9,2) |
| THLY_CUMULATIVE_DAILY_SALES_AMT | DECIMAL(9,2) |
| THTY_CUST_TXN_CNT | INTEGER |
| THLY_CUST_TXN_CNT | INTEGER |
| THTY_CASH_AMT | DECIMAL(9,2) |
| THLY_CASH_AMT | DECIMAL(9,2) |
| THTY_DC_AMT | DECIMAL(9,2) |
| THLY_DC_AMT | DECIMAL(9,2) |
| THTY_CC_AMT | DECIMAL(9,2) |
| THLY_CC_AMT | DECIMAL(9,2) |
| THTY_OTHER_AMT | DECIMAL(9,2) |
| THLY_OTHER_AMT | DECIMAL(9,2) |

HOURLY_DEPT_STORE_SALES

| | |
|---|---|
| STORE_ID | SMALLINT |
| OPER_DEPT_NBR | INTEGER |
| ACCT_DT | TIMESTAMP |
| HOUR_CODE | INTEGER |
| THTY_GROSS_SALES_AMT | DECIMAL(9,2) |
| THLY_GROSS_SALES_AMT | DECIMAL(9,2) |
| THTY_CUST_TXN_CNT | INTEGER |
| THLY_CUST_TXN_CNT | INTEGER |
| THTY_CASH_AMT | DECIMAL(9,2) |
| THLY_CASH_AMT | DECIMAL(9,2) |
| THTY_DC_AMT | DECIMAL(9,2) |
| THLY_DC_AMT | DECIMAL(9,2) |
| THTY_CC_AMT | DECIMAL(9,2) |
| THLY_CC_AMT | DECIMAL(9,2) |
| THTY_OTHER_AMT | DECIMAL(9,2) |
| THLY_OTHER_AMT | DECIMAL(9,2) |

NOTE:
THLY=This Hour Last Year
THTY=This Hour This Year
TDLY=This Day Last Year
TDTY=This Day This Year
DC=Discount
CC=Credit Card

DAILY_STORE_SALES

| | |
|---|---|
| STORE_ID | SMALLINT |
| ACCT_DT | TIMESTAMP |
| TDTY_GROSS_SALES_AMT | DECIMAL(15,2) |
| TDLY_GROSS_SALES_AMT | DECIMAL(15,2) |
| TDTY_GROSS_PROFIT_AMT | DECIMAL(15,2) |
| TDLY_GROSS_PROFIT_AMT | DECIMAL(15,2) |
| TDTY_MARKDOWN_AMT | DECIMAL(15,2) |
| TDLY_MARKDOWN_AMT | DECIMAL(15,2) |
| TDTY_WAGES_AMT | DECIMAL(15,2) |
| TDLY_WAGES_AMT | DECIMAL(15,2) |
| TDTY_CUST_TXN_CNT | INTEGER |
| TDLY_CUST_TXN_CNT | INTEGER |
| TDTY_CASH_AMT | DECIMAL(15,2) |
| TDLY_CASH_AMT | DECIMAL(15,2) |
| TDTY_DC_AMT | DECIMAL(15,2) |
| TDLY_DC_AMT | DECIMAL(15,2) |
| TDTY_CC_AMT | DECIMAL(15,2) |
| TDLY_CC_AMT | DECIMAL(15,2) |
| TDTY_OTHER_AMT | DECIMAL(15,2) |
| TDLY_OTHER_AMT | DECIMAL(15,2) |
| TDTY_CNTL_EXPENSE_AMT | DECIMAL(15,2) |
| TDLY_CNTL_EXPENSE_AMT | DECIMAL(15,2) |
| TDTY_UNCNTL_EXPENSE_AMT | DECIMAL(15,2) |
| TDLY_UNCNTL_EXPENSE_AMT | DECIMAL(15,2) |

DAILY_REGION_SALES

| | |
|---|---|
| REGION_ID | SMALLINT |
| DIVISION_ID | INTEGER |
| ACCT_DT | TIMESTAMP |
| TDTY_GROSS_SALES_AMT | DECIMAL(15,2) |
| TDLY_GROSS_SALES_AMT | DECIMAL(15,2) |
| TDTY_GROSS_PROFIT_AMT | DECIMAL(15,2) |
| TDLY_GROSS_PROFIT_AMT | DECIMAL(15,2) |
| TDTY_MARKDOWN_AMT | DECIMAL(15,2) |
| TDLY_MARKDOWN_AMT | DECIMAL(15,2) |
| TDTY_WAGES_AMT | DECIMAL(15,2) |
| TDLY_WAGES_AMT | DECIMAL(15,2) |
| TDTY_CUST_TXN_CNT | INTEGER |
| TDLY_CUST_TXN_CNT | INTEGER |
| TDTY_CASH_AMT | DECIMAL(15,2) |
| TDLY_CASH_AMT | DECIMAL(15,2) |
| TDTY_DC_AMT | DECIMAL(15,2) |
| TDLY_DC_AMT | DECIMAL(15,2) |
| TDTY_CC_AMT | DECIMAL(15,2) |
| TDLY_CC_AMT | DECIMAL(15,2) |
| TDTY_OTHER_AMT | DECIMAL(15,2) |
| TDLY_OTHER_AMT | DECIMAL(15,2) |
| TDTY_CNTL_EXPENSE_AMT | DECIMAL(15,2) |
| TDLY_CNTL_EXPENSE_AMT | DECIMAL(15,2) |
| TDTY_UNCNTL_EXPENSE_AMT | DECIMAL(15,2) |
| TDLY_UNCNTL_EXPENSE_AMT | DECIMAL(15,2) |

DAILY_DEPT_STORE_SALES

| | |
|---|---|
| STORE_ID | SMALLINT |
| OPER_DEPT_NBR | INTEGER |
| ACCT_DT | TIMESTAMP |
| TDTY_GROSS_SALES_AMT | DECIMAL(15,2) |
| TDLY_GROSS_SALES_AMT | DECIMAL(15,2) |
| TDTY_GROSS_PROFIT_AMT | DECIMAL(15,2) |
| TDLY_GROSS_PROFIT_AMT | DECIMAL(15,2) |
| TDTY_MARKDOWN_AMT | DECIMAL(15,2) |
| TDLY_MARKDOWN_AMT | DECIMAL(15,2) |
| TDTY_WAGES_AMT | DECIMAL(15,2) |
| TDLY_WAGES_AMT | DECIMAL(15,2) |
| TDTY_CUST_TXN_CNT | INTEGER |
| TDLY_CUST_TXN_CNT | INTEGER |
| TDTY_CASH_AMT | DECIMAL(15,2) |
| TDLY_CASH_AMT | DECIMAL(15,2) |
| TDTY_DC_AMT | DECIMAL(15,2) |
| TDLY_DC_AMT | DECIMAL(15,2) |
| TDTY_CC_AMT | DECIMAL(15,2) |
| TDLY_CC_AMT | DECIMAL(15,2) |
| TDTY_OTHER_AMT | DECIMAL(15,2) |
| TDLY_OTHER_AMT | DECIMAL(15,2) |

DAILY_DEPT_REGION_SALES

| | |
|---|---|
| REGION_ID | INTEGER |
| DIVISION_ID | INTEGER |
| OPER_DEPT_NBR | INTEGER |
| ACCT_DT | TIMESTAMP |
| TDTY_GROSS_SALES_AMT | DECIMAL(15,2) |
| TDLY_GROSS_SALES_AMT | DECIMAL(15,2) |
| TDTY_GROSS_PROFIT_AMT | DECIMAL(15,2) |
| TDLY_GROSS_PROFIT_AMT | DECIMAL(15,2) |
| TDTY_MARKDOWN_AMT | DECIMAL(15,2) |
| TDLY_MARKDOWN_AMT | DECIMAL(15,2) |
| TDTY_WAGES_AMT | DECIMAL(15,2) |
| TDLY_WAGES_AMT | DECIMAL(15,2) |
| TDTY_CUST_TXN_CNT | INTEGER |
| TDLY_CUST_TXN_CNT | INTEGER |
| TDTY_CASH_AMT | DECIMAL(15,2) |
| TDLY_CASH_AMT | DECIMAL(15,2) |
| TDTY_DC_AMT | DECIMAL(15,2) |
| TDLY_DC_AMT | DECIMAL(15,2) |
| TDTY_CC_AMT | DECIMAL(15,2) |
| TDLY_CC_AMT | DECIMAL(15,2) |
| TDTY_OTHER_AMT | DECIMAL(15,2) |
| TDLY_OTHER_AMT | DECIMAL(15,2) |

**WEEKLY_STORE_SALES**

| | |
|---|---|
| STORE_ID | SMALLINT |
| WK_END_DT | DATE |
| TDTY_GROSS_SALES_AMT | DECIMAL(15,2) |
| TDLY_GROSS_SALES_AMT | DECIMAL(15,2) |
| TDTY_GROSS_PROFIT_AMT | DECIMAL(15,2) |
| TDLY_GROSS_PROFIT_AMT | DECIMAL(15,2) |
| TDTY_MARKDOWN_AMT | DECIMAL(15,2) |
| TDLY_MARKDOWN_AMT | DECIMAL(15,2) |
| TDTY_WAGES_AMT | DECIMAL(15,2) |
| TDLY_WAGES_AMT | DECIMAL(15,2) |
| TDTY_CUST_TXN_CNT | INTEGER |
| TDLY_CUST_TXN_CNT | INTEGER |
| TDTY_CASH_AMT | DECIMAL(15,2) |
| TDLY_CASH_AMT | DECIMAL(15,2) |
| TDTY_DC_AMT | DECIMAL(15,2) |
| TDLY_DC_AMT | DECIMAL(15,2) |
| TDTY_CC_AMT | DECIMAL(15,2) |
| TDLY_CC_AMT | DECIMAL(15,2) |
| TDTY_OTHER_AMT | DECIMAL(15,2) |
| TDLY_OTHER_AMT | DECIMAL(15,2) |
| TDTY_CNTL_EXPENSE_AMT | DECIMAL(15,2) |
| TDLY_CNTL_EXPENSE_AMT | DECIMAL(15,2) |
| TDTY_UNCNTL_EXPENSE_AMT | DECIMAL(15,2) |
| TDLY_UNCNTL_EXPENSE_AMT | DECIMAL(15,2) |

**WEEKLY_REGION_SALES**

| | |
|---|---|
| REGION_ID | INTEGER |
| DIVISION_ID | INTEGER |
| WK_END_DT | DATE |
| TDTY_GROSS_SALES_AMT | DECIMAL(15,2) |
| TDLY_GROSS_SALES_AMT | DECIMAL(15,2) |
| TDTY_GROSS_PROFIT_AMT | DECIMAL(15,2) |
| TDLY_GROSS_PROFIT_AMT | DECIMAL(15,2) |
| TDTY_MARKDOWN_AMT | DECIMAL(15,2) |
| TDLY_MARKDOWN_AMT | DECIMAL(15,2) |
| TDTY_WAGES_AMT | DECIMAL(15,2) |
| TDLY_WAGES_AMT | DECIMAL(15,2) |
| TDTY_CUST_TXN_CNT | INTEGER |
| TDLY_CUST_TXN_CNT | INTEGER |
| TDTY_CASH_AMT | DECIMAL(15,2) |
| TDLY_CASH_AMT | DECIMAL(15,2) |
| TDTY_DC_AMT | DECIMAL(15,2) |
| TDLY_DC_AMT | DECIMAL(15,2) |
| TDTY_CC_AMT | DECIMAL(15,2) |
| TDLY_CC_AMT | DECIMAL(15,2) |
| TDTY_OTHER_AMT | DECIMAL(15,2) |
| TDLY_OTHER_AMT | DECIMAL(15,2) |
| TDTY_CNTL_EXPENSE_AMT | DECIMAL(15,2) |
| TDLY_CNTL_EXPENSE_AMT | DECIMAL(15,2) |
| TDTY_UNCNTL_EXPENSE_AMT | DECIMAL(15,2) |
| TDLY_UNCNTL_EXPENSE_AMT | DECIMAL(15,2) |

**WEEKLY_DEPT_STORE_SALES**

| | |
|---|---|
| STORE_ID | SMALLINT |
| OPER_DEPT_NBR | INTEGER |
| WK_END_DT | DATE |
| TDTY_GROSS_SALES_AMT | DECIMAL(15,2) |
| TDLY_GROSS_SALES_AMT | DECIMAL(15,2) |
| TDTY_GROSS_PROFIT_AMT | DECIMAL(15,2) |
| TDLY_GROSS_PROFIT_AMT | DECIMAL(15,2) |
| TDTY_MARKDOWN_AMT | DECIMAL(15,2) |
| TDLY_MARKDOWN_AMT | DECIMAL(15,2) |
| TDTY_WAGES_AMT | DECIMAL(15,2) |
| TDLY_WAGES_AMT | DECIMAL(15,2) |
| TDTY_CUST_TXN_CNT | INTEGER |
| TDLY_CUST_TXN_CNT | INTEGER |
| TDTY_CASH_AMT | DECIMAL(15,2) |
| TDLY_CASH_AMT | DECIMAL(15,2) |
| TDTY_DC_AMT | DECIMAL(15,2) |
| TDLY_DC_AMT | DECIMAL(15,2) |
| TDTY_CC_AMT | DECIMAL(15,2) |
| TDLY_CC_AMT | DECIMAL(15,2) |
| TDTY_OTHER_AMT | DECIMAL(15,2) |
| TDLY_OTHER_AMT | DECIMAL(15,2) |

**WEEKLY_DEPT_REGION_SALES**

| | |
|---|---|
| REGION_ID | INTEGER |
| DIVISION_ID | INTEGER |
| OPER_DEPT_NBR | INTEGER |
| WK_END_DT | DATE |
| TDTY_GROSS_SALES_AMT | DECIMAL(15,2) |
| TDLY_GROSS_SALES_AMT | DECIMAL(15,2) |
| TDTY_GROSS_PROFIT_AMT | DECIMAL(15,2) |
| TDLY_GROSS_PROFIT_AMT | DECIMAL(15,2) |
| TDTY_MARKDOWN_AMT | DECIMAL(15,2) |
| TDLY_MARKDOWN_AMT | DECIMAL(15,2) |
| TDTY_WAGES_AMT | DECIMAL(15,2) |
| TDLY_WAGES_AMT | DECIMAL(15,2) |
| TDTY_CUST_TXN_CNT | INTEGER |
| TDLY_CUST_TXN_CNT | INTEGER |
| TDTY_CASH_AMT | DECIMAL(15,2) |
| TDLY_CASH_AMT | DECIMAL(15,2) |
| TDTY_DC_AMT | DECIMAL(15,2) |
| TDLY_DC_AMT | DECIMAL(15,2) |
| TDTY_CC_AMT | DECIMAL(15,2) |
| TDLY_CC_AMT | DECIMAL(15,2) |
| TDTY_OTHER_AMT | DECIMAL(15,2) |
| TDLY_OTHER_AMT | DECIMAL(15,2) |

MONTHLY_STORE_SALES

| | |
|---|---|
| STORE_ID | SMALLINT |
| MO_ID | SMALLINT |
| TDTY_GROSS_SALES_AMT | DECIMAL(15,2) |
| TDLY_GROSS_SALES_AMT | DECIMAL(15,2) |
| TDTY_GROSS_PROFIT_AMT | DECIMAL(15,2) |
| TDLY_GROSS_PROFIT_AMT | DECIMAL(15,2) |
| TDTY_MARKDOWN_AMT | DECIMAL(15,2) |
| TDLY_MARKDOWN_AMT | DECIMAL(15,2) |
| TDTY_WAGES_AMT | DECIMAL(15,2) |
| TDLY_WAGES_AMT | DECIMAL(15,2) |
| TDTY_CUST_TXN_CNT | INTEGER |
| TDLY_CUST_TXN_CNT | INTEGER |
| TDTY_CASH_AMT | DECIMAL(15,2) |
| TDLY_CASH_AMT | DECIMAL(15,2) |
| TDTY_DC_AMT | DECIMAL(15,2) |
| TDLY_DC_AMT | DECIMAL(15,2) |
| TDTY_CC_AMT | DECIMAL(15,2) |
| TDLY_CC_AMT | DECIMAL(15,2) |
| TDTY_OTHER_AMT | DECIMAL(15,2) |
| TDLY_OTHER_AMT | DECIMAL(15,2) |
| TDTY_CNTL_EXPENSE_AMT | DECIMAL(15,2) |
| TDLY_CNTL_EXPENSE_AMT | DECIMAL(15,2) |
| TDTY_UNCNTL_EXPENSE_AMT | DECIMAL(15,2) |
| TDLY_UNCNTL_EXPENSE_AMT | DECIMAL(15,2) |

MONTLY_REGION_SALES

| | |
|---|---|
| REGION_ID | INTEGER |
| DIVISION_ID | INTEGER |
| MO_ID | SMALLINT |
| TDTY_GROSS_SALES_AMT | DECIMAL(15,2) |
| TDLY_GROSS_SALES_AMT | DECIMAL(15,2) |
| TDTY_GROSS_PROFIT_AMT | DECIMAL(15,2) |
| TDLY_GROSS_PROFIT_AMT | DECIMAL(15,2) |
| TDTY_MARKDOWN_AMT | DECIMAL(15,2) |
| TDLY_MARKDOWN_AMT | DECIMAL(15,2) |
| TDTY_WAGES_AMT | DECIMAL(15,2) |
| TDLY_WAGES_AMT | DECIMAL(15,2) |
| TDTY_CUST_TXN_CNT | INTEGER |
| TDLY_CUST_TXN_CNT | INTEGER |
| TDTY_CASH_AMT | DECIMAL(15,2) |
| TDLY_CASH_AMT | DECIMAL(15,2) |
| TDTY_DC_AMT | DECIMAL(15,2) |
| TDLY_DC_AMT | DECIMAL(15,2) |
| TDTY_CC_AMT | DECIMAL(15,2) |
| TDLY_CC_AMT | DECIMAL(15,2) |
| TDTY_OTHER_AMT | DECIMAL(15,2) |
| TDLY_OTHER_AMT | DECIMAL(15,2) |
| TDTY_CNTL_EXPENSE_AMT | DECIMAL(15,2) |
| TDLY_CNTL_EXPENSE_AMT | DECIMAL(15,2) |
| TDTY_UNCNTL_EXPENSE_AMT | DECIMAL(15,2) |
| TDLY_UNCNTL_EXPENSE_AMT | DECIMAL(15,2) |

MONTLY_DEPT_STORE_SALES

| | |
|---|---|
| STORE_ID | SMALLINT |
| OPER_DEPT_NBR | INTEGER |
| MO_ID | SMALLINT |
| TDTY_GROSS_SALES_AMT | DECIMAL(15,2) |
| TDLY_GROSS_SALES_AMT | DECIMAL(15,2) |
| TDTY_GROSS_PROFIT_AMT | DECIMAL(15,2) |
| TDLY_GROSS_PROFIT_AMT | DECIMAL(15,2) |
| TDTY_MARKDOWN_AMT | DECIMAL(15,2) |
| TDLY_MARKDOWN_AMT | DECIMAL(15,2) |
| TDTY_WAGES_AMT | DECIMAL(15,2) |
| TDLY_WAGES_AMT | DECIMAL(15,2) |
| TDTY_CUST_TXN_CNT | INTEGER |
| TDLY_CUST_TXN_CNT | INTEGER |
| TDTY_CASH_AMT | DECIMAL(15,2) |
| TDLY_CASH_AMT | DECIMAL(15,2) |
| TDTY_DC_AMT | DECIMAL(15,2) |
| TDLY_DC_AMT | DECIMAL(15,2) |
| TDTY_CC_AMT | DECIMAL(15,2) |
| TDLY_CC_AMT | DECIMAL(15,2) |
| TDTY_OTHER_AMT | DECIMAL(15,2) |
| TDLY_OTHER_AMT | DECIMAL(15,2) |

MONTLY_DEPT_REGION_SALES

| | |
|---|---|
| REGION_ID | INTEGER |
| DIVISION_ID | INTEGER |
| OPER_DEPT_NBR | INTEGER |
| MO_ID | SMALLINT |
| TDTY_GROSS_SALES_AMT | DECIMAL(15,2) |
| TDLY_GROSS_SALES_AMT | DECIMAL(15,2) |
| TDTY_GROSS_PROFIT_AMT | DECIMAL(15,2) |
| TDLY_GROSS_PROFIT_AMT | DECIMAL(15,2) |
| TDTY_MARKDOWN_AMT | DECIMAL(15,2) |
| TDLY_MARKDOWN_AMT | DECIMAL(15,2) |
| TDTY_WAGES_AMT | DECIMAL(15,2) |
| TDLY_WAGES_AMT | DECIMAL(15,2) |
| TDTY_CUST_TXN_CNT | INTEGER |
| TDLY_CUST_TXN_CNT | INTEGER |
| TDTY_CASH_AMT | DECIMAL(15,2) |
| TDLY_CASH_AMT | DECIMAL(15,2) |
| TDTY_DC_AMT | DECIMAL(15,2) |
| TDLY_DC_AMT | DECIMAL(15,2) |
| TDTY_CC_AMT | DECIMAL(15,2) |
| TDLY_CC_AMT | DECIMAL(15,2) |
| TDTY_OTHER_AMT | DECIMAL(15,2) |
| TDLY_OTHER_AMT | DECIMAL(15,2) |

# Further Reading

Biehl, Bernd. "Information für alle" and "Die Praxisrelevanz zählt," *Lebensmittel Zeitung*, pp. 50–52, September 26, 1997.

Biehl, Bernd. "Alles wissen—alles managen," *Lebensmittel Zeitung* #9, pp. 52–56, February 27, 1998.

Biester, Silke. "Wal-Marts effektive Sortimentssteuerung basiert auf einer Data-Warehouse-Technologie," *Lebensmittel Zeitung*, pp. 32, October 5, 1999.

Compaq Computers, Inc. "Introduction to NonStop SQL/MP," technical manual, Tandem division.

Compaq Computers, Inc. "Introduction to Tandem S-Series," technical manual, Tandem division.

Compaq Computers, Inc. "Introduction to Transaction Manager," technical manual, Tandem division.

Compaq Computers, Inc. "Introduction to Transaction Processing," technical manual, Tandem division.

Compaq Computers, Inc. "Nonstop SQL/MP Query Guide," technical manual, Tandem division.

Compaq Computers, Inc. "Nonstop SQL/MP Reference Manual," technical manual, Tandem division.

Compaq Computers, Inc. "Tandem Directional Consulting," Compaq Computers white paper, Tandem division, 1997.

Gersting, Judith L. *Mathematical Structures for Computer Sciences*, W. H. Freeman and Company, 1982.

Inmon, William H., Imhoff, Claudia (contributor), and Battas, Greg (contributor). *Building the Operational Data Store*, John Wiley & Sons, October 1995.

Kimball, Ralph. *The Data Warehouse Toolkit: Practical Techniques for Building Dimensional Data Warehouses*, John Wiley & Sons, 1996.

NCR Corporation. "Teradata Concepts and Facilities," technical manual, January 25,1996.

NCR Corporation. "Teradata Database Reference Manual," technical manual.

Walton, Sam, with John Huey. *Sam Walton: Made in America*, Doubleday Publishing, 1992.

Westerman, Paul. "Entscheidungs-Unterstützung im Einzelhandel," Compaq Computers GmbH, white paper, 1997.

Westerman, Paul. "Retail Decision Support—A White Paper of Successful Retail Analyses," Compaq Computers, January 27, 1997.

Westerman, Paul, "Wal-Mart: Wettbewerbsvorteil durch Data Warehouse," *Dynamik im Handel*, Heft 9, pp. 30–34, September 1997.

Westerman, Paul. "Concepts of Micro-merchandising," Compaq Europe white paper, Business Intelligence Series: Retail Decision Support—Executive Level, June 1998.

Westerman, Paul. "Merchandising," Compaq Europe white paper, Business Intelligence Series: Retail Decision Support—Technical Level, June 1998.

Westerman, Paul. "Store Operations," Compaq Europe white paper, Business Intelligence Series: Retail Decision Support—Technical Level, June 1998.

Westerman, Paul. Translation by Silke Biester. "Erfolgreicher Einstieg ins Data Warehousing: Der sinnvolle Einsatz neuer Technik sollte am Return-on-Investment orientieren/ teil 1," *Lebensmittel Zeitung*, pp. 38–40, June 19, 1998.

Westerman, Paul. Translation by Silke Biester. "Kampf gegen Out-of-Stock/ teil 2," *Lebensmittel Zeitung*, pp. 42–43, June 26, 1998.

Westerman, Paul. Translation by Silke Biester. "Kein Geld verschenken: Preisabschriften sind ein guter Start ins Data Warehousing/ teil 3," *Lebensmittel Zeitung*, p. 34, July 10, 1998.

Westerman, Paul. Translation by Silke Biester. "Zur rechten Zeit am rechten Ort: Die Zuteilung am Bedarf auszurichten, ist ein zentrales Ziel von Data Warehousing/ teil 4," *Lebensmittel Zeitung*, p. 28, July 31, 1998.

Westerman, Paul. Translation by Silke Biester. "Dauerbrenner Sortiment: Ein Data Warehouse legt die Beziehung der Produkte offen/ teil 5," *Lebensmittel Zeitung*, pp. 38–39, August 7, 1998.

Westerman, Paul. Translation by Silke Biester. "Jeder Kunde kauft anders: Micromarketing erfordert Informationen über die Kunden/ teil 6," *Lebensmittel Zeitung*, pp. 48–50, August 21, 1998.

Westerman, Paul. Translation by Silke Biester. "Herzstück der un-denorientierung: Wal-Marts Warenwirtschaft automatisiert die lokale Anpassung der Sortimente," p. 42, February 12, 1999.

# Index

287

| Date Due → | 12/11/14 | | |
|---|---|---|---|
| | 2/2/16 | | |
| | 2/10/17 | | |
| | | | |
| | | | |
| | | | |
| | | | |
| | | | |
| | | | |
| | | | |